STUDIES IN EASTERN RELIGIONS

STUDIES IN EASTERN RELIGIONS

BY

ALFRED S. GEDEN, M.A.

TUTOR IN HEBREW AND BIBLICAL LITERATURE AT THE
WESLEYAN COLLEGE, RICHMOND
AUTHOR OF "STUDIES IN COMPARATIVE RELIGION"

GYAN

Published by

Gyan Publishing House
5, Ansari Road
Daryaganj, New Delhi-110002
Phone: 011-47034999, 9811692060
E-mail: books@gyanbooks.com

Distribution Network
gyanbooks.com
India, USA, Canada, UK, Australia, France

ISBN : 978-81-212-1321-9 (HB)
First Published, 1900

2nd Impression 2021

Printed at: Gyan Press, Delhi.

Studies in Eastern Religions
Author: Alfred S. Geden

STUDIES

IN

EASTERN RELIGIONS

BY

ALFRED S. GEDEN, M.A.

TUTOR IN HEBREW AND BIBLICAL LITERATURE AT THE

WESLEYAN COLLEGE, RICHMOND

AUTHOR OF "STUDIES IN COMPARATIVE RELIGION"

London:

CHARLES H. KELLY

2, CASTLE ST., CITY RD.; AND 26, PATERNOSTER ROW, E.C.

1900

To

My Fellow-Students

Past and Present

of Richmond College

PREFACE

THE interval of two years which has elapsed since the publication of *Studies in Comparative Religion* has been longer than was anticipated. The unavoidable delay has been caused partly by the pressure of regular College duties, and partly by the difficulty of comprehending a readable account of the great Eastern Religions within the narrow limits of a small volume. Of the incompleteness of the following Studies no one can be more conscious than the author. I can only repeat the hope to which I ventured to give expression in an earlier Preface that these pages may be to some a not unwelcome introduction to a subject of perpetual charm and of the most serious importance,—a stimulus also and help in its pursuit. It is becoming increasingly impossible and I trust increasingly rare for a Christian minister, still less a missionary in foreign countries, to regard himself as adequately equipped for his work, while he remains in ignorance of the habits and thoughts of alien peoples, who with different preconceptions and from different standpoints have stretched out their hands towards God. And to others also whose daily work lies on lines that diverge widely from those of a Theological College or the routine of a Christian Pastorate I trust that the following brief Studies may not be found without interest.

In the transliteration of Sanskrit and other words the usual rules have been observed. Consonants are to be pronounced ordinarily as in English, vowels as in Italian. The use of diacritical marks has been as far as possible avoided. *C'* is the English *ch* in *church*; *s'* is *sh*; *g* is always hard. In compound consonants, the second element of which is an aspirate, the component parts are separately and distinctly heard; *e.g.*, *th* is pronounced neither as in *th*orn nor as in *th*at, but as in foo*th*old; *c'h*, as in chur*ch-h*ouse; *ph*, as in u*ph*ill. Where the second member of the compound is *v*, the *v* is equivalent to *w*, except after *r*; *d* is usually English soft *th*, as in *th*ough: *dvish* therefore is to be pronounced *thw*ish. Of the vowels *e o* are always long: *ai au* are the diphthongs in *ai*sle, lo*u*d. The three simple vowels *a i u* are short, unless marked long. *Ă* however is never the English short *a* as in *rat*, a sound which does not exist in the Indian languages; but always the obscure vowel sound heard in *come*, *utter*. *Ri* is also a vowel, and is pronounced in South India at least as *rü*, nearly as in *cru*et, or as in T*rü*bner. German authors have largely adopted for the letter the single sign ṛ, and in this practice some English writers have followed their example. The drawback to this mode of representation is that it obscures the vowel character of the sound. In the following pages *ri* the vowel is distinguished where possible from ri the consonant and vowel by printing the former in italics.

No attempt has been made to supply a complete bibliography; neither are the titles of books on Religion in general already referred to in my earlier Studies again quoted here. There have merely been named a few of the best and most complete works, such as will probably be found most readily accessible. Those interested in the subject will have no difficulty in adding to the list. A long catalogue of authorities is more likely to be confusing than helpful, except to the expert; and for him it is unnecessary. Naturally very many more works have been consulted than are here set down. For the same reason except in rare instances I have abstained from citing other than English books.

The fascination which the religions and peoples of the East exert on all who have come into intimate relations with them is one to be felt rather than put into words. Its adequate expression defies the power of language. The charm of their gentleness and patience, the amazement at the volcanic force of passion that lies hidden beneath a quiet exterior, the perpetual surprise of the new and unexpected, the amused despair which overtakes all efforts to understand them, and which is scarcely lessened by the experience of years; these elements and many others combine to form a whole which for attractiveness and interest has never been surpassed. The intricate puzzle of the Eastern mind is like that of a woman; their charm also is womanly. The attempt to force them, whether in outward habit of life or in inward conviction and thought, into a masculine or Occidental mould is as certain of failure as the endeavour to confound the offices and functions of the two sexes in Western society. To sit at the feet of an Eastern sage is to listen to words of cunning and insight, tender and yet hard, sympathetic and yet singularly wanting in generous outlook or comprehension, individualistic and self-centred, full of warmth and colouring, rich in imagination and details, but withal as disconnected as the flashes of lightning. To feel the touch and glamour of the thought of the East will be an incalculable enrichment to the life of the West, and the best antidote to British insularity that even a world-wide Empire can command. The stimulant of Western justice straightforwardness and lofty ideals of purity and brotherhood is the only tonic that can restore the shattered and prostrate civilisations and society of the Orient.

If these Studies may in some measure contribute to a better understanding of the East, so hauntingly picturesque, so deeply religious, and of the spell which it lays upon all who have come into contact with its marvels, or entered the charmed circle of its strange and much misread thought,—thought as intense as its own blue skies,—the many hours devoted to the work will have been more than justified.

ALFRED S. GEDEN.

RICHMOND,
March 1900.

CONTENTS

INTRODUCTION AND SURVEY

INTRODUCTION AND SURVEY

DEFINITIONS and Limitations.—The religious systems and beliefs that enter here into consideration would be perhaps more accurately described as the Religions of India and the Far East. The term Eastern Religions, although convenient, is too broad and comprehensive. It would include for example Muhammadanism Zoroastrianism and Christianity itself; and except incidentally, these do not fall within the range of subjects now proposed. More difficult indeed would it be to set limits to its comprehensiveness, as regards those Religions at least which have crystallized into a formed and enduring system. For it is in the East, more broadly considered, that all the great Religions of the world have come into existence. In no instance has there been initiated and developed among a Western people any considerable body of religious beliefs and customs that has shown itself possessed of vitality and power of growth. The religious systems of the old Western world, so far as they can be termed systems at all, are dead. Their influence has been comparatively slight and indirect, and has never extended to the building up of a reasoned and influential body of opinions or rules. Eastern Religions on the contrary live. In the East also may be recognised, still speaking broadly, certain prominent centres of religious activity and diffusion:—Arabia, with which Persia in historical times at least has linked its fortunes; Syria; and Northern India. Further, it is usual to enumerate four great Religions of the world,—great in the number of their adherents, and in the influence they have exerted on the history of mankind. These are all from the East. The West stands aside, to a limited extent receptive, never initiating on any large or important scale. Following the chronological order of their appearance, the four referred to are Brâhmanism or Hinduism with its various branches, Buddhism, Christianity, and finally Muhammadanism. With this classification, as with any other, it would be easy to find fault on the side of defect, that it omits much which is important. These four however are of permanent interest, have been most widely influential, and have practically divided the world between them at the present day.

Religion on Racial Lines.—It is not without interest also to notice how closely the forms of religion have followed the lines of cleavage of race. Christianity and Brâhmanism are Aryan faiths. The former has scarcely touched Semitic or Mongol peoples, and its great missionary triumphs have been won among the low and the outcaste, who have held no definite place in the scale of nations and no clearly articulated system of belief. Brâhmanism has absorbed from the same classes, although it has never proselytised. Muhammadanism at the present day is almost conterminous with the Semitic peoples, and except in Persia has made no impression upon Aryan thought or life. Judaism, on the other side, is the standing exception. And both exceptions tend to prove the rule. The peoples again of Mongol birth and descent are Buddhist. If the traditions concerning its founder may be trusted its origin was Aryan. But it has abandoned the Aryan and Semitic fields to successful rivals. With the religion of Muhammad Buddhism never came into serious conflict. With Christianity it has twice entered into rivalry, in China and in Tibet; and in both instances from a competition on its own ground Buddhism issued victorious. Whatever the ultimate explanation may be, the fact of a tripartite religious and racial division of mankind along practically the same lines is one not to be overlooked, but demands serious consideration.

Contrasted History of Christianity.—Regarded as an Eastern Religion Christianity at once differentiates itself from the other three, in that it alone has been found capable of spreading and gaining for itself a place and home amongst the nations of the West. Brâhmanism or Hinduism was born in Asia, and has remained within modern times at least confined to India. Buddhism, cradled in India and driven forth from her early home, has spread widely Eastwards, but never, or only in an infinitesimal degree, to the West. Muhammadanism, which comes nearest in character and belief to Christianity, made strenuous and long-continued attempts to establish herself in Europe; but all her endeavours sooner or later have met with failure. And the little world of Muhammadanism, that still lingers by sufferance on the European shores of the Bosphorus, is only a fragment of Asia, of the East, transplanted to the opposite side of the Straits, which by its very presence there may be said to form the exception that establishes the rule. Christianity alone from the beginning turned her face Westwards; gave early and decisive evidence of her ability to satisfy Western modes of thought and experience; and won her most permanent conquests among the nations of Europe. Now she is returning to the East; to prove that she has not forgotten the land of her nativity, and to set forward her title to world-wide supremacy. In this respect also will she be unique, if she can make good her claim to perfect adaptability to every country and people upon the face of the earth.

Study of Particular Religions a Preparation for the Study of Comparative Religion.—It is however distinctly as illustrating a larger theme that the study of these two great religions of Brâhmanism and Buddhism deserves attention; less therefore for their own sake, interesting and important as they are, than for that which lies beyond and above them, the wide and fascinating subject of Comparative Religion. This can hardly be studied to greater advantage than in the development and history of the Religions of India. Thence was derived the first impulse towards a comparative view of religious thought and organisation and life; and there, in a rich and marvellously complex past, and in a present that has far outgrown the narrow geographical limits of the country of its birth, such a comprehensive view finds its best illustration and exponent. Youngest born as the science of Comparative Religion may be, it is rapidly growing to a most fruitful manhood; and yields to none of the older sciences in magnitude and importance. It must however vindicate its claim to the title by sobriety of method and permanence of results. Mere speculation or an *a priori* dogmatism that developes a preconceived theory at the cost of facts has neither part nor lot in the matter. A definition of the term therefore will in the first instance look at ascertained or ascertainable facts. By Comparative Religion is to be understood in general the science which examines the various religions of mankind, views side by side their beliefs, doctrines, customs, and ritual, tabulates their similarities and divergences, traces historically their origin, growth, and if necessary decline, and from the accumulated *data* before it draws legitimate inferences as to the religious needs and capacities of the human race, and the form of religion best adapted to meet those needs. Christianity at least has nothing to fear from such an examination. Every search for truth, rightly conducted, can only lead to Him who is the truth; and misses its way if it fail to point to Christ. Those who revere the Christ will or ought to welcome truth in other religions also,—as much truth as can be discovered there; confident that a faith which is high and pure can never suffer from comparison with other creeds, or from a full and frank recognition of that which is good in other forms of belief.

Demands and Method of the Study.—Christianity therefore will here enter mainly by way of comparison and illustration. With a limitation however to the two great systems of Brâhmanism or Hinduism with its diverse forms and wide ramifications on the one hand, and Buddhism on the other with its stern theory and easy practice, there presents itself a field too wide to be surveyed in detail, a subject too vast to be perfectly mastered in a lifetime. Something like a bird's-eye view will be all that is possible; but a view that will tax all the powers of memory, of sober reasoning, of realistic and constructive imagination, of philological acuteness, or of mathematical subtlety and precision. In harmony with a just conception of the requirements of an exact Comparative Religion, it will be necessary to endeavour to lay hold of and dwell upon the salient points in the origin, rise, progress, and if the evidence warrants such a conclusion the decay of these religions, noting especially the features of similarity or contrast they present to one another and to Christianity, and seeking to form for ourselves a lively and faithful picture of their past history, their present position and influence, and so far as forecast is admissible or possible their future prospects and destiny. The study thus prosecuted will be far from fruitless, if it do no more than enlarge our knowledge of our fellow-men, and give the power to trace more clearly the hand of a Divine Father in religious history, leading into the light, and declaring the way to Himself.

Characteristics of Oriental Thought.—One or two preliminary thoughts lie ready to hand on points of introduction and detail. The religions to be considered are *Oriental*; they are cast therefore wholly in *Oriental* modes of thought, and suited to impress *Oriental* minds. And it may well prove to be the case that for the ordinary European an effort is needed, before he can place himself at the stand-point of the Eastern, think his thoughts, or appreciate his mental or spiritual dispositions. The fact that except Christianity not one of these religions of the East has ever had any success among European nations, or is ever likely to have, suggests at once a profound difference of character, which renders the people susceptible to very dissimilar arguments and methods of appeal. Unquestionably this is the case. Oriental habits of thinking and reasoning differ widely from European. A logical syllogism, be it never so formal, is powerless against an Eastern mind, entrenched within preconceived ideas and customs. Truth to an Oriental is relative, not absolute; relative to himself, his own capacities, circumstances, and wishes; and what is true for one man is by no means necessarily or even probably true for another. The thought of the East, while possessing a certain logic of its own,—and let it be remembered that India had her system or systems of logic at least as early as Aristotle, —appears to the Occidental to be incomplete, disjointed, intensely illogical, as the term is understood in the West; refuses to carry out a principle to its conclusion, or even sometimes to admit that it has any conclusion at all. In the train also of their thinking comes of course their philosophy, their religion, practice, and the whole fabric of the intellectual and social life. One of the first difficulties to be overcome in comprehending and sympathizing with Eastern religions is that the Western mind anticipates a well-ordered and articulated frame-work, with its nerves and muscles and joints, each having its due place and function, and meets instead with an infinitely complicated and perplexing system, apparently without beginning or end, the parts of which, so far from working harmoniously together, seem often to be in the most hopeless contradiction. Speaking broadly,—possibly a little too broadly, but the illustration will serve at least to make clear the absolute difference of character and view,—the fundamental axiom of European thought, that a thing cannot both be and not be at the same time and in the same sense, has no force or authority to an Oriental mind: which sees no reason at all for accepting Hamlet's famous dilemma "to be or not to be" as presenting alternatives by any means mutually exclusive.

Effectiveness of Illustration and Memory.—Further, and perhaps almost as a consequence of this characteristic of the thought of the East, an apt illustration or a happy simile is more effective than the most clearly reasoned argument. A parallel drawn from daily life, the more familiar the better, drives home the truth it is sought to convey more forcibly than the most elaborate and formal eloquence. A train of reasoning may be lost in a cloud of words;

the end may either not be reached at all, or, if it is reached, the beginning and the steps by the way are alike forgotten. But an illustration photographs itself on the mind, and remains. With their literature the case is very much the same. This is usually florid and diffuse, rich in imagery and digressions, plays about its subject, and finds a difficulty in coming to the point. The Oriental loves discussion, and never wearies of the play of repartee; but it is a comparatively minor matter, whether the discussion lead to any result or no. He will be ready to begin *de novo* with equal zest, ignoring all previous conclusions. On the other hand, their patience is exhaustless, and their memory, trained by centuries of necessity and practice, has reached a very high degree of excellence. Upon this power of memory they are accustomed to rely much more than Europeans, who have been possessed of abundant and easily accessible printed books; with the result that the mind acquires by rote and retains with a facility almost unknown amongst us.[1] Some of these characteristics will

[1] Those who are best acquainted with the colleges and schools of India report that by the students of the present day this extraordinary faculty is being rapidly lost. With the growth of a printed literature the great need for its exercise has passed away; and with the passing of the need and remission of the practice decay of the faculty itself has set in. The tendency

in the sequel explain features in their religious life and practice, which appear strange and contradictory to our sober, less warm imagination and modes of thought.

Christianity also an Eastern Religion.—Christianity however it must not be forgotten is also an Oriental Religion, although it has taken deepest root and spread most widely among the peoples of the West. The fact that while other great systems of belief are Eastern and Eastern only the Christian faith is cosmopolitan, and has hitherto prevailed in the West rather than the East, among men of Western hardihood rather than Eastern flexibility, must not blind us to the fact that by origin and character, as well as by the nationality of its first Apostles and preachers and of the Founder Himself, Christianity speaks the language of the East. Its Western garb is to a certain extent strange and unnatural. It is we who have read into it Western ideas, and imposed upon it Western interpretations. And were it possible to divest it and ourselves of such accretions and modes of presentment it would without question come with

is to be regretted, but appears inevitable. The older generation of pandits, who could repeat by heart the Sanskrit sacred books, is dying out; and none come forward to take their place.

much more homeliness and convincing power to the nations of the East, to whom we endeavour to explain and commend it. Many things in the Hebrew and Greek Scriptures are best, perhaps only understood, when it is remembered that they were devised in an Oriental mind and addressed to an Oriental people. It may be that some of the scholars of our own day, who so ably dictate to us terms as to the date and circumstances of composition of the books of the Bible, would see cause to modify their conclusions, especially as to what is possible in the way of repetition or even apparent contradiction, could they spend two or three years in close personal contact with peoples of the East. Oriental writings cannot justly be judged or appreciated from an entirely Occidental stand-point.

Comparative Statistics of Chief Religions.—A brief statement may fitly be added here as to the respective prevalence of these and the other chief religions of the world at the present day. The assertion has frequently been made, and until recent times was in all probability correct, that the followers of Buddhism numerically exceeded those of any other faith. There can however be very little doubt that within the present century this has ceased to be true. In the number of its adherents Christianity, including both the Greek and Roman as well as the Reformed Churches, now stands at the head; and Buddhism does not occupy even the second place. It is difficult to attain to precision of statistics in matters such as these; not in all countries is an exact religious census carried out every ten years. The total population of the world however is estimated to be not less than fifteen hundred millions,[1] about a third of whom are professed Christians. With some hesitation Confucianism is placed second, having regard to the large population of the Chinese Empire. In the preface to his work on Buddhism Sir Monier Williams, whose authority on all matters of Comparative Religion is deservedly high, brings forward evidence to show that the great majority of the Chinese would, if required to tabulate their own belief, put themselves down as Confucianists.[2] This is however a point upon which none but practical experts have a right to give

[1] Europe, 360 millions; Asia, 832 millions; Africa, 171 millions; Australasia, 6 millions; America, North and South, 131 millions. Compare an article by A. H. Keane in *Church Missionary Intelligencer* for 1894, pp. 721 ff., from which the above figures are taken. The article is reprinted in the *C. M. S. Atlas*, London, 1896.

[2] Sir Monier Williams died in the spring of 1899, since these words were written. The same view was held by the late Dr. Legge; see his *Fâ-Hien*, p. 8.

their opinion; and in the present state of unrest and change, it can perhaps hardly be regarded as proved. The third place is taken by Hinduism, a very elastic term, which covers a multitude of widely different beliefs, with over two hundred millions of adherents. The latest census has shown that of the inhabitants of India including Burma nearly three-quarters are Hindus [1]; and that they have increased at about the same rate as the population, or a little short of eleven per cent. within the years 1881–91. This growth seems to be due largely to the absorption of wild and jungle tribes, of primitive belief and backward in civilisation. Fourth in order comes Muhammadanism, with a total very variously estimated, scattered over the greater part of Asia and the northern half of Africa; forming twenty per cent. of the population of India, and still holding their own there, with a percentage of increase during the last decade slightly less than that of Hinduism. There are said to be thirty millions of Muhammadans in China,[2] and from forty to forty-five millions in Africa.

[1] 207,731,727 out of a total of 287,223,431. See *Report of the Census of India* 1891, London, 1893, pp. 158 ff., 174, and Table vi. The same table gives the number of Muhammadans in India as 57⅓ millions, and of Christians 2¼ millions.

[2] Stanford's *Compendium of Geography*, Asia, vol. i. p. 370.

If we concede fifty millions for Europe and the rest of Asia, it would seem to be a not illiberal estimate. This would give a total number of about a hundred and eighty millions; which cannot be very far from the truth.[1] Buddhism stands fifth, with scarcely one hundred million adherents, mainly in China, Japan, Burma, and Ceylon. From statements made on apparently good authority, it is doubtful whether Japan now contains many real Buddhists. It is clear also that in all comparative statistics such as these, much depends upon the religious description that is to be given of the inhabitants of China, who often worship impartially and with equal zeal in the temples of rival sects. Lastly would come Taoism, Jainism, Judaism, and other minor faiths; some of which are of course of an importance far exceeding their small numerical following.[2]

Summary of Course of Studies.—Returning to Hinduism, a slight and brief sketch may be given of the order and method to be hereafter followed. Beginning with the most ancient

[1] Sir Monier Williams, *Buddhism*, pp. xvii., xviii., strangely reckons the number of Muhammadans at less than a hundred millions, allowing to the Turkish Empire only fourteen millions, and to Africa the same number. This can hardly be correct.

[2] The table page 21 *infra* is taken from the article by Professor A. H. Keane, already referred to.

known form of the religion, the first subject will naturally be the Hindu sacred book or books, the *Veda*,—that storehouse of ancient thought and belief which is to the majority of the inhabitants of India the sum and expression of all knowledge, the foundation of all the vast structure of their philosophy and practice, the court of appeal in all matters religious and civil, the sole repository of all wisdom, the one unequivocal self-revelation of the Supreme. A survey of the early literature will naturally lead to the consideration of the Vedic religion or religions, its character and pretensions, its ritual and its gods. There will follow a brief account of the Upanishads, the books containing the mystical esoteric doctrine evolved as a kind of commentary upon or vast corollary from the earlier Veda, with the six official systems of Hindu philosophy. Founded upon these is *Brâhmanism*, the religion of the Brâhmans, combining all these elements into one whole, the sole but mighty bond of union being the supremacy of the sacred caste. Later in the order of time is Hinduism proper, under which will be comprehended the history and nature of the two principal Hindu sects, the Vaishnavites and the S'aivites, with the respective offshoots of these; including also a description of the great Epic poems of India, from which so many elements in Hindu religions are derived, the Mahâbhârata and the Râmâyana. Here perhaps will be found an opportunity to pause for a moment to note certain broad features of Hinduism, which are illustrated alike by its literature and its history, namely its immobility combined with incessant change, its power of resistance and ability to absorb the most incongruous elements, and finally its vitality, triumphing over all the attempts of open violence or secret aggression. Modern or popular Hinduism must be placed next, comprising the later literature, the Purânas and numerous other works; demonology and nature worship; popular Hindu beliefs, indicative of Hindu character, its weakness and strength; and finally Hindu attempts at reform from within, the Brâhma-Samâj, and other eclectic sects. And in conclusion an attempt may be made, which must necessarily be brief and imperfect, to sum up our knowledge and results, and to place side by side, to compare and contrast the two faiths of Hinduism and Christianity.

	Europe	Asia with E. Archipelago	Africa	America	Australia with Polynesia and New Guinea	Total
Jews	5,500,000	260,000	430,000	300,000	15,000	6,505,000
Muhammadans	5,750,000	160,000,000	40,000,000		25,000	205,775,000
Hindus and Sikhs		207,000,000	300,000	100,000		207,400,000
Buddhists, Jains, Shintus, Taoists, and followers of Confucius	160,000	430,000,000			14,000	430,174,000
Religions not specified, and sundries	350,000	250,000		200,000	30,000	830,000
Pagans	20,000	15,000,000	125,000,000	14,000,000	1,600,000	155,620,000
Total non-Christians	11,780,000	812,510,000	165,730,000	14,600,000	1,684,000	1,006,304,000
Roman Catholics	156,000,000	8,500,000	1,200,000	57,000 000	850,000	223,550,000
Protestants	86,000,000	1,000,000	820,000	59,000,000	3,135,000	149,955,000
Orthodox Greeks	92,000,000	6,000,000	30,000			98,030,000
Armenians, Syrians, Malchites, Copts, and Abyssinians	300,000	3,000,000	3,000,000			6,300,000
Other Christians not specified	14,000,000	1,000,000			30,000	15,030,000
Total Christians	348,300,000	19,500,000	5,050,000	116,000,000	4,015,000	492,865,000
Grand Total	360,080,000	832,010,000	170,780,000	130,600,000	5,699,000	1,499,169,000

BRÂHMANISM AND HINDUISM

LITERATURE. GENERAL.—A. Barth, *Religions of India*, third edition, London, 1891; F. Max Müller, *History of Ancient Sanskrit Literature*, second edition, London, 1860; Sir Monier Monier-Williams, *Indian Wisdom*, fourth edition, London, 1893; and *Brâhmanism and Hinduism*, fourth edition, London, 1891; E. W. Hopkins, *Religions of India*, London, 1896; R. W. Frazer, *Literary History of India*, London, 1898; A. Weber, *History of Indian Literature*, third edition, London, 1891.

SPECIAL.—A. A. Macdonell, *Vedic Mythology*, Strassburg, 1897; A. E. Gough, *Philosophy of the Upanishads*, second edition, London, 1891; F. Max Müller, *Six Systems of Indian Philosophy*, London, 1899; and *Vedânta Philosophy*, London, 1894; M. Bloomfield, *The Atharva Veda*, Strassburg, 1899; Papers on *Religious Reform*, four parts, Madras, 1887–88. Brief accounts of the leading native Indian Reformers of the present century will be found in F. Max Müller, *Auld Lang Syne*, second series, London, 1899.

TRANSLATIONS.—J. Muir, *Original Sanskrit Texts*, five vols., second and third editions, London, 1873–90; F. Max Müller and H. Oldenburg, *Vedic Hymns*, two vols., Oxford, 1891 and 1897; F. Max Müller, *The Upanishads*, two vols., Oxford, 1879 and 1884; M. Bloomfield, *Hymns of the Atharva-Veda*, Oxford, 1897.

THE VEDA

NECESSITY of a Study of the Veda.—Every serious attempt to understand the ancient religions of India must begin from the Veda. The life and thought of the people are so saturated with the teaching of their sacred books, more often indirectly than directly received, that to withdraw these from consideration would be to take away the foundation upon which all rests. Much,—to follow up for a moment the metaphor,—has been built in besides, cloisters and wings have been attached, even entire tenements, originally independent, have been incorporated; but the Vedic writings are the strong under-lying base, without which the house would never have stood. It is not too much to say that the Veda, with all that springs from it and depends upon it, has played as important a part in the formation of Indian character and life as the Bible in the development of the nations of the West. As the history of Great Britain cannot be rightly read apart from the English Bible, so in her Veda has India found the one bond, which however loosely has held together the heterogeneous peoples that dwell between the Himalayas and Cape Comorin, and moulded them into a real if incomplete likeness of thought and conviction.

Meaning and Contents of the Term.—The term *Veda* signifies knowledge, from a root *vid*, to know, and is equivalent to the Greek *οἶδα*, *ἰδεῖν*, and the Latin *video*. The name is given collectively to the sacred writings of the Hindus, which like our own Bible constitute rather a library of books than a single treatise dealing with a single subject; and which, again like the Bible, are due to many authors, and have been composed at widely separated intervals of time. These works are written in Sanskrit, for the most part of an ancient and difficult type, long obsolete, with a highly elaborate grammar and an almost exhaustless vocabulary. For a long period they were handed down mainly if not entirely by oral tradition, being committed to memory in the various schools of learning. It was not apparently until the eleventh century of our era that the practice began of writing down the sacred books, lest the accurate remembrance of them should be lost; but the belief still held its ground after it had ceased to be reasonable, that the memory formed a safer as well as a purer repository of the sacred lore than ink and paper.[1]

What then is the *Veda?* The question is not one readily and at once answered. The books themselves it is comparatively easy to enumerate; but in a few sentences to describe their varied and miscellaneous character, or to tabulate the subjects of which they treat, is hardly possible. It may however be said in brief that the Veda is *knowledge,* wisdom embodied and concrete, containing in the estimation of the orthodox Hindu all that needs to be known for this life or for the next. What is written in the Veda is wisdom; what is not so written is foolishness, or at least is superfluous and of no material consequence. This conception of the sacred writings represents the average Hindu belief of the last two thousand years, untouched by European literature and thought. On the other hand the influence of modern education, its science philosophy and religion, is modifying, and has profoundly modified the attitude of

[1] Cp. Max Müller, *Physical Religion,* new edition, 1898, pp. 33 ff.; who quotes Al-Birûnî as stating that the prohibition against writing was enforced in his day. It seems not improbable that the need for reliable transcripts was first felt in the confusion and destruction incident to the Muhammadan invasion. The art of writing itself was of course known and practised in India for many centuries before this date.

mind of the younger generation in India; so that the theories and doctrines which their fathers received on authority do not satisfy them. Moreover the *rishis* or authors of the Veda were believed to have received the books by a direct revelation from heaven,—verbal inspiration, in its most literal and rigid form. This revelation came to them not through the ear, but through the eye. They actually *saw*,—for such is the technical and doubtless in its origin merely poetical term,—the compositions attributed to them.[1] Although not a few of them claim in so many words to have been the authors of their own works, their claim is ignored, as far as the play of individual mind or character is concerned. And thus while a religious homage and worship is paid to them, the theory concerning their place and function reduces them to simple machines, through whose eyes and pens the words of the gods have been faithfully transmitted to men. They are to be honoured accordingly as the vehicles, but in no sense whatever the originators, or even the shapers of the literary works

[1] The term *rishi* was supposed to be derived from the root *dris'*, to see; compare Heb. חֹזֶה, and Eng. *seer*. So that a popular etymology gave rise to the belief in question. The rea origin of the word is uncertain; but it probably comes from a root *ric'*, to praise.

attributed to them, and handed down from them by oral tradition. This sacred literature is also termed *S'ruti*, heard, that which comes by direct revelation from the Deity, as distinguished from later uninspired works called *Smriti*, remembered, or that which owes its origin and continuance to the initiative and instrumentality of man.[1] This conception of a direct revelation of Himself made by God to man, so unfamiliar in this wide and general form at least to Greek and Roman thought, is met with continually in the religions of Eastern nations; who seem to have lived in closer communion as it were with the unseen and supernatural than the peoples of the West.

Divisions of the Veda.—The Veda, or more strictly speaking the Vedas, the most ancient documents of the religions of India, consist if the nature of their contents be considered of three parts:—

(1) *Mantra*, or liturgical texts, hymns of prayer and praise, for the most part written in poetry.

(2) *Bráhmana*, formulæ and precepts referring

[1] Cp. Manu, ii. 10:—"By S'ruti is meant the Veda, and by Smriti the Institutes of the sacred law; those two must not be called into question in any matter, since from those two the sacred law shone forth." *S. B. E.*, vol. xxv. p. 31.

to ritual and sacrifice, in prose generally of an archaic character.

(3) *Upanishad*, mystical or secret doctrine, esoteric philosophy and theological speculation, in prose or verse.

By the side of this triple classification according to subject-matter there was a quadruple arrangement, not perhaps so ancient as the other, of the Vedic writings into four different collections, of which the first is the oldest and by far the most important. These are:—

(1) *Rig-Veda*, containing the greater number of the hymns, and forming the ceremonial textbook of the *Hotri* priests.

(2) *Yajur-Veda*, or Veda of sacrifice and ritual; a collection of texts, not independent but for the most part taken with slight changes from the Rig-Veda. It is divided into two parts, the *Taittirîya* and *Vâjasaneyin*, named also the Black and White Yajur-Veda.[1] Its appropriate priests are the *Adhvaryus*.

(3) *Sâma-Veda*, which again borrowed most of its verses from the Rig-Veda, and is merely

[1] White, *s'ukla*, because here the mantra and brâhmana portions are kept distinct. In the Black, *krishna*, they are mingled together. The latter is probably the more ancient. See Max Müller, *History of Ancient Sanskrit Literature*, p. 350 f.; H. Baynes in *Indian Antiquary*, xxvi. p. 213.

a compilation of liturgical forms for use by the *Udgâtri* priests in the ceremonies connected with the sacred Soma plant.[1]

(4) *Atharva-Veda*, in general more recent than the others and more independent. It is a collection of hymns like the Rig-Veda, about five-sixths of which are original. The remainder, which are common to the two, are supposed by many authorities to have been adapted and employed in a different worship,—a worship more of the nature of incantations and popular magic. Hindu writers say that the Atharva-Veda was designed especially for the use of the Brâhmans; but of this there seems to be no proof, or any indication of such a limitation in practice.

That the Atharva-Veda is in fact the most recent collection, or at least most recently gained currency and recognition, is shown also by the habitual employment by the most ancient writers of the term "triple Veda." It is only later that a fourth is added.[2] The character of individual

[1] Cp. Macdonell, *Vedic Mythology*, p. 3 f.

[2] Compare for example the commentator on the Veda quoted by Max Müller, *History*, p. 122:—"As there are three different branches of the ceremonial, the Veda is, for the better performance of the sacrifices, divided into three: the Rig-Veda, Yajur-Veda, and Sâma-Veda. The ceremonial of the Hotri priests is performed with the Rig-Veda; that of the Adhvaryu priests

hymns of the collection often suggests a considerable antiquity.

Rig-Veda. — The Rig-Veda consists of ten *mandalas*, or books, with a total of 1028 hymns. Of these, eleven that are added at the end of the eighth book are a later addition. The *mandalas* form independent collections belonging to one or other of the great Vedic families, the names of which are given by tradition.[1] The ninth book consists of hymns in praise of the Soma plant; and the tenth is miscellaneous, suggesting a gathering up of the fragments, and consequently a later origin than the others. With the exception of the eighth and ninth, all the mandalas begin with a hymn in praise of Agni, and in the case of the first seven this is immediately followed by a hymn to Indra. Not only the hymns themselves, but the verses and words they contained were counted and carefully registered by the Sanskrit grammarians.[2] Of the 1549 verses of the Sâma-Veda only seventy-eight are not already found in the Rig-Veda, as it

with the Yajur-Veda; that of the Udgât*ri* priests with the Sâma-Veda. The duties of the Brâhman priests, and of him for whom the sacrifice is offered, are also contained in these three Vedas. The Atharva-Veda is not used for solemn sacrifices, and is very different from the others."

[1] Max Müller, *Physical Religion*, p. 59 f.

[2] See Max Müller, *ut supra*, App. vii.

is now extant. The hymns at the Soma worship were intended to be chanted or sung, while those of the Rig-Veda on the contrary were simply recited. The sacrificial formulæ of the Yajur-Veda were to be muttered as incantations or prayers, during the time of the presentation of the offering.

These collections of hymns are termed *Samhitâs*; and besides the *Samhitâs*, each Veda comprises one or more *Brâhmanas*, or prose directions for ceremonial observance. The Yajur and Sâma-Vedas indeed contain little else than Brâhmana. Attached to each Brâhmana as a kind of exposition or supplement was an *Upanishad*, treating of doctrine philosophy and speculative themes in general. These three divisions were however by no means always maintained clearly distinct.

Recensions of the Vedas.—Finally of each Veda there were several recensions, called *S'âkhâs*, probably for use in different schools of thought and in different localities. Of the Rig-Veda there is extant only one, that of the S'âkalas; of the Yajur-Veda five, three Black and two White; of the Sâma-Veda three; and of the Atharva-Veda two.[1] These are all included under the term S'ruti, and are regarded as authoritative and inspired.

[1] Cp. Barth, p. 4 and notes.

Date.—As to the date of these writings the widest possible variety of opinion has prevailed, and only general and approximate limits can be assigned, leaving still a somewhat wide margin of doubt. That the mantra portion is the oldest, the evidence of style and language, as well as of subject-matter prove. On these hymns and texts the rest is founded, assumes their existence and authority, and derives from them its inspiration. A similar relation holds between the Brâhmanas and Upanishads. The descending order in time would therefore be mantra, including the ancient hymns, brâhmana, upanishad. On the other hand the teaching, perhaps even the language of some at least of the Upanishads is certainly presupposed by Buddhism; whose rise is fixed to the fifth century before our era. Parts of the Brâhmanas are generally regarded as not earlier than this date. This gives a period anterior to which the larger portion of the sacred literature of India must have come into existence. The whole question however is surrounded with difficulty; and it is hardly likely that an entirely satisfactory settlement will ever be reached. The tendency of modern research is to reduce within more moderate limits the excessive antiquity claimed by some Sanskrit scholars for the

Veda. But the opposite extreme of its comparatively modern character can certainly not be maintained in the light of history.[1]

[1] Dr. Haug, for instance, assigns the beginning of Vedic literature to as early a date as 2000–2400 B.C.; cp. Muir, *Sanskrit Texts*, vol. i. p. 4 f. Professor Max Müller distinguishes four great periods of Sanskrit literary composition:—

(1) The *Sûtra* period, extending to about 600 B.C. "Several of the most eminent among the authors of Sûtras or aphorisms lived prior, if not to the origin, at least to the spreading and the political ascendency of Buddhism."

(2) The *Brâhmana* period, 600–800 B.C.

(3) The *Mantra* period, comprising the "later sacrificial hymns, and the collection of these, together with the older hymns, into separate books, and afterwards into a complete body of sacred and liturgical poetry"; 800–1000 B.C.

(4) The *Chhandas* period, the last and most important of the four, being that in which the great *ri*shis lived and flourished; 1000–1200 B.C. *Circa* 1200 B.C. is therefore the latest date that can be assigned to the settlement of the Vedic poets in northern India.

See Max Müller, *Rig-Veda*, Pref. to vol. iv., 2nd ed., pp. vii. ff.; *History of Sanskrit Literature*, pp. 67–70, 572, and *passim*; *Physical Religion*, Lecture v. Most authorities consider that the limits here laid down are too narrow, and do not allow sufficient time for the development of thought and language. The periods moreover almost certainly overlap. Professor Max Müller himself claims nothing more for them than that they are approximations to the truth. Periods three and four pass into one another, and are incapable of any very precise differentiation. Other well-known writers have carried back the age of the earliest hymns to the twentieth century before Christ.

Attempts have been made to determine the age of these works by the help of astronomy. The latest of these as far as my

Religion and Gods of the Vedic Hymns: Indra.— The religious belief expressed and embodied in these ancient hymns is nature worship, the personification of the visible phenomena and forces of the world around and of the sky above, with appropriate homage and devotion paid to each. In the extreme zones of the earth much more than in the temperate, there has always been manifest the tendency to credit with consciousness and life the physical powers of the universe: for there they are seen working on a vaster and more impressive scale. The poets of the Veda accordingly looked out upon the forces of nature by which they were encompassed, imagining each as living and sentient; and the more majestic and imposing

knowledge goes are the researches of F. K. Ginzel, referred to in a note in the *Athenæum* of September 1894. It is there laid down that of four eclipses mentioned in the sacred books, three are to be probably identified with the eclipses of March 4th. 1250 B.C., November 17th. 1301 B.C., and May 26th. 1386 B.C.; the last two of these were nearly, and the first quite total, presumably in the north of India. The earliest of the four is identified with an annular eclipse of October 5th. 1978. The fact however that the central line of this eclipse crossed southern India puts the identification practically out of court. Considering moreover the risks which beset the accurate transmission of numbers and dates, all such calculations and inferences are very precarious, even if reliance could always be placed on the original observations.

the power displayed, the greater the god who wielded it. There was *Indra*, the most popular and widely honoured divinity of the Veda, to whose praise more than two hundred and fifty hymns are dedicated, and who indeed approaches the character of a national god. He is the mighty lord of the rain and the thunderstorm, the giver of good gifts when he sends his fertilising showers upon the burnt-up and thirsty soil; but also the terrible king, who commissions and guides the floods in their destructive course. He is further the god of battle, who wields the thunderbolt, and rides forth on his golden car, accompanied by the *Maruts*, the storm-deities, sons of *Rudra*, lord of healing and of the arts. *Indra* is perhaps the most completely personified of the great divinities of the Veda. His appearance is described, and his vast size. He holds the earth in the hollow of his hand, spreads out and supports the sky, bestowing his bountiful gifts upon all who reverence him; and himself in turn revels in the offerings of his worshippers, especially the intoxicating drink of the Soma plant, in which he indulges to excess, and which strengthens him to go forth in terrible might, and to rout the opposing demons. The mythical combat in which he is most frequently engaged is with *Vritra*, the malignant demon of darkness and drought, whom he again and again defeats and slays. As the deity of the air and the winds *Indra* holds the second place in the earliest Vedic triad of gods, the other members of which are Agni and Sûrya. In later Hindu mythology however he passes almost altogether out of sight. The following are illustrations of hymns in his praise[1]:—

Thou, O Indra, with the swift Maruts, who break even through the stronghold, hast found even in their hiding-place the bright ones (days or clouds).
The pious singers (the Maruts) have, after their own mind, shouted towards the giver of wealth, the great, the glorious (Indra).
Mayest thou (host of the Maruts) be verily seen coming together with Indra, the fearless: you are both happy-making, and of equal splendour.
With the beloved hosts of Indra, with the blameless hasting (Maruts), the sacrificer cries aloud.
From yonder, O traveller (Indra), come hither, or from the light of heaven; the singers all yearn for it;—
Or we ask Indra for help from here, or from heaven, or from above the earth, or from the great sky.[2]

O Indra, a thousand have been thy helps accorded to us, a thousand, O driver of the bays, have been thy most

---

[1] The translations here as elsewhere are those of Professors F. Max Müller and H. Oldenburg, in *Sacred Books of the East*, vols. xxxii. and xlvi.; to the former of whom especially students of Indian literature and religion, whether they agree with all his conclusions or not, owe an incalculable debt.

[2] *S. B. E.*, vol. xxxii. p. 14 f.

delightful viands. May thousands of treasures richly to enjoy, may goods come to us a thousandfold.

May the Maruts come towards us with their aids, the mighty ones, or with their best aids from the great heaven, now that their furthest steeds have rushed forth on the distant shore of the sea.

. . . .

No people indeed, whether near to us, or from afar, have ever found the end of your strength, O Maruts! The Maruts, strong in daring strength, have, like the sea, boldly surrounded their haters.

May we to-day, may we to-morrow in battle be called the most beloved of Indra. We were so formerly, may we truly be so day by day, and may the lord of the Maruts be with us.

May this praise, O Maruts, this song of Mândârya, the son of Mâna, the poet, ask you with food for offspring for ourselves! May we have an invigorating autumn, with quickening rain![1]

He who, immediately on his birth, the first, the wise, surpassed the gods in force; at whose might the two worlds shook, through the greatness of his strength, he, O men, is Indra.

He who fixed the quivering earth; who gave stability to the agitated mountains; who measured the vast atmosphere; who propped up the sky, he, O men, is Indra.

. . . .

He who has been a counterpart of the Universe; who casts down the unshaken, he, O men, is Indra.

. . . .

The sky and the earth bow down to him; at his might the mountains are afraid.[2]

---

[1] *S. B. E.*, vol. xxxii. pp. 272 f.

[2] Rig-Veda, ii. 12. 1, translated in Muir, *Sanskrit Texts*, iv. p. 87. Cp. Macdonell, *Vedic Mythology*, pp. 54–66; *Vedic Hinduism*, p. 26 ff.

Soma.—This *Soma*, in which Indra indulges, properly the fermented juice of a plant, was itself deified and hymns composed in its honour. The entire ninth book of the Rig-Veda, consisting of one hundred and fourteen hymns, is devoted to celebrating its virtues and power. It was the favourite libation to the gods, and had a mystical life in the third heaven. Like the nectar of the Greeks, it was the drink of the gods, through partaking of which they became immortal; and men also will win immortality, when they quaff the Soma in the abode of the blessed. In the representation of Soma there is less anthropomorphism than in that of Indra; and the consciousness appears never to have been entirely lost that the name denoted the sap or juice of a plant. This plant however was semi-mythical or divine; it grew in heaven as well as upon earth; and had indeed originally been brought down from the sky, a gift from the gods to men. Soma is termed a warrior and king, lord of plants and lord of the wood. In the later literature it is identified with the moon, and of this identification there are certainly intimations, brief and obscure, in the Rig-Veda itself.[1] By some scholars however it is

[1] The principal passages referred to are vi. 44, 21: viii. 71, 8: x. 85, 2, 3; 123, 8: cp. Macdonell, *Vedic Mythology*, p. 112 f.

maintained that throughout the Veda, and from the very beginning, Soma is to be understood as referring to the moon. If this had been so, it is at least strange that all native commentators should have gone so entirely astray with respect to the meaning of the word.[1]

Varuna.—The most important deity of the Veda, second only to Indra, if indeed second to him, is *Varuna*, the Greek *Οὐρανός*, the wide-spreading heavens,[2] in whom is embodied the ancient Indian conception of justice and right. To him comparatively few hymns are directly addressed. These few however set forth with almost unequalled force his majesty and power. He is the moral ruler of the universe, whose ordinances not even the gods may with impunity disregard; and who is represented at times as possessing all the attributes of supreme authority and unerring righteousness, omniscient and omni-

[1] The leading advocate of this view is, I believe, Professor A. Hillebrandt, *Vedische Mythologie*, Breslau, 1891; cp. Macdonell, *ut supra*, and Barth, *Indian Antiquary*, xxiii. p. 364.

[2] That the identity of Varuna and Οὐρανός has been strongly disputed, mainly on philological grounds, is of course well known. The arguments in favour of the substantial accuracy of the view which explains the character and attributes of Varuna from the all-encompassing, all-surveying vault of heaven appear to me considerably stronger than any that have been advanced against it. Cp. Macdonell, p. 27 f.; Max Müller, *Contributions to the Science of Mythology*, vol. i. p. 416 ff.

potent, the maker of all and the preserver of all. Varuna sees all things, the future as well as the present and past, and calmly overlooks all in the quiet consciousness of strength, punishing the wrong-doer, but forgiving and merciful to the man who repents of his sin. In all the hymns that bear his name there is found a prayer for forgiveness. He takes note of every action, "far-sighted and thousand-eyed" is acquainted with every thought; and his numberless messengers go to and fro throughout the whole universe. Of him it has been well said, if perhaps a little too strongly, that "with Varuna the religion of the Veda goes down into the depths of the conscience, and realises the idea of holiness."[1] Certainly Varuna is the least earthly, the most heavenly of the Vedic deities; and in strong contrast with Indra, he is never made the subject of any myth or story. He is therefore pre-eminently the upholder of order, the lord of day and night and of the seasons in their regular succession, as distinguished from all that is disorderly and out of course. In the later mythology Varuna shares the fate of so many of the Vedic deities, and becomes reduced to comparative insignificance, in the character of a god of the sea. The follow-

[1] Barth, *Religions of India*, p. 17.

ing is part of one of the best-known hymns addressed to him:—

However we break thy laws from day to day, men as we are, O god, Varuna,
Do not deliver us unto death, nor to the blow of the furious; nor to the anger of the spiteful!
To propitiate thee, O Varuna, we bind thy mind with songs, as the charioteer a weary steed.
Away from me they flee dispirited, intent only on gaining wealth; as birds to their nest.
When shall we bring hither the man who is victory to the warriors, when shall we bring Varuna, the wide-seeing, to be propitiated?

. . . .

He who knows the place of the birds that fly through the sky, who on the waters knows the ships,—
He, the upholder of order, who knows the twelve months, with the offspring of each, and knows the month that is engendered afterwards,[1]—
He who knows the track of the wind, of the wide, the bright, and mighty; and knows those who reside on high,—
He, the upholder of order, Varuna sits down among his people; he, the wise, sits there to govern.
From thence perceiving all wondrous things, he sees what has been and will be done.
May he, the wise son of time, make our paths straight all our days; may he prolong our lives!

. . . .

O hear this my calling, Varuna, be gracious now; longing for help, I have called upon thee.
Thou, O wise god, art lord of all, of heaven and earth: listen on thy way.[2]

---

[1] Explained as the thirteenth or intercalary month.

[2] Max Müller, *Sanskrit Literature*, p. 535 ff.

In his *Indian Wisdom* Professor Monier Williams gathers together in metrical form a number of the texts referring to this god. The passage is worth quoting, although of course it is a paraphrase rather than a translation, and moreover belongs to the Atharva-Veda:—

The mighty Varuna, who rules above, looks down
Upon these worlds, his kingdom, as if close at hand.
When men imagine they do aught by stealth, he knows it.
No one can stand or walk or softly glide along
Or hide in dark recess, or lurk in secret cell,
But Varuna detects him and his movements spies.
Two persons may devise some plot, together sitting
In private and alone; but he, the king, is there—
A third—and sees it all. This boundless earth is his,
His the vast sky, whose depth no mortal e'er can fathom.
Both oceans find a place within his body, yet
In that small pool he lies contained. Whoe'er should flee
Far, far beyond the sky, would not escape the grasp
Of Varuna, the king. His messengers descend
Countless from his abode—for ever traversing
This world and scanning with a thousand eyes its inmates.
Whate'er exists within this earth, and all within the sky,
Yea all that is beyond, king Varuna perceives.
The winkings of men's eyes are numbered all by him.
He wields the universe, as gamesters handle dice.
May thy destroying snares, cast sevenfold round the wicked,
Entangle liars, but the truthful spare, O king![1]

Agni.—The most popular of the Vedic gods next to Indra, judging from the number of

[1] *Op. cit.*, p. 16; cp. Bloomfield, *Atharva-Veda*, *S. B. E.*, vol. xlii. pp. 88, 389 f., where references are given to other translations of the same hymn.

hymns dedicated to him, was *Agni*, the Latin *ignis*, the god of fire, son of heaven and earth, the friend and protector of mankind; who is said to have had a three-fold origin as the lightning in heaven, the kindled fire upon earth, and in the waters of the sky. More than two hundred hymns are addressed to him, and, with the exception of the eighth and ninth, all the ten books of the Rig-Veda begin with a hymn in his praise. With Soma he is the only great god of whom it may fairly be said that he has preserved in the main in the Veda his physical characteristics. The myths moreover related of him concern themselves more with his origin and functions than with his deeds. He has the right to claim from men reverence and fear, inasmuch as he attends upon them daily at the hearth, bears their sacrifices and offerings to heaven, gives them kindly warmth and makes their crops to grow. But the same beneficent power strikes and scorches in the lightning and the tropical sun those who oppose him and neglect to render him his due. Thus Agni was one of the first and greatest of the Vedic deities, the eldest of the gods, a priest and seer in heaven as well as on earth, messenger and intermediary between god and man, author and preserver, yet terrible to his foes as he rides in his flaming form on a golden car. If Indra is the type of the hero and warrior, Agni is the high priest, uniting in himself the functions of all inferior and human priests, and making acceptable the worship and service of men to the gods. To the latter the opening hymn of the Rig-Veda is addressed:—

> I magnify Agni, the Purohita,[1] the divine ministrant of the sacrifice, the Hot*ri* priest, the greatest bestower of treasures.
>
> Agni, worthy to be magnified by the ancient *Ri*shis and by the present ones,—may he conduct the gods hither.
>
> May one obtain through Agni wealth and welfare day by day, which may bring glory and high bliss of valiant offspring.
>
> Agni, whatever sacrifice and worship thou encompassest on every side, that indeed goes to the gods.
>
> May Agni the thoughtful Hot*ri*, he who is true and most splendidly renowned, may the god come hither with the gods.
>
> Whatever good thou wilt do to thy worshipper, O Agni, that (work) verily is thine, O Angiras.
>
> Thee, O Agni, we approach day by day, O (god) who shinest in the darkness; with our prayer bringing adoration to thee—
>
> Who art the king of all worship, the guardian of *Ri*ta,[2] the shining one, increasing in thy own house.
>
> Thus, O Agni, be easy of access to us, as a father is to his son. Stay with us for our happiness.[3]

[1] Household or family priest.

[2] Fixed or settled order, law; the appropriate order of the sacrificial rite.

[3] *S. B. E.*, vol. xlvi. p. 1.

I worship with good cheer Agni the steward of all treasures, whom the seven ladles (of the priests), the worshippers choose as the Hot*ri*, the last sacrificer at the rites, and I pray for treasure.

Son of strength, great like Mitra, grant to-day flawless protection to us who magnify thee. Agni! guard from distress with strongholds of iron him who praises thee, O offspring of vigour!

Be a shelter to him who praises thee, O resplendent one; be protection, generous giver, to the generous. Agni! guard him who praises thee from distress. May he who gives wealth for our prayer, come quickly in the morning.[1]

Agni, thou art for ever the wise son of Heaven and of the Earth, the all-wealthy one. In thy peculiar way sacrifice here to the gods, O intelligent one!

Agni, the knowing, obtains (for his worshipper) heroic powers; he obtains (for him) strength, being busy for the sake of immortality. Bring then the gods hither, O (Agni), rich in food.

Agni, the wise, shines on Heaven and Earth, the two immortal goddesses who encompass all people—he who rules through his strength, and who is full of light through adoration.

Agni and Indra, come hither to the sacrifice in the house of the worshipper rich in pressed (Soma), never failing, ye two gods, at the drink of Soma.

Agni, thou art kindled in the house of the waters, (our) own (god), O son of strength, Jâtavedas, who exaltest the abodes (in which thou dwellest) by thy blessing.[2]

The following is a joint hymn to Agni and the Maruts:—

[1] *S. B. E.*, vol. xlvi. p. 46.

[2] *Ibid.*, p. 291; cp. *Indian Wisdom*, p. 18.

Thou art called forth to this fair sacrifice for a draught of milk; with the Maruts come hither, O Agni!
No god indeed, no mortal, is beyond the might of thee, the mighty one; with the Maruts come hither, O Agni!

. . . .

The strong ones who sing their song, unconquerable by force; with the Maruts come hither, O Agni!
They who are brilliant, of terrible designs, powerful and devourers of foes; with the Maruts come hither, O Agni!
They who in heaven are enthroned as gods, in the light of the firmament; with the Maruts come hither, O Agni!
They who toss the clouds across the surging sea; with the Maruts come hither, O Agni!
They who shoot with their darts (lightnings) across the sea with might; with the Maruts come hither, O Agni!
I pour out to thee for the early draught the sweet (juice) of Soma; with the Maruts come hither, O Agni![1]

Sûrya.—Closely connected with Agni, sometimes apparently identified with him, was *Sûrya*, the son of *Dyaus* or the sky, the foremost of the solar deities, to whom ten hymns of the Rig-Veda are dedicated. He is worshipped under many names and forms, as *Savitri*, the vivifier, who awakens the universe and men in the morning from sleep: as *Vishnu*, the all-pervader, who traverses the three worlds in three strides, who bears the standing epithet of "wide-going" or "wide-stepping," and of whom indeed little else is recorded, for he occupies in

[1] Translated by Max Müller, *S. B. E.*, vol. xxxii. p. 53.

the older literature an altogether subordinate position, although destined to develop later into one of the most important and widely known of India's gods: and as *Pûshan*, the guardian and preserver of cattle, the companion of travellers, and guide of the soul on its way to the lower world.

Other Gods.—These are the most important divinities of the Veda. It would be easy to extend the list. Others that do not there occupy so prominent a position, are interesting because of their associations or subsequent history. *Vâyu* or *Vâta*, the wind, was another impersonation of the rain-storm, fabled to be the husband of the earth. *Brihaspati*, or *Brahmanaspati*, is the lord of prayer, divine priest of the gods like Agni, with whom indeed he is sometimes identified. He intercedes for men with the gods, and protects the good against the wicked. *Ushas*, Aurora, the dawn, receives praise in about twenty hymns. She is the daughter of heaven ever bright and ever young. Borne on her car, she opens the gates of the sky, and keeps far away hurtful or malicious spirits. In her is seen perhaps the most attractive and beautiful personification to be found in the Veda. Other well-known deities are the *As'vins*, twin gods of the morning, children of the sun, who have often been compared to the Dioscuri of Greece. In their honour more than fifty hymns are composed. They bestow gifts, and drive away sickness and ill from men. In later times accordingly they came to be worshipped as divine physicians. But their original nature and character has been much in dispute. The most probable view appears to be that they represent the morning and evening stars, conceived by primitive man to be separate and independent bodies, but so evidently alike in their functions and course in the sky as to be regarded as twins.[1] Lastly there is *Yama*, the grim stern god of death, son of the sun, who though immortal chose to die, and having been the first to tread the road to the lower world was appointed its king. There he holds his court, and before him the souls of the dead appear and are judged according to their deeds. The good drink of the Soma, and ascend into heaven, there to be themselves worshipped as gods under the name of *Pitris*, fathers or ancestors. The wicked are hurled down into

[1] Others have thought that the *As'vins* symbolized the morning and evening twilights, or even the sun and moon. See Macdonell, *Vedic Myth.*, p. 53. The word is properly an adjective, signifying "belonging to horses." The As'vins are the two charioteers, who conduct the car of the dawn through the sky.

one of the twenty-one hells, in which they make expiation for their crimes. Those who believe that Yama also is a personification of some natural power or phenomenon hold that he represented the setting sun, or perhaps the day as it passed away into darkness. In the legends however of Yama, and the conception of his office, there seems to be a foreshadowing of the doctrine of metempsychosis, that so pervades and dominates all later Hindu religious belief.

Tone and Character of Hymns.—Some of these ancient hymns of the Veda have already been quoted, in whole or in part. It may be worth while to add two or three more examples. Many of them have been translated into English and other modern languages more than once, and the translations are easily accessible. No rendering however can adequately reproduce the combined dignity and terseness of the original. Their simplicity, often almost childishness of conception, recalls to mind the Iliad and Odyssey; but in beauty and warmth of expression they fall far behind Homer. On the other hand there is present in them a subtlety and originality of thought, scarcely to be matched in the ancient literature of any religion. The following hymn is from the sixth mandala of the Rig-Veda, addressed to Soma and Rudra:—

> Soma and Rudra, may you maintain your divine dominion, and may the oblations reach you properly. Bringing the seven treasures to every house, be kind to our children and our cattle.
>
> Soma and Rudra, draw far away in every direction the disease which has entered our house. Drive far away Nirriti,[1] and may auspicious glories belong to us!
>
> Soma and Rudra, bestow all these remedies on our bodies. Tear away and remove from us whatever evil we have committed, which clings to our bodies.
>
> Soma and Rudra, wielding sharp weapons and sharp bolts, kind friends, be gracious unto us here! Deliver us from the snare of Varuna, and guard us, as kind-hearted gods![2]

Hymns of the Creation.—The tenth book of the Rig-Veda, though later in date than the others, contains some of the most interesting compositions. The 129th Hymn has been termed the "Hymn of the Creation," and is thus translated or paraphrased by Sir Monier Williams:—

> In the beginning there was neither nought nor aught,
> Then there was neither sky nor atmosphere above.
> What then enshrouded all this teeming Universe?
> In the receptacle of what was it contained?
> Was it enveloped in the gulf profound of water?
> Then there was neither death nor immortality,

---

[1] Goddess of destruction. [2] *S. B. E.*, vol. xxxii. p. 434.

Then there was neither day, nor night, nor light, nor darkness.
Only the Existent One breathed calmly, self-contained.
Nought else than him there was—nought else above, beyond.
Then first came darkness hid in darkness, gloom in gloom.
Next all was water, all a chaos indiscreet,
In which the One lay void, shrouded in nothingness.
Then turning inwards he by self-developed force
Of inner fervour and intense abstraction grew.
And now in him Desire, the primal germ of mind,
Arose, which learned men, profoundly searching, say
Is the first subtle bond, connecting Entity
With Nullity. This ray that kindled dormant life,
Where was it then? before? or was it found above?
Were there parturient powers and latent qualities,
And fecund principles beneath, and active forces
That energized aloft? Who knows? Who can declare?
How and from what has sprung this Universe? the gods
Themselves are subsequent to its development.
Who then can penetrate the secret of its rise?
Whether 'twas framed or not, made or not made; he only
Who in the highest heaven sits, the omniscient lord,
Assuredly knows all, or haply knows he not.[1]

A similar hymn, embodying curious speculation on the origin of the universe from the primæval man *Purusha*, is given in a literal prose translation by Dr. J. Muir:—

Purusha has a thousand heads, a thousand eyes, a thousand feet. On every side enveloping the earth, he overpassed (it) by a space of ten fingers. Purusha himself is this whole (universe), whatever has been and whatever shall be. He is also the lord of immortality, since (or, when) by food he expands.

[1] *Indian Wisdom*, p. 22 f.

Such is his greatness, and Purusha is superior to this. All existences are a quarter of him; and three-fourths of him are that which is immortal in the sky. . . . When born he extended beyond the earth, both behind and before. When the gods performed a sacrifice with Purusha as the oblation, the spring was its butter, the summer its fuel, and the autumn its (accompanying) offering. This victim, Purusha, born in the beginning, they immolated on the sacrificial grass. . . . From that universal sacrifice sprang the *rich* and sâman verses, the metres, and the yajush. From it sprang horses, and all animals with two rows of teeth; kine sprang from it; from it goats and sheep. When (the gods) divided Purusha, into how many parts did they cut him up? what was his mouth? what arms (had he)? what (two objects) are said (to have been) his thighs and feet? The Brâhman was his mouth; the Râjanya was made his arms; the being (called) the Vais'ya, he was his thighs; the S'ûdra sprang from his feet. The moon sprang from his soul, the sun from his eye, Indra and Agni from his mouth, and Vâyu from his breath. From his navel arose the air, from his head the sky, from his feet the earth, from his ear the (four) quarters: in this manner (the gods) formed the worlds.[1]

Hymn to the Unknown God.—A further hymn of great interest is the "Hymn to the Unknown God":—

In the beginning there arose the Golden Child (Hiranyagarbha); as soon as born, he alone was the lord of all that is. He stablished the earth and this heaven:—Who is the God to whom we shall offer sacrifice?

He who gives breath, he who gives strength, whose command all the bright gods revere, whose shadow is immortality, whose shadow is death:—Who is the God to whom we shall offer sacrifice?

---

[1] *Sanskrit Texts*, vol. i. p. 9 f.

> He who through his might became the sole king of the breathing and twinkling world, who governs all this, man and beast:—Who is the God to whom we shall offer sacrifice?
>
> . . . .
>
> He through whom the awful heaven and the earth were made fast, he through whom the ether was stablished, and the firmament; he who measured the air in the sky:—Who is the God to whom we shall offer sacrifice?
>
> He to whom heaven and earth, standing firm by his will, look up, trembling in their mind; he over whom the risen sun shines forth:—Who is the God to whom we shall offer sacrifice?
>
> . . . .
>
> He who by his might looked even over the waters which held power (the germ) and generated the sacrifice (light), he who alone is God above all gods:—Who is the God to whom we shall offer sacrifice?
>
> May he not hurt us, he who is the begetter of the earth, or he, the righteous, who begat the heaven; he who also begat the bright and mighty waters:—Who is the God to whom we shall offer sacrifice?[1]

Gâyatrî.—Finally may be quoted the *Gâyatrî*, the brief formula of supplication on the lips of every Brâhman in India in his daily prayers:—

> On the surpassing splendour of that divine Vivifier let us meditate; and may he enlighten our minds.[2]

Number and Inter-relation of Gods.—The

[1] *S. B. E.*, vol. xxxii. pp. 1, 2.

[2] *Tat Savitur varenyam bhargo devasya dhimahi, dhiyo yo naḥ prac'odayât.* Rig-Veda, iii. 62, 10.

number of gods and goddesses thus invoked, the deified forms and powers of nature in her changing moods, is indefinitely great. They have been variously estimated by native writers as from thirty-three to upwards of a million. To reckon up their names and titles alone would be a serious task; and would afford no safe guide to the real number of the divinities, since each god makes his appearance under different names. They interchange with one another with bewildering Protean rapidity. Now one and now another seems to be supreme, and invests himself with all the powers and dignities of the rest; only to sink again into a second or lower place, as another claimant to sovereign rank comes forward.[1] There is no settled hierarchy, no fixed and acknowledged gradation of authority. All is floating, liable to change. The one god for the moment addressed by the poet looms as it were through the crowd of his companions, apparently so great as to exclude or dwarf all the others; then himself retires into the background. And in this variety, uncertainty, want of definiteness of agreement

[1] Cp. Max Muller, *Sanskrit Literature*, p. 533:—"It would be easy to find, in the numerous hymns of the Veda, passages in which almost every single god is represented as supreme and absolute."

or of outline, it is easy to recognise the features of a young religion, the childhood of a nature worship, with the beauty and elasticity of childhood; one however which has not yet attained to a fixed position or character, or laid down for itself strict lines of development, upon which it shall steadily and consistently proceed.

Monotheism and Polytheism of the Vedic Hymns.—The question may fairly be raised whether the religious beliefs disclosed in these most ancient hymns of the Veda inclined to the side of polytheism or of monotheism. Did the men of Vedic times worship many gods or one alone? Strange as it may seem after the preceding enumeration of the many deities to whom invocations were addressed, the inquiry has been and is seriously made; and with equal conviction and sincerity precisely opposite answers have been returned. It ought to be added however that with wider, more definite knowledge there seems to be some approach now to a common agreement on the subject. On the one hand it has been maintained that the numerous gods of whom the hymns make mention were intended by the poets themselves, and were understood by their hearers or readers to be but adumbrations of the reality, the manifold forms in which the one supreme being, invisible intangible inapprehensible, clothed himself in order that he might declare his name and his nature unto men. Not a little support seemed to be lent to this view by the fact that in some, especially the later hymns, there appeared to be presented such a mysterious personality, most vague and abstract, shadowing himself forth behind and amidst the crowd of lesser deities, undefined and undefinable,—one who passed under many names, as *Hiranyagarbha* the golden embryo, *Svayambhû* the self-existent one, *Vis'vakarman* the maker of all things, and especially *Prajâpati* the lord of creatures. In reply to this it was contended that the idea of one God, alone and supreme, who manifested himself in varying forms, was the creation entirely of a later age, altogether alien to the simplicity and directness of an early faith; that of evidence of such a belief amongst the peoples who lived in India in this the dawn of history, as distinct from mere supposition, there was none; and that there was therefore no ground for rejecting the *primâ facie* and natural conclusion from the mention of many gods, that as a matter of fact the people did actually worship all these separate divinities.

Probably the true answer, and that which is now generally accepted, is that the men of Vedic times were to a certain extent both polytheists and monotheists, with perhaps a larger share of the former creed. The line of distinction between the two forms of belief wavered, inclining now to this and now to that side. Ideas, which appear to us to be contradictory or mutually exclusive, were found to be by no means so in practice. The apparent incompatibility of the worship of the one and the many presented no difficulty to Oriental thought. It is not difficult to understand how a twofold tendency should exist; a tendency which, starting always from a personification of the natural forces around, moved on the one hand towards the simple pantheism of later times, which identified everything with God; and on the other, in the direction of a purer loftier creed, which with deeper more spiritual reflection and insight represented to itself all these external and visible things as but manifestations of the one supreme unknowable Lord.[1] The mass of the people, as in India to-day, were pure pagans, polytheists, nature worshippers. The elect souls,

[1] Cp. *e.g. Brihadâranyaka-Upanishad*, i. 4, 6:—"When they say, 'Sacrifice to this or sacrifice to that god,' each god is but his manifestation, for he is all gods." Of this latter tendency the philosophy and theology of the Upanishads is the outcome and logical conclusion.

amongst the poets and elsewhere, questioned as to the origin of these powers of nature, the birth and apparition of this crowd of gods, if gods they were, endeavoured to peer through the infinite mists, and to solve the great problem, Whence come we and the world in which we live? The germs of almost all the later developments of Indian speculation are to be found in the Veda; among the rest, that which goes back in vague and ever-increasing abstraction, through ranks upon ranks of divinities, until it ends in blankness and mystery, the great Unknown.

Henotheism.—This also perhaps may be said, that the poet who invested with all the attributes of supreme dignity and power the god whom at the moment he was addressing, and expressly subordinated all others to him, was virtually and for the time being a monotheist, although the object of his monotheistic worship might and in fact did vary. Such an attitude of mind has been aptly termed *henotheistic.* This is the better, more spiritual side of the Vedic religion. And upon this aspect of the faith that finds expression in these hymns it is worth while to lay stress, yet not to the exclusion of the other,—upon the element of simplicity, the spark of the divine; lest it should be altogether lost sight of in what appears to be the merest folly of a riotous polytheism. The pure, the noble, the elevated in these religious beliefs and aspirations will be found after all to be but the small wheat-grain well-nigh lost in the heap of the chaff. The grain does not lie upon the surface, or present itself unsought. But the carefully conducted search will always repay the seeker, and prove that even in these far-off ages men persistently and honestly reached out their hands unto the truth.

Ritual.—Of the ritual or ceremonial observance of the Vedic hymns not much need or perhaps can be said. Minutely elaborate and carefully guarded in later times, the worship was probably simple enough in form in the earliest ages. The offerings made to the gods chiefly consisted of melted butter, curds, rice, cakes, etc., with the Soma juice mingled with milk poured out as a libation morning, noon, and evening. These were consumed in the fire, which was conceived as bearing them to heaven. Animal sacrifices also were presented, buffaloes, cows, rams, or goats, but especially the horse. The *As'vamedha*, or sacrifice of a hundred horses, was the most powerful means of approaching the gods; and by it rightly performed the sacrificer became the equal of Indra himself, the ruler of the heavens. Some writers also have believed that they found traces of the practice of human sacrifice in the

Veda. The inference however is a very precarious one, drawn from hints and descriptions which may be no more than the play of a poetic fancy, never intended to be literally understood. Upon these offerings the gods are represented as eagerly feeding, Indra especially delighting himself in the Soma drink; and by them they are strengthened for their daily labours in resisting the attacks of the demons.

Prayer: Brahman.—Of pre-eminent importance moreover was the invocation or prayer, with which every offering was accompanied. In the uttered word there lay a secret spell or energy, which gave to the act of worship its efficacy, and without which the sacrifice was incomplete and valueless. Hence *Vâc'*, sacred speech, is personified in the Veda, and she is represented as the wife of Prajâpati. By the power of *Vâc'* the sacrificer obtained the benefits he desired, not excepting the destruction of his foes. In the later literature *Vâc'* is identified with *Sarasvatî*, the goddess of learning. This subtle, almost magical energy subsisting in the formula employed or the mantra spoken was termed *brahman*, a word often used in the Veda to signify prayer, hymn, or even spell; and which has had a long and singular history. Derived from a root *vrih* or *brih*, meaning to grow, increase, it indicates properly the religious feeling of reverence or devotion, as growing and developing within the soul, and then the outward expression of this devotion in prayer or hymn of praise. This is the explanation of the term given by Sâyana, the great native commentator on the Veda. The word is then employed to denote a sacred text or mantra used as an adjuration for dispelling evil influences, or a formula for securing good. Especially is it used for the sacred syllable Om, of which Manu writes, "The monosyllable (Om) is the highest Brahman."[1] It is then further extended to signify in general the inspired word, the sacred text, the Veda itself. From this meaning of the sacred text it passed to its contents, religious knowledge or theology, especially the higher theoretical or speculative wisdom as opposed to the lower and practical, the merely external life of works of the unenlightened lay worshipper or the mendicant, which at its best consisted only in formal observances, or in self-mortification and austerities. And finally, in its loftiest most abstract signification, that with which we are most familiar, the word is used to denote the great object of religious knowledge, Brahma, the self-existent supreme being, from whom all souls

[1] Manu, ii. 83.

come and to whom all souls return. Nor does this brief outline by any means exhaust all the ideas conveyed by the term, or trace to their issue the various ramifications connected with it. In truth the conception of prayer as a kind of magical invocation, possessing magical power, is one of the most ancient and highly elaborated in Vedic literature.

Sacrifice.—The sacrifice thus offered and accompanied was primarily at least regarded as of the nature of a ransom, or a price paid for an expected benefit. The sacrificer presented something to the gods in order to obtain from them in return a gift, the fulfilment of his wish. This is sometimes expressed plainly and without disguise, as in the invocation to Indra, "Give to me, and I will give to thee; bring to me, and I will bring to thee,"[1] or in more forcible if coarser fashion, "Here is butter, give us cows." Further, this act of sacrifice was also in a loftier and more spiritual sense of a highly mysterious character, with an inherent virtue so great and indispensable that on the continuance and right performance of sacrifice depended the whole course of nature. Were the offerings to cease, the rain would not fall, the sun shine, or the crops grow. Even the gods were begotten of

[1] Cp. esp. Barth. p. 35 f. and note 1.

sacrifice, and derived all their strength from the food and gifts provided by their worshippers. They are themselves represented as offering sacrifice; although it is not said to whom. By the power of sacrifice they in the beginning rescued the world from chaos, and by the same power prevent it from falling back into confusion. The dismemberment of the primæval man Purusha was the first act of sacrifice.[1] Sometimes also in an excess of refinement, since the gods themselves are thus dependent on sacrifice, it is concluded that sacrifice must have existed antecedent even to the gods. And the climax of paradox and extravagance seems to be reached when the Supreme, the Self-Existent One, is represented as sacrificing himself in order to create. Thus the idea of sacrifice, simple enough in its origin, became exceedingly complex, and gave rise to a vast train of ritual and symbolical observance, of myths and types and legends.

Ethics of the Veda.—On the ethical and moral practice of Vedic times no definite or altogether precise evidence is available. Mere ritual and sacrifice occupied the attention of the authors of the Hymns, and but little information is con-

[1] Muir, *Sanskrit Texts*, i. p. 9 f.; *supra*, p. 53 f.

veyed by them on the subject of their duties and relations to God in moral behaviour and life, or on the obligations they acknowledged towards their fellow-men. So large a portion of their writings is taken up with the externals of religion,—it would seem as though the external and pressing circumstances of their physical life so entirely filled their thoughts,—that little time or space was left for ethical rule or principle. And the few details that can be learnt are rather matter of inference than actual statement of fact. By some scholars a very high tone of morality has been claimed for these early settlers by the Indus and on the plains of the Panjâb. Positive evidence however is scanty. It is noticeable that the Hymns acknowledge no evil divinities. All if not actively good are at least neutral. They speak indeed of demons, whose powers are exercised for evil and malicious ends; but as yet these are not gods. It seems fair therefore to conclude that on the whole, as would naturally be expected to be the case, the moral character of the worshipper is reflected in the moral character of the deities he worshipped, the creations of his own fancy.

The Hymns however declare with much reiteration the obligations of service under which men lie to the gods, and the reality and closeness of the ties by which they are bound to this service. A sacrifice offered without sincerity or purity of heart will not be acceptable. Apart from *s'raddhâ*, faith, all gifts and prayers are unavailing. It is on the duty of man to man in the relations of ordinary life that few and scanty conclusions can be drawn. In one passage at least kindness towards the suffering and needy is enjoined; elsewhere witchcraft and idolatry are denounced, and men are exhorted to live in harmony one with another. On the other hand there are not wanting traces of a darker faith and of usages prevalent always and such as we should expect to find amongst a primitive nature-loving people,—habits of demon worship, sorcery, incantations, with all the licentiousness impurity and crime which are wont to accompany savage ignorance and credulity. Such practices are in general quietly ignored or judiciously kept in the background by the Vedic poets, the advocates of a more refined and elevating cult. Doubtless there were good and evil amongst the early settlers in India, noble and ignoble souls. The loftier, more ethereal tendency has found expression in words and songs that have lived; the baser and grovelling is glossed over, perishes, and as far as the literature is concerned is largely forgotten.[1] The broad conclusion therefore is that in the hymns of the Rig-Veda ritual is the chief thing. And the great end and aim of man as here presented is the worship of the gods in the appointed way of sacrifice and prayer.

Eschatology.—The early poets of the Veda therefore reflected much about the beginnings of all things, the constitution and government of the universe. They endeavoured to unlock the secrets of an eternal past, and framed theories to account for the origin of the world and of the gods themselves. But with regard to the future and a possible life to come very little is said. There is no consistent or reasoned eschatology in the Vedic hymns. Often as the writers have asked themselves and tried to answer the question, Whence; the question which fills so large a place in the later speculations and literature, Whither, appears but little if at all to have occupied their attention. Chiefly in the legends concerning Yama, the god of death, there is contained what scanty information is available with regard to Vedic beliefs concerning a future existence. These legends moreover belong almost entirely to the last book and the

[1] The Atharva-Veda is the chief exception,—the *vade-mecum* of the spell-workers and the mystery men.

latest period of the age of the Hymns. While therefore it must be remembered that the chronology of the Vedic writings is admittedly obscure, and the argument from silence accordingly is here more than usually unsafe; yet unless the inferences as to date that are drawn from indications of language, subject-matter, and the pre-supposed conditions of existence are entirely misleading, the earliest strata of the literature refuse wholly, or almost wholly, to bear testimony on the subject of a life after death.

THE BRÂHMANAS

DEFINITION and Date.—From the consideration of the Hymns of the Veda it is natural to pass to the *Brâhmanas*, those portions of the Vedic writings which are devoted to the explanation of the sacrifices and ceremonies, and to the laying down rules for ritual observance. They further occupy themselves with mystical and philosophical expositions, and record strange legends and traditions, which reappear with new details exaggerated and distorted in the later literature. To clearly define the subject-matter of the *Brâhmanas* was a difficulty to the ancient Indian commentators themselves. The title in itself denotes merely that they are appropriate to, or the possession of the Brâhmans. In part they are hardly to be distinguished from the earlier *mantra*; and at the other extreme, they shade off into the later *Âranyakas*, which are religious hand-books for the use of or composed by devotees in the forest, and into the philosophical

Upanishads.[1] Their date also, and order of succession, it is not easy to determine. That they are subsequent to the Hymns is proved by the constant use they make of these, and by the fact that they apply themselves to the explanation of the mantras.[2] Some of the oldest are assigned to the seventh or eighth century B.C.; others, and probably the majority, are consider-

[1] Various definitions are suggested by Sâyana, who is quoted by Max Müller, *Sanskrit Literature*, p. 342 ff.:—"The only means by which Mantras can be distinguished from Brâhmanas lies in their general sacrificial appellation, which comprehends the most different things under the one common name of Mantras. . . . Knowing, however, that the Veda consists only of two parts, we may say that whatever does not come under the name of Mantra is Brâhmana, whether it contain reasons, explanations, censures, recommendations, doubts, commandments, relations, old stories, or particular determinations. Not one of these subjects belongs to the Brâhmanas exclusively, but they occur more or less frequently in the Mantras also, and could therefore not be used as definitions of the Brâhmanas." This is not very satisfactory. Professor Tiele writes of them:—"The Brâhmanas contain here and there occasional elevated thoughts, and not a few antique traditions of the highest importance, but they are in other respects marked by narrow formalism, childish mysticism, and superstitious talk about all kinds of trifles, such as may be expected where a pedantic and power-loving priesthood is invested with unlimited spiritual authority." *Outlines of the History of Religion*, p. 123.

[2] See Muir, *Sanskrit Texts*, i. p. 3, and the commentator there cited:—"Although the Veda is formed both of Mantra and Brâhmana, yet as the Brâhmana consists of an explanation of the Mantras, it is the latter which were at first recorded."

ably later. The period 600–800 B.C. may be provisionally and generally accepted as the Brâhmana era of Sanskrit literature;[1] but almost certainly these limits are too narrow. In particular the composition of works in the spirit of the Brâhmanas was carried on at a much less remote age. Details however are uncertain, authorities differ, and a relative not an absolute dating is often all that is attainable.

Language of the Brâhmanas: Relation to the Hymns: Contents.—These works are written in prose, in a language somewhat less archaic than that of the Hymns or the Mantras. Their relation to these has often been compared to that of the Talmud to the canonical books of the Old Testament, or the Muhammadan Sunnat to the Qurân. The illustration must not be pressed; inasmuch as the Brâhmanas are equally S'ruti, revealed truth, and are acknowledged to stand on the same level of inspiration and authority with the Hymns themselves. Each Samhitâ, or collection of Hymns, has one or more Brâhmanas attached to it, devoted especially to the exposition of the ceremonial, and the instruction of the priests to whose school or cult it belongs. Thus the Rig-Veda has the *Aitareya* and the *Kaushîtaki* Brâhmanas. With

[1] *Supra*, p. 35.

the Black Yajur-Veda is associated the *Taittirîya* Brâhmana, and with the White the *S'atapatha* Brâhmana, the last being the most interesting and important of the Brâhmanas for the early ritual and practice of the Vedic priests. The Sâma-Veda has eight Brâhmanas, of which the best known are perhaps the *Tândya* and the *Shadvims'a*, the latter of comparatively modern date. And the Atharva-Veda has the *Gopatha* Brâhmana.[1] As an illustration may be quoted the Hindu legend of the Flood, contained in its earliest form in the S'atapatha Brâhmana, i. 8, 1, 1 :—

In the morning they brought to Manu water for washing, as men are in the habit of bringing it to wash with the hands. As he was thus washing a fish came into his hands (which spake to him), "Preserve me; I shall save thee." (Manu enquired), "From what wilt thou save me?" (The fish replied), "A flood shall sweep away all these creatures; from it I will rescue thee." (Manu asked), "How (shall) thy preservation (be effected)?" The fish said: "So long as we are small, we are in great peril, for fish devours fish; thou shalt preserve me first in a jar. When I grow too large for the jar, then thou shalt dig a trench, and preserve me in that. When I grow too large for the trench, then thou shalt carry me away to the ocean. I shall then be beyond the reach of danger." Straightway he became a large fish; for he waxes to the utmost. (He said), "Now in such and such a year, then the flood will

---

[1] Complete lists are given in Barth, p. 2 ff. and notes; Max Müller, *Sanskr. Liter.*, p. 345 ff.; and elsewhere.

come; thou shalt therefore construct a ship, and resort to me; thou shalt embark in the ship when the flood rises, and I shall deliver thee from it." Having thus preserved the fish, Manu carried him away to the sea. Then in the same year that the fish had enjoined, he constructed a ship and resorted to him. When the flood rose, Manu embarked in the ship. The fish swam towards him. He fastened the cable of the ship to the fish's horn. By this means he passed over this northern mountain.[1] The fish said, "I have delivered thee; fasten the ship to a tree. But lest the water should cut thee off whilst thou art on the mountain, as much as the water subsides, so much shalt thou descend after it." He accordingly descended after it as much (as it subsided). Wherefore also this, namely, "Manu's descent," is (the name) of the northern mountain. Now the flood had swept away all these creatures; so Manu alone was left here. Desirous of offspring, he lived worshipping and toiling in arduous religious rites. Among these he also sacrificed with the *pâka*[2] offering. He cast clarified butter, thickened milk, whey and curds, as an oblation into the waters. Thence in a year a woman was produced. . . . With her he lived worshipping and toiling in arduous religious rites, desirous of offspring. With her he begat this offspring, which is this offspring of Manu.[3]

A noteworthy example of speculation of another kind is found in the Aitareya Brâhmana, iii. 44:—

The sun never sets nor rises. When people think to themselves the sun is setting, he only changes about after reaching

---

[1] *I.e.*, the Himâlayas.

[2] Defined as a simple or domestic sacrifice; the precise nature of which is uncertain.

[3] Muir, *Sansk. Texts*, vol. i. p. 182 ff.; cp. Max Muller, *Sansk. Lit.*, p. 425 ff.

the end of the day, and makes night below and day to what is on the other side. Then when people think he rises in the morning, he only shifts himself about after reaching the end of the night, and makes day below and night to what is on the other side. In fact, he never does set at all. Whoever knows this that the sun never sets, enjoys union and sameness of nature with him and abides in the same sphere.[1]

Doctrine.—While however there is no precise system of theology or clearly marked philosophy in the Brâhmanas, there is a real if slight advance in religious thought. That this took place under the guidance of the priests, and was in the first instance intended to further priestly designs and assumptions, may be regarded as certain. The doctrine of a future life has become more definitely an article of faith, and it is more plainly taught that in this next life the good are rewarded, and the wicked punished according to their deeds on earth. But the nature of the reward or punishment is not set forth in any very explicit terms. It is left to a future generation to elaborate and expound the great Hindu doctrine of the perpetual transmigration of souls, the most distinctive feature of Indian speculation concerning a life to come; the foreshadowings of which only are found in the Brâhmanas.

Characteristics of Religion of the Brâhmanas.—

[1] Sir Monier Williams, *Indian Wisdom*, p. 35.

Thus in general the religion of the Brâhmanas and of this later period of the Vedic literature has been found to be a religion of externals, of punctilious and elaborate ritual. The changes that have taken place since the age of the Hymns do but illustrate and accentuate this essential character. Some of these changes have been already noticed. New deities are recognised, or come into prominence; of whom the chief is *Prajâpati*, the lord of creatures, now the acknowledged head of the Hindu pantheon. His very name however and nature emphasize the advance in religious thought that has been made. No longer a god of the storm or the light, he is abstracted from all natural phenomena, and is placed above and behind them,—a mental conception and an effort of reason, rather than a personification of force. Many also of the older divinities of the Hymns suffer eclipse, and are seldom if ever mentioned by name. On the other hand for the first time there is distinguished a *triad* of gods, a group of three, Agni Vâyu and Sûrya, the fire the air and the sun, regarded as comprehending all the forces and attributes of nature;[1] an attempt as it were to lift the conception of the gods into a higher, a

[1] Contrast the *local* triads of Babylonia, *Studies in Comparative Religion*, pp. 100 f., 108 f.

more unearthly sphere, by uniting together the attributes and functions of each. These new deities, with new or more comprehensive powers and rights, required a new or at least more highly cultivated ceremonial for their worship. And in the Brâhmanas were elaborately conceived and set forth the directions for this worship, which later were again crystallized into a number of codes and rules and mnemonic formulæ, called *sûtras*, that in substance are widely observed in India at the present day. Moral teaching and precepts, as has been seen, were not entirely absent. But the outward organisation, the mere ritual of sacrifice, held the first place.

Rise of Brâhmanical Priesthood.—In proportion then to the complexity of the outward and obligatory ceremonial, this art of practical religion, would be the necessity for a trained and instructed class, who should be able to carry it out discreetly and accurately, with minute and faultless attention to detail. As the letter usurped authority over the spirit, and the due observance of the rites of religion became of more importance than the moral character and life of the worshipper, there arose an order of men whose business it was to master the letter of the religious law, and to be able for themselves and for others efficiently and faultlessly to conduct its ritual and sacrifice. It will readily be seen how such a class would tend to advance into the possession of exclusive rights and privileges. In their hands was the practical control not only of the destiny of a man after death, but also of his well-being in the present life. They wielded all the terrors of divine threatened vengeance for the non-fulfilment of religious obligations. An unlearned and ignorant man could not so sacrifice as to be well-pleasing to heaven. If he did not sacrifice, or if he erred in his sacrifice, the gods would assuredly visit him with pains and penalties, both temporal and eternal. He must therefore employ a member of the learned enlightened class to perform the sacrifice in his name and stead. There is abundant evidence to prove that it was by these or similar means that the great caste of the Brâhmans gained in India its unique ascendency and sacred inviolable character. Originally a hereditary priesthood, set apart for the study of the sacred books and the due performance of religious rites and ceremonies, the members of this caste used the spiritual influence and authority thus placed in their hands as a stepping-stone to temporal dignity and power. The parallel example in the West at once suggests itself of the growth of the Papal authority in Europe during the Middle Ages. In India also the struggle lasted in all probability for several hundred years. But the advantage which the possession of the key of sacred knowledge gave in each case prevailed. It was this possession which, aided by a long and dogged persistence and a jealous closing of the door against any outside of their own narrow circle, enabled the Brâhmans to rivet fast the fetters of caste assumption and tyranny upon the necks of the subject races of India.

Schools of Learning: Sûtras.—The same necessity for a trained and educated priesthood gave rise to the Brâhmanical schools of learning. A teacher famed for his piety and knowledge attracted to himself disciples often from great distances, who sat at his feet and received from him oral instruction in the Vedas, their meaning and observances. In these schools appear to have been formed the collections of sacred writings, the *S'âkhâs* or recensions of the Veda, which have been more or less completely preserved, and afterwards the commentaries and works on criticism and grammar, philosophy, science and art.[1] From them also emanated in later times

[1] The schools of the prophets held a similar position in the national life of Israel, except in so far as the actual carrying

the manuals of ritual observances, the *Sûtras*, or collections of rules for the due performance of ceremonial either public or private. Soon it became legally impossible for any but a Brâhman to offer sacrifice, or to celebrate any religious rite. This was not however the case in the earliest times. And on the strict and accurate fulfilment of the formalities of the ritual, and on the special qualification of the priest, much more stress was laid than on the moral character of the worshipper. Of the latter only two things seem to have been in general required, namely freedom from any legal impurity, and a full persuasion of the efficacy of the rite. The fees exacted on these occasions by the officiating Brâhmans have gone far to bring about the general state of indebtedness and poverty among the lower classes of the Indian peoples. The *Sûtras* are arranged according as they have to do with the more elaborate public ceremonial, animal sacrifices and the like, or the simpler private observances of every individual and household. The former are almost entirely, if not entirely obsolete in India at the present

out of the detail of the ritual was concerned; and may be quoted as a perhaps nearer parallel than is often supposed. They were at least centres of religious and literary culture in the land.

day; and have been so for a long time past. The latter, including the ordinary daily acts of worship, special ceremonies on anniversaries and feast-days, rites of initiation and purification at births marriages and deaths, reiterated and multiplied on every conceivable occasion, make up now the larger part of the routine of daily life to the orthodox Brâhman from the Himâlayas to Cape Comorin.

THE UPANISHADS

CHARACTER and Importance.—That part of the Vedic literature which is included under the name of Upanishad is in many respects the most interesting and important part. There are many treatises which by their form and contents lay claim to the title. Of these some are of recent date. But the name is technically and usually confined to the few of acknowledged authority and antiquity. Both chronologically, and in the course of the natural development of thought, these works are later than the mantra and brâhmana portion of the Veda; but from the latter they are not separated by any very definite line. In them is to be found the most subtle and elevated thought and the most refined speculation, mingled with apparently irrational and puerile fancies. They are however comparatively free from the sophistries and grotesque exaggerations to which a later age abandoned itself. And it is by the Upanishads alone that in the ultimate resort native Indian students whether of philosophy or of religion establish their reasonings and justify their opinions. They have therefore been described by a scholar whose knowledge of the Indian faiths has been scarcely surpassed as "practically the only Veda of all thoughtful Hindus in the present day."[1] It is from them that all attempts at religious reform from within have taken their rise in India; and to them all orthodox native reformers have turned, as presenting their religion in its purest fairest form. It is not however easy by means of brief extracts to convey a just impression of the general doctrine and teaching of these works. Their style is diffuse, full of returns and repetitions, and does not readily lend itself to comprehensive summary. Complete renderings moreover of all the principal Upanishads into English are easily accessible. The best and most exact is that by Professor Max Müller, in vols. i. and xv. of the *Sacred Books of the East*, published at Oxford. In the place therefore of lengthy quotations, which might only mislead or set in false proportion, it will be of greater advantage to attempt to gain in the first instance some conception of what the Upanishads really

[1] Sir Monier Williams, *Indian Wisdom*, p. 35 ; cp. the opinion of Râmmohun Roy, the great Indian Reformer, as given by Max Müller, *S. B. E.*, vol. i. p. lxii. ff.

are; and secondly to endeavour to present in as connected and consistent a form as possible a brief account of their religious ideas and teaching as lying at the basis of all later developments of Hindu thought and practice.

Meaning of the Term.—As concerns the word itself, the term *Upanishad* is fancifully derived by native grammarians from a root *sad,* to perish. Thus through the knowledge conveyed in these works ignorance and passion in the soul is destroyed by the revelation of the supreme being and source of all. The true explanation appears to be that the word has its origin in a root *sad*, meaning to sit down, with the prefixed prepositions *upa* and *ni*; and therefore signifies properly the sitting down at the feet of a teacher to hear his words.[1] In ordinary usage however the term is not employed in this its literal meaning; but by a natural association of thought it comes to denote the mystical or secret doctrine received at the lips of a teacher, or through the study of sacred books. Thus regarded, the term

[1] Cp. Max Müller, *Anc. Sanskr. Lit.*, p. 319:—"There can be little doubt that Upanishad meant originally the act of sitting down near a teacher, of submissively listening to him; and it is easy to trace the steps by which it came to mean implicit faith, and at last truth or divine revelation."

would seem to be equally applicable to the whole of the Veda. In practice however, and in all the extant literature, it is confined to the highest and most abstract teaching or knowledge, the involved and elaborate doctrines and speculations, which form the third part of S'ruti or sacred revelation. It is therefore often equivalent to another term, celebrated in Hindu philosophy, *jnânakânda*, the method or department of knowledge, the path that leads to emancipation and blessedness by the way of spiritual insight and intelligence, which only the truly wise can tread. Thus *Upanishad* is the philosophical and speculative portion of the Veda, as distinguished from the *karmakânda*, which is the practical method of works, intended for and suited to the multitude, who need for their religion the tangible support of rites and ceremonies, and cannot rise to the purely intellectual stand-point of the reasoner and sage. In the usage therefore of the Vedic writings themselves the word *Upanishad* may be said to have four distinct significations as follows [1] :—

[1] It does not follow that the chronological order of development of the various meanings was as stated above. In all probability the speculative philosophy was at first entirely independent, and was only later fitted to the ritual.

(1) Mystical exposition of ceremony and ritual.

(2) Knowledge received through such exposition.

(3) Rules of living prescribed for those who have attained to this knowledge.

(4) A treatise or book in which this knowledge is contained.

Age of the Upanishads, and Relation to the Brâhmanas.—These treatises are attached to the Brâhmanas, and extend and develop their thought and teaching in the direction of free speculation. They also themselves sometimes form part of larger works called *âranyakas,* writings designed for use in the seclusion of the forest, or perhaps so named because composed there by men who had retired from the world for the sake of meditation and prayer. The subject-matter of the *âranyakas* is not however different from that of the *upanishads.* In the latter are often quoted or incorporated verses from the hymns, which are then made the texts for philosophical or legendary expositions. The number of works that bear the character of Upanishads has been estimated, probably erroneously, as high as 250.[1]

[1] See Barth, p. 65 f., who says "nearly 250"; where also a list is given of the principal Upanishads and litera-

But it certainly exceeds the half of this total, and to the list new names are even now occasionally added, as our knowledge extends. Much uncertainty still hangs over the date and chronological order of these writings. The most ancient are prior to the rise of Buddhism in the sixth century B.C.; or if not prior in their present form at least embody an earlier tradition. The latest originated in comparatively recent times. The period during which these speculations struck deepest root and flourished most widely may perhaps be placed with Professor Max Müller from the sixth to the eighth century before Christ. They contain, however, elements which appear to lay just claim to a greater antiquity, and they have all been modified and ruthlessly interpolated by the hands of more modern revisers. The diction is less archaic than that of the

ture quoted. Cp. Max Müller, *Sanskr. Lit.*, pp. 325 ff.; and *S. B. E.*, vol. i. p. lxviii. f., vol. xv. p. xi. f. The Upanishads translated in these two volumes are the eleven referred to by S'ankara, and which are supposed to be the oldest, namely the C'hândogya, Kena, Aitareya, Kaushîtaki, Îs'â or Vâjasaneyi, Katha, Mundaka, Taittirîya, Brihadâranyaka, S'vetâs'vatara, and Pras'na. They have often been edited in the original, for example in the Bombay Sanskrit Series, or later in a small and convenient edition at Benares in 1889. The texts published at Poona, in the Ânandâs'rama Series, are said to be the latest and most accurate.

mantras or hymns, approximating to the classical Sanskrit; but employs words and grammatical forms and construction foreign to the style of the later language. The most ancient and most modern are written in prose; a few lying in point of date between these are in verse; and all usually adopt the form of dialogue.

Contents and Doctrine.—The instructed disciple of the Upanishads accordingly pursues this path of knowledge, *jnânakânda*; and endeavours to apprehend and make his own the great mystical truth there expounded, to know which will secure for him deliverance from the bondage of nature and ignorance, and bring him into union with the one source of all life. To set forth this truth in its simplest form is comparatively easy, however difficult may be its complete and logical apprehension. All individual souls are only parts, reflections as it were of the great universal Soul. He therefore who knows this is truly wise. There is but one being in the universe, who comprehends all and is himself all, one only without a second, *ekam evâdvitîyam*, he whom men call Brahma, the existent one, *sat*, τὸ ὄν. To him or it,—for Brahma in this sense is neuter,—all men and things owe their being. Each individual exists only by virtue of a life derived from Brahma, and is in reality a portion of his essence. As it is briefly and antithetically expressed, *Âtmânam âtmanâ pas'ya*, Discern the Self by the self; a saying which has been erroneously compared with the Greek *Γνῶθι σεαυτόν*, but which in reality has its root in entirely different ideas. It is rather to be interpreted or paraphrased, Learn to recognise in thyself an image, a reflection of the one great Self, which is Brahma. This is the central conception of the Upanishads; and to quote all the passages which set it forth and illustrate it from different points of view would be to quote the larger portion of their text. A few examples will be sufficient to make clear at once the real profundity of the thought of these ancient writers, and the peculiarity of their mode of expression, so diverse from that of European philosophers. The whole however, diffuse and full of repetitions as it may appear to be, well deserves and will repay careful study. The following is from the *C'hândogya-Upanishad*, iii. 14[1]:—

[1] The translations are those of Professor Max Müller in the volumes referred to above. The slight alterations made in one or two instances have been in the hope of conveying more simply the meaning without sacrifice of fidelity. They do not diminish my obligation to the translator.

All this is Brahma. Let a man meditate on that (visible world) as beginning, ending, and breathing in it.

. . . .

The intelligent, whose body is spirit, whose form is light, whose thoughts are true, whose nature is like ether, from whom all works, all desires, all sweet odours and tastes proceed; he who embraces all this, who never speaks, and is never surprised,

He is my self within the heart, smaller than a corn of rice, smaller than a corn of barley, smaller than a mustard seed, smaller than a canary seed or the kernel of a canary seed. He also is my self within the heart, greater than the earth, greater than the sky, greater than heaven, greater than all these worlds.

He from whom all works, all desires, all sweet odours and tastes proceed, who embraces all this, who never speaks and who is never surprised, he, my self within the heart, is that Brahma. When I shall have departed from hence, I shall obtain him (that Self). He who has this faith has no doubt.

. . . .

There is one ruler, the Self within all things, who makes the one form manifold. The wise who perceive him within their Self, to them belongs eternal happiness, not to others.

There is one eternal thinker, thinking non-eternal thoughts, who though one fulfils the desires of many. The wise who perceive him within their Self, to them belongs eternal peace, not to others.[1]

. . . .

In the beginning Brahma was all this. He was one and infinite; infinite in the east, infinite in the south, infinite in the west, infinite in the north, above and below and everywhere infinite. East and the other regions do not exist for him, nor across, nor below, nor above. The Highest Self is not to be fixed, he is unlimited, unborn, not to be reasoned about, not

---

[1] *Katha-Up.*, ii. 5. 12, 13.

to be conceived. He is like the ether (everywhere), and at the destruction of the universe he alone is awake.[1]

In the beginning this was Self alone, in the shape of a person (purusha). He looking round saw nothing but his Self. He first said, "This is I"; therefore he became I by name.[2]

Non-duality, the unity of principle and life throughout the whole universe, is taught in the following passages, and in many others:—

"In the beginning, my good sir, there was that only which is (τὸ ὄν), one only without a second. Others say, in the beginning there was that only which is not (τὸ μὴ ὄν), one only without a second; and from that which is not that which is was born."

"But how indeed, my good sir, could this be?" he said. "How from that which is not could that which is be born? That only which is, my good sir, this was in the beginning, one only without a second."[3]

He is the one God, hidden in all beings, all-pervading, the self within all beings, watching over all works, dwelling in all beings, the witness, the perceiver, the only one, free from qualities.

He is the one ruler of many who (seem to act, but really) do not act; he makes the one seed manifold. The wise who perceive him within their self, to them belongs eternal happiness, not to others.

He is the eternal among eternals, the thinker among thinkers, who though one fulfils the desires of many. He who has known that cause which is to be apprehended by Sânkhya (philosophy) and Yoga (religious discipline), he is freed from all fetters.[4]

---

[1] *Maitrâyana-Brâhmana-Up.*, vi. 17.

[2] *Brihadâranyaka-Up.*, i. 4. 1. Cp. *ib.* 10; *Katha-Up.*, i. 2. 20.

[3] *C'hând.-Up.*, vi. 2. 1, 2. [4] *S'vetâs'vatara-Up.*, vi. 11–13.

When there is as it were duality, then one sees the other, one smells the other, one tastes the other, one salutes the other, one hears the other, one perceives the other, one touches the other, one knows the other; but when the Self only is all this, how should he see another, how should he smell another, how should he taste another, how should he salute another, how should he hear another, how should he touch another, how should he know another? How should he know Him by whom he knows all this? That Self is to be described by No, no! He is incomprehensible, for he cannot be comprehended; he is imperishable, for he cannot perish; he is unattached, for he does not attach himself; unfettered, he does not suffer, he does not fail. How, O beloved, should he know the Knower? Thus, O Maitreyî, thou hast been instructed. Thus far goes immortality.[1]

Pantheism of the Upanishads.—The thought and teaching therefore of these books is in its essence pantheistic. If the soul of every living being is identical with God, is really but a part of Him, then God is in everything and everything is God. It must not however be supposed that the doctrines inculcated here are always consistent with themselves, or form in any sense a homogeneous whole. The different periods and perhaps localities to which they are to be ascribed, no less than the genius of the writers, forbid this. A home is found amongst them for the most diverse and contradictory

[1] *Brih.-Up.*, iv. 5. 15: cp. *Kath.-Up.*, quoted above, p. 90; *Aitareya-Âranyaka*, iii. 4. 1. 1; *Brih.-Up.*, iii. 9. 26; iv. 2. 4, 4. 22.

speculations. All the great and opposing systems of Indian philosophy, of which it is usual to enumerate six in particular, trace their parentage to the Upanishads; and the lines of thought on which they will develop are here already indicated, if not distinguished or separately pursued. The same therefore is true of these works, which is true more or less of all Oriental thinking, that there is to be found in them rather a confused eclecticism, various trains of fancy and reasoning interlacing with one another and often at apparently cross purposes, than a clear and consistent scheme of philosophy with definite beginning and middle and end.

Nevertheless the principle here laid down may be considered to be the true centre of upanishad philosophy, as far as it can be said to have a centre. This conception predominates over all, and often appears to comprehend all. Hindu thought, whether ancient or modern, rests on a foundation of pantheism, although into the superstructure much is built that would seem to have no place there. Starting from the endeavour to interpret to themselves God and the universe, the authors of the Upanishads arrived at a complete identification of these two. The principle at work everywhere and present in all, the *ātman* or self, they found in man in the breath, *prâna*; in nature it was expounded to be the air, or ether. And these two are not different but essentially one and the same.[1] An alternative or physical explanation of the *âtman* was offered in the conception of a small being, a *purusha*, of the size of a thumb, seated within the heart of man, and thence controlling his entire nature and life. A similar *purusha* dwells within, and rules the sun, moon, stars, etc. During the life of the man the *purusha* looks forth through his eye, and may there be seen in the pupil. At his death it escapes through a small hole at the top of the skull, and rejoins or is re-absorbed into the great Universal Soul. Hints or pre-intimations of this curious doctrine of the *purusha* are found in the Rig-Veda itself. The doctrine is often referred to in the Upanishads; and in accordance with the general teaching of these books, it is explained that the human *purusha* or *âtman* and the *purusha* of the sun etc. are in reality identical.

> The person (purusha), of the size of a thumb, stands in the middle of the self, as lord of the past and the future, and thenceforward fears no more. This is that.

---

[1] Brahma is identical with the breath, *Kaushîtaki-Up.*, ii. 1, 2; with the *âkâs'a*, or ether, *C'hând.-Up.*, iii. 12. 7–9. Cp. for the breath the essential element of the body, *Aitar.-Ârany.* iv., *Pras'na-Up.*, ii.

That person, of the size of a thumb, is like a light without smoke, lord of the past and the future, he is the same to-day and to-morrow. This is that.

. . . .

As pure water poured into pure water remains the same, thus, O Gautama, is the self of a thinker who knows.[1]

The person not larger than a thumb, the inner self, is always settled in the heart of men. Let a man draw that Self forth from his body with steadiness, as one draws the pith from a reed. Let him know that Self as the bright, as the immortal; yes, as the bright, as the immortal.[2]

Now the person who is seen in the eye, he is *Ric'*, he is Sâman, Uktha, Yajus, Brahman. The form of that person (in the eye) is the same as the form of the other person (in the sun), the joints of the one (*Ric'* and Sâman) are the joints of the other, the name of the one (ut) is the name of the other.[3]

Now what is the true, that is the Âditya (the sun), the person that dwells in yonder orb, and the person in the right eye. These two rest on each other, the former resting with his rays in the latter, the latter with his prânas (senses) in the former.[4]

Earth fire food and the sun (these are my forms, or forms of Brahman). The person that is seen in the sun, I am he, I am he indeed.

. . . .

The person that is seen in the moon, I am he, I am he indeed.

. . . .

---

1 *Katha-Up.*, ii. 4. 12–15. 2 *Ib.* ii. 6. 17.

3 *C'hând.-Up.*, i. 7. 5. Uktha is explained as a collection of hymns to be recited, the Sâman to be sung, and the Yajus muttered.

4 *Brihad.-Up.*, v. 5. 2.

The person that is seen in the lightning, I am he, I am he indeed.

. . . .

The person that is seen in the eye, that is the Self. This is the immortal, the fearless, this is Brahman.[1]

To this doctrine of the supposed identity of the human soul, of all souls, with the divine, was given the name, famous in Hindu philosophy, of *advaita*, non-dualism.

Mâyâ.—In the teaching thus set forth there was at once seen to be a contradiction both in theory and in experience; to the resolution of which early Hindu philosophy appears to have bent all its energies, but without adequate or satisfactory result. This âtman,—or *jîvâtman*, as it was sometimes called for the sake of distinction from the *paramâtman*, the universal soul,—was both identical with and separate from the one supreme. Its identity with the paramâtman is not absolute or consistently maintained, for it is represented as thinking and willing, and promotes of its own free and enlightened will its return into the bosom of the paramâtman. Yet with almost wearisome reiteration this identity is insisted on, as the most fundamental and all-important truth, to know which is the

[1] *C'hând.-Up.*, iv. 11–15: cp. *ib.* i. 6. 6; viii. 7. 3; *S'vetas'.-Up.*, iii. 12 ff. The same doctrine is found in the *Bhagavad-Gîtâ, passim*; compare *infra*, p. 151.

foundation and essence of all wisdom. Further, by intense meditation, by self-abstraction from all care and all thought, man may gain power over his own âtman, and may thus bring himself into conscious union with the eternal source of all. A release from this fundamental difficulty seems to have been sought in two directions. On the one hand there were those who, though they denied the absolute and real existence of the jîvâtman, yet allowed to it a kind of relative practical existence. And between the human âtman, thus conceived, and the great universal soul they interposed a personal god, *Îs'vara*, ruler of the world but distinct both from it and from the paramâtman, and serving in some sort as intermediary between them. The other and more popular solution invoked the aid of *Mâyâ*, illusion, and thus laid the foundations of or expounded a notable doctrine which played a large part in later Hindu speculation. *Mâyâ* in the mythology is the mother of Death, and is somewhat strangely said to have been from all eternity. Only Brahma however really exists; all else, the universe and the creatures therein are illusory, a shadow and a show. To have learned this truth that everything is unreal is to have become indeed wise. Both these doctrines, foreshadowed or outlined in the

Upanishads, reappear in definite and organised form in the great systems of Indian philosophy.

Ethics of the Upanishads. — Barren theory however or speculation is not all that is to be found in the Upanishads. If it were beyond the general interest of the bearing and growth of human thought, there would be little to invite study. There is however in this literature a large element of earnest religious and practical teaching, of lofty exhortations to morality and devotion, of commendation of self-denial and soberness and truth. Beyond a doubt it is this ethical content that has given to the Upanishads their unique position in the history of religious thought in India, the most widely known and influential of the sacred books of the Hindus. It was Râmmohun Roy, perhaps the greatest and most enlightened of native Indian reformers, who declared that in his judgement a selection from the Upanishads, published and largely circulated, would contribute more than anything else to the moral and religious elevation of his fellow-countrymen. These books with the doctrines derived from them are, if not the only, certainly the main source from which Buddhism has derived those precepts of moral law and conduct which have been so justly commended. A brief notice of this element of ethical teaching may fitly bring to a close the present survey of the Vedic literature proper, as it bears upon the history of religion.

The individual soul finds itself existing in a state of separation from the great Universal Soul, to which it belongs, and from which it has originally come forth. This alienation is the source and cause of all moral evil, as well as of all intellectual darkness and error. The soul of man is entangled in the world of matter, involved in a ceaseless round of changes and re-births, the "samsâra," or circuit of existences, deliverance from which with its necessary attendance of ignorance and misery can only be attained by re-absorption into the Supreme. Evil is traced to ignorance; and ignorance culminates or is summed up in the delusion of the human spirit, which fails to know itself as a portion of the *paramâtman*, the great spirit of the universe. This doctrine of the *samsâra* is here first fully expounded; and it may be said without exaggeration to be the key to all subsequent developments of Hindu philosophy and practice, the fundamental pre-supposition of all Hindu religion. A similar doctrine is found in the Brâhmanas, but with an important difference. In these earlier treatises to be born again in a new body is a punishment for wrong-doing in a former existence. Here it is the natural and inevitable result of action of any kind, good or bad; and all that, theoretically at least, can be achieved by just and righteous dealing is to ensure that the next life shall be in a higher form and under more desirable conditions than the last, a step upwards in the scale of being. If therefore to this theory of *punarbhava*, of the incessant inevitable transmigration of souls, there be joined the teaching that every man's lot in a given state of existence is determined by the sum-total of his deeds in former lives,—the great doctrine of *karma*, of action,—we have the two fundamental articles of the creed of a devout follower of the Upanishads. To escape from this vicious circle, or in other words to cease to be born again and again, is the supreme object of his desire. And this deliverance can only be attained through the cessation of his personal individual existence, the re-absorption of the soul into Brahma.

Yoga.—Hence on their practical and devotional side the Upanishads give themselves up to teaching the way of salvation through *yoga*, or union of the soul with the one absolute being. As long as action continues, of necessity its fruit continues also; and this fruit is re-birth into another state of existence. Abandon all action therefore, and the separate life of the soul will come to an end, it will reach its natural home in an unconscious eternal union with God. Accordingly the morality of these books is rather negative than positive. It has been well termed a "morality of renunciation."[1] Abstinence is the highest good, abstinence from deed, from word, even from thought. And the ideal of a devout life is that of the *sannyásí*, the complete ascetic, who renounces everything, withdraws himself from every occupation, and is absorbed in a meditation that counts itself perfect when the mind can meditate on nothing.[2] Somewhat later in time, and especially in connection with the Yoga system of philosophy, dreams and visions, unusual or ecstatic conditions of mind, were regarded as evidences of this union with the one absolute being, either attained or in course of attainment; and rules were given for the production of such states. The path therefore to

[1] Barth, p. 79.

[2] Cp. *Bhag. Gítá*, ch. vi.:—"A devotee should constantly devote his self to abstraction, remaining in a secret place, alone, with his mind and self restrained, without expectations and without belongings. . . . Thus constantly devoting his self to abstraction, a devotee whose mind is restrained, attains that tranquillity which culminates in final emancipation and assimilation with me (*i.e.* Krishna, the deity). . . . Abandoning without exception all desires . . . one should by slow steps become quiescent, with a firm resolve coupled with courage; and fixing the mind upon the self, should think of nothing." *S. B. E.*, vol. viii². p. 68 ff. It is a curious illustration of the contradictory or apparently

final and complete blessedness lay in the renunciation and avoidance of all action whether of the body or mind. And this blessedness when gained does not seem practically to differ from personal and individual annihilation.

Ethical Precepts.—Formal and adequate illustrations again drawn from the Upanishads are not readily given; examples that is to say of a moral teaching, which is so closely wedded to philosophical theory that it does not easily lend itself to separate statement. The following is from the C'hândogya-Upanishad:—

> There are three branches of the law. Sacrifice, study, and charity are the first.
>
> Austerity the second, and to dwell as a Brahmac'ârin[1] in the house of a tutor, always mortifying the body in the house of a tutor, is the third. All these obtain the worlds of the blessed; but the Brahmasamstha alone (he who is firmly grounded in Brahma) obtains immortality.[2]

---

contradictory theories that find a place in these books that elsewhere in the *Bhagavad Gîtâ* a strenuous and active life is eulogized:—"A man does not attain freedom from action merely by not engaging in action; nor does he attain perfection by mere renunciation. . . . Do you perform prescribed action, for action is better than inaction," etc. "Renunciation and pursuit of action are both instruments of happiness; but of the two, pursuit of action is superior to renunciation of action." *Loc. cit.* pp. 52 ff., 63; cp. *ibid.* pp. 59, 67.

[1] Student of religion, or of the Veda.

[2] *C'hând.-Up.*, ii. 23. 1, 2.

The three-fold descendants of Prajâpati, gods men and Asuras (evil spirits), dwelt as Brahmac'ârins with their father Prajâpati. Having finished their studentship the gods said: "Tell us (something), Sir." He told them the syllable Da. Then he said: "Did you understand?" They said: "We did understand. You told us 'Dâmyata,' Be subdued." "Yes," he said, "you have understood."

Then the men said to him: "Tell us something, Sir." He told them the same syllable Da. Then he said: "Did you understand?" They said: "We did understand. You told us 'Datta,' Give." "Yes," he said, "you have understood."

Then the Asuras said to him: "Tell us something, Sir." He told them the same syllable Da. Then he said: "Did you understand?" They said: "We did understand. You told us 'Dayadham,' Be merciful." "Yes," he said, "you have understood."

The divine voice of thunder repeats the same, Da Da Da, that is, Be subdued, Give, Be merciful. Therefore let that triad be taught, Subduing, Giving, and Mercy.[1]

Religious and Ethical Defects.—To us however the whole appears to present a cheerless and unpromising creed; enjoining stagnation and atrophy of all the faculties of the soul and body, and offering personal extinction as its goal. Not then without reason is his doleful religious faith to a great extent held chargeable for the strongly marked tinge of melancholy that runs through all Hindu life and character. At the same time it ought to be remembered again that theory and practice by no means always or necessarily went hand in hand; that these doctrines

[1] *Brihad.-Up.*, v. 2.

were perhaps largely speculative, and influenced less than we are apt to imagine the lives of those who professed them. Certainly on the testimony of the books themselves, even at so early a period as this, a free-thinking scepticism did not fail to make its voice heard. And its votaries, so far from practising asceticism, appear to have acted consistently up to the old Epicurean maxim, Let us eat and drink, for to-morrow we die.

BRÂHMANISM

VARIETY and Comprehensiveness of Hinduism.—With the Upanishads the survey of the early sacred literature comes to its natural conclusion. In these Vedic writings, beginning with the hymns of the Rig-Veda and advancing to the more modern treatises on philosophy and doctrine, has been preserved with more or less fidelity a record of the primitive beliefs, the mythology, the ritual, and the speculations of the Hindus. They form the original source from which have been developed all the manifold forms of Indian religions and philosophies at the present day. The period of growth has been long, and the results reached are often as widely divergent as it is possible to conceive from the first principles. But the root of the matter is there, however overlaid it may be or contaminated by outside influences. It is however misleading and, except in a very limited sense, incorrect to speak of a Hindu religion, whether as contained in sacred books, or built up upon these as a foundation. There is no

Hindu creed, no defined or definable body of doctrines or practices, accepted by all alike. There is only an assemblage of varying not seldom contradictory beliefs, held with greater or less tenacity, evolved by the aid of active and highly-strung mental capabilities, and profoundly modified by all manner of external movements indigenous and foreign. The history of Hinduism,—to use the term for want of a better,—has been a continuous history of absorption and assimilation, as well as of internal growth and progress. And the contest still being maintained in India between rival creeds is on the part of the native religion of the country carried on by old methods, when Hinduism attempts to repeat on a larger scale the process that has been so successful in the past, to disarm or to destroy by a wide comprehension, and to enrich her pantheon with the adopted gods of her sometime foes.

Brâhmanism.—The name of *Brâhmanism* is usually and conveniently given to this earliest and purest form of Indian religious observance, while the term *Hinduism* is confined to later and modern developments. Brâhmanism, founded on these sacred books and claiming to fulfil their precepts, is the religion of *Brahmâ*, the great creator, or of the *Brâhmans*, the priestly and privileged class, charged with the preservation of doctrine and the maintenance of the rites. A further classification has sometimes been made into the four phases or sub-divisions of Ritualistic, Philosophical, Mythological, and Nomistic Brâhmanism.[1] As an aid to memory such an arrangement may be, and in practice is helpful. But it has of course no justification in the usage of the Hindus themselves. In the case of Eastern beliefs and forms of worship, hard and fast lines of division in a European sense of the term can never be drawn. The different classes shade off imperceptibly into one another, and borrow from one another ideas and technical expressions; they are neither mutually exclusive nor orderly in their chronological development. With this qualification however it may be noted that by ritualistic Brâhmanism is to be understood that phase or aspect of the priestly religion which occupied itself with sacrifices and rites and ceremonies. Philosophical Brâhmanism, neglecting and partly despising external observance, speculated widely and profoundly on all manner of themes, with results formulated chiefly in the Upanishads. Mythological Brâhmanism threw itself into the arms of an exuberant popular mythology, with its legends and fairy-

[1] Monier Williams, *Brâhmanism and Hinduism*, pp. 21 ff.

tales of gods and goddesses and heroes, in which India has ever been peculiarly rich; taking under its protection especially the great epic poems, the *Mahâbhârata* and the *Râmâyana*, and making these as it were its book of books, thus approaching nearest to the every-day creed of an ordinary Hindu at the present time. It may fairly be regarded as open to question, whether such a specialised form of Brâhmanism as this, detached from or in any sense independent of the ritual and philosophy, ever in reality existed. At the most it was only a by-product, co-existent with but of later origin or at least later adoption than the others; and if at all separated from them, then so degenerate as scarcely to have any claim to the title of Brâhmanism. Finally there was Nomistic Brâhmanism, the creed or cult that concerned itself with νόμος or law, and whose text-books were the great *dharmas'âstras*, or law-codes, containing the detailed rules for Brâhmanical practice in ritual and daily life. Of these books the most widely known and reverenced is the Code of Manu; which originally the private code of a sect or tribe of Brâhmans called Mânavas, living probably in a district of the North-West Provinces, has spread and won general acceptance throughout the whole of India.[1]

[1] Cp. *infra*, p. 124 f.

The Brâhman Caste.—*Brâhmanism* then is the general and somewhat indefinite name for the earliest form or forms into which the religious ideas of the Veda and succeeding writings crystallized; of which, both as concerned doctrine and practice, the hereditary caste of the Brâhmans became the sole priests and trustees, and which in turn gave to them unrivalled cohesion and strength, enabling them to triumph over all opponents and to secure for the members of their caste undisputed power and prestige. It was a significant and important advance upon primitive nature worship, and itself became the foundation and strength of the highly elaborated and complex systems of later times. The formal laws of its religious observance were laid down in the Brâhmanas, the ritualistic treatises already considered; its philosophy found expression in the Upanishads; its mythology and legal enactments in epic poems and dharmas'âstras. The historical importance however of the system does not rest exclusively or even mainly upon any of these; but upon its practical consequences in the establishment of a caste domination of unparalleled efficiency and permanence. This importance is indicated in the very name which has been given to their creed. *Brâhmanism* is so called as being the possession of the *Brâhmans*, the authorised exponents of the religion of Brahmâ, and the sole depositories of the sacred lore which taught concerning the gods. This deposit they guarded with jealous care, and defended successfully against the unhallowed touch of a man of alien caste. Their unique and privileged knowledge of things divine, their position as the sole intermediaries between god and man, became the foundation of their caste strength, and the lever by which they removed all obstacles to their own undisputed supremacy. Thus the earliest dawn of history reveals the Brâhmans as a caste gradually asserting their authority over the other castes, and arrogating to themselves as their peculiar heritage rights and privileges which others had originally shared with them.

Brahmâ.—The supreme object of this worship, nominally at least, was Brahmâ. To him as the primary source and final end of all, the other gods as well as men were subject. Here again is indicated a certain advance in religious thought, and a change in the religious stand-point. The ancient ill-defined deities of the Veda, especially Prajâpati, suffer loss of rank and position, and their place is taken by a new personification of the great universal all - pervading soul of the universe. This is *Brahmâ*, masculine, the Creator and Father of all, who is the old *Brahma*, neuter, the mysterious all-comprehending *paramâtman*, brought forward into the light, and clothed with a living personality and attributes. Even so he has never been more than half defined and realised,—a working force rather than an intelligent ruler; and therefore in his turn has been dispossessed by figures in the pantheon more vividly pictured and conceived, until at the present day there is only one temple exclusively dedicated to his worship in the whole of India.[1] And while the rites of his service are described with much minuteness in some of the later books, they would seem never to have been very widely reduced to practice.

Changes and Modifications.—From its very birth, and during a long subsequent period, the religion of Brâhmanism is found on its defence against so-called sectarian or popular beliefs, springing up or already existing by its side, and challenging its claim to universal acceptance and homage. These beliefs were for the most part entirely rudimentary and unformed, with no pretensions to the dignity of ecclesiastical

[1] At Pushkar, near the town of Ajmîr, in Râjputâna. See Barth, pp. 92, 93; Hunter, *Gaz. of India*, *s.v.*

systems; and therefore the more readily succumbed to the concerted efforts of Brâhmanical orthodoxy, or were adopted within the elastic bounds of its theology and ritual. The greatest, perhaps the only real exception, was Buddhism, of early Brâhmanism unquestionably the most formidable opponent and rival, the history of whose profound and lasting influence upon contemporary faiths has yet to be written. The others were in their origin mainly forms of nature or fetich worship belonging to non-Aryan tribes, which yet were effective in largely modifying or enriching Brâhmanism with their own peculiar rites and deities. It is a proof of the marvellous strength and vitality of the Brâhmanical religion that it has survived all these attacks, assimilated to itself all these diverse elements, and to-day remains, transformed indeed but recognisable, the backbone and essence of every variety of Hindu belief.

To trace the history of these changes, or to assign a precise value to each element in the total result, is in most instances beyond our power. Generally it is impossible even to approximately determine the time and place of the introduction of innovations, or the disuse of practices long sanctioned by custom or authority. A bare statement must suffice of some of the most striking modifications in observance and faith accepted under the pressure of foreign conceptions or usages. It is of value rather as illustrating the contrast between past and present, than as marking periods of growth or development.

(1) In the most ancient books there is no mention of pilgrimages, or ablutions in sacred streams, as efficacious to procure merit or wash away sin. Under present conditions these form a large part of the religious duties of every pious Hindu.

(2) In the orthodox writings Brâhmans are prohibited from serving in connection with temples or idols. Now it is rare to find a non-Brâhman in any of the higher offices at least associated with the temple duties or worship.

(3) Living sacrifices, which take so large a place in Vedic ritual, have gradually been superseded by offerings of flour paste etc., often moulded into animal shape. There is evidence that the great sacrifices were observed at least occasionally as late as about the eighth century of our era. Since that period they have been rare, and have now for some time altogether ceased.[1] Gifts to Brâhmans have come to be a

[1] Sacrifices of living animals, especially goats, are of course common in parts of India, although decreasing in number every

surer as well as an easier means of obtaining the favour of the gods than the most costly and elaborate sacrifices.

(4) The practice of *satî*,[1] or as it is properly termed *sahamarana*, that the widow should burn herself on the funeral pile of her late husband, finds no place or sanction in the most ancient sacred literature. Instances are said still to occur in distant and isolated parts of India, although the custom has for many years been forbidden by the British Government.

(5) The prohibition of widow re-marriage also meets with no recognition in the ancient sacred books.

These are features of the old religion presented at its best. It is moreover easy to see what a support such facts give to the native Hindu reformer, who protests against the introduction

year. They are all however in connection with sectarian temples or aboriginal worship, not with the true Brâhmanical rites.

[1] *Vulgo*, suttee. The word is simply a feminine adjective, meaning good or virtuous, and is applied to the woman who allows herself or is compelled to be burnt with her dead husband. *Sahamarana* signifies "accompanying in death," and denotes the act. Another Hindu term is *anumarana*, "following in death," which is used when for any reason the corpse of the husband is not on the pyre, and the widow suffers alone. She must then by law take with her some part of his clothing.

into his country of Christianity or any other alien faith. The plea for a return to the true primitive form of his own religion, free from later additions and disguises and stripped of all admixture of foreign creeds, is familiar to those who have to do with the most earnest and thoughtful Hindus at the present day. The claim of such men that when the husk is removed the inner kernel will then be found to be sweet and good, and all-sufficing for their spiritual needs, is one deserving of respectful sympathy and fair examination. If Hinduism fails under the test invited by its most sincere and open-minded supporters it will have failed finally and for ever.

PHILOSOPHICAL SYSTEMS

IN the history and development of Indian religions, philosophy and speculative thought have played a larger part than perhaps in any other country outside of Greece. The reasoning faculty, as distinguished from the emotional, may be said to have led the way in the regulation of practice, as well as in the formulating of creed. No real appreciation of the religious feeling or aspiration of the Hindu is possible which does not take account of his philosophy. Hence of the sub-Vedic literature of India, or that which immediately succeeds in time and is scarcely inferior in authority to the revealed Veda, the most important part is the six recognised philosophical systems, all of which are derived more or less directly from the Upanishads. The names of these, with the names of their reputed founders or authors, are given as follows:—

The Vedânta, founded by Vyâsa.
The Mîmâmsa, „ Jaimini.
The Sânkhya, „ Kapila.

The Yoga, founded by Patanjali.
The Nyâya, „ Gotama.
The Vais'eshika, „ Kanâda.

The origin and early history of these are lost in obscurity, and of the authors to whom they are traditionally ascribed little or nothing is known beyond the bare names. Like so much beside of the ancient precept and thought of India, they are conveyed to us at the present day in *sûtras*, collections of brief rules or statements, frequently obscure and unintelligible without a commentary, and which are indeed often mere *memoriae technicae*, designed in this case to assist the memory to retain philosophical ideas and dogmas. Of the six systems however only two are of importance or interest here for the influence they have exerted on religious thought; and these it is the less necessary to discuss at length, because in substance the more important of them formulates a doctrine identical with the main teaching of the Upanishads. The *Nyâya* and the *Vais'eshika* are rather systems respectively of logic and literary criticism, and of natural philosophy. The *Yoga* is a hand-book of religious exercises and austerities, by means of which the soul of man may attain to union with the divine soul, and is in reality only a development and application of the Sânkhya. While the *Mîmâmsa* has little claim to be independent of the Vedânta, consisting chiefly of explanatory comments on the ritualistic portion of the Veda.

Sânkhya.—There remain the Sânkhya and Vedânta systems, full and accessible expositions of which will be found in Sir Monier Williams' *Indian Wisdom*, or in any work dealing with Hindu literature or religion. Briefly the *Sânkhya*[1] philosophy is so called from a root *sankhyâ*, meaning to count up, to enumerate, because it enumerates twenty-five *tattvas* or principles[2]; of which *purusha*, the person or soul, is the twenty-fifth, and is wholly distinct in nature from the rest. The aim which the philosophy then contemplates is to show the way by which the soul may be set free from its connection with matter and material things. Of the remaining twenty-four tattvas the first eight are *prakritis* or producers, and sixteen are

[1] On the significance of the term see Max Müller, in *S. B. E.*, vol. xv. p. xxxv.

[2] These are *avyaktum*, the "unperceived," the primitive element or material source of all; *buddhi*, intelligence; *ahankâra*, individuality; the five *tan-mâtras*, or subtle elements, viz. sound, touch, form, taste, and smell; the five *mahâ-bhûtas*, or gross elements, products of the tan-mâtras, viz. ether, air, fire, water, and earth; the eleven organs including *manas* or mind; and *purusha*. Compare *Brâhmanism and Hinduism*, p. 30 f.

productions. The former create or evolve, the latter are evolved. Of the eight producers again the first is the supreme *Prakriti*, the original blind unintelligent principle from which all existing things have come forth. This *Prakriti* is identified with Brahma, and has various names, of which the most significant perhaps and famous is Mâyâ, the mighty power of illusion, which deludes men into a belief in the reality of the external universe. *Prakriti* however is by itself inert and powerless. Only by union with the soul, *purusha*, does it obtain the power to create. The system therefore is essentially materialistic and dualistic, ascribing the formation of the world to two distinct principles, both existing from eternity, that of matter *prakriti*, and that of soul *purusha*; and has no place in its philosophy for a God. Whether this dualistic character is really primitive, or merely a later development or accretion, is perhaps open to question. Of all Hindu schools of thought the Sânkhya has the greatest affinity with Buddhism.

Vedânta.—Opposed to this is the *Vedânta* doctrine, which has on the whole most commended itself to the Hindu mind, and which with its various ramifications and extensions is the most popular and widely spread philosophy in India at the present day. The Vedânta is the *advaita* teaching of the Upanishads, non-dualism, expounded and formulated into a system; and is the popular pantheistic creed of the cultivated Brâhman wherever he may be found. To a large extent moreover it lies at the base of the polytheistic developments into which the beliefs of the common people have shaped themselves. So far from denying that there is a God, this system identifies everything with Him. From the one supreme soul, Brahma, Paramâtman, all created beings and things have taken their rise. Human souls are in reality but parts of the one great soul. Their ignorance of this truth keeps them separate from him for a time. But when that ignorance is removed, they will be re-absorbed into the divine essence, to which they belong. This is practically the doctrine of the greater portion of the Upanishads. And it may be said to be the philosophical tenet that is most distinctively characteristic of the people and country of India at the present day. The conceptions of every Hindu appear to be coloured more or less consciously and avowedly by pantheistic ideas; and he builds his working systems of thought on pantheistic foundations. While therefore he takes pleasure in an eclectic philosophy, and in weaving a mosaic which borrows its colours and patterns from every school, the underlying tracery and outline will generally be found to be in harmony with the conceptions and teaching of the Vedânta. Thus of the two great and influential philosophies of India, the one the Sânkhya is atheistic, materialistic, and dualistic; the other the Vedânta, at least in its simplest form, is a pure monism and pantheism.

Epic Poems.—The Epic Poems most widely known and popular in India, and which are most closely interwoven with the life and thought of the people, somewhat in the same manner as the songs of Homer entered into the national life of Greece, or the poetry and imagery of Milton have influenced English religious ideas, are the two to which reference has already been made,[1] the *Mahâbhârata* and the *Râmâyana.* These form the great storehouse of mythology and popular belief, on which the later *Purânas* and other legendary accounts of gods and heroes have drawn; and the vast and unwieldy mass of later mythological literature gathers round these as its source and kernel. They have been therefore and are to-day the ultimate literary source of the usages and beliefs of large numbers of the Hindu peoples, much as Homer appears to have been a kind of Bible to the Greeks. The

[1] *Supra*, p. 108.

later mythological writings largely owe to them their inspiration and character, although they in their turn have surpassed their original in grotesqueness and extravagance of detail. For a full account of this probably the earliest epic poetry in existence it must be sufficient to refer to works dealing especially with Hindu literature and history.[1] Here it can only be briefly said that both the Mahâbhârata and the Râmâyana are extant in slightly varying recensions, the precise relations of which have not been determined, and which present many problems of great difficulty to the historian and student of comparative mythology. The latter, which is the more finished production, sets forth the virtues of noble woman in the person of Sîtâ, wife of Râma, faithful under all manner of

[1] A brief and readable description and outline of the two poems will be found in the first two chapters of J. Talboys Wheeler's *Short History of India.* Cp. R. W. Frazer, *Lit. Hist. of India*, ch. x.; Monier Williams, *Indian Wisdom*, chh. xii.-xiv. The Râmâyana is usually understood as celebrating in heroic and legendary form the conquest of Southern India by the Aryans. Frazer however expresses doubt on this point, or at least holds that it is not proven, on the ground that in the Mahâbhârata there are more traces of an acquaintance with the South than in the very vague Râmâyana. *Op. cit.*, p. 305 f. Verse translations of parts of both epics by Romesh Dutt have recently been published in the *Temple Classics*, London, 1898 and 1899.

temptation and suffering, and in the end triumphantly vindicated and restored to happiness. The Mahâbhârata in most lengthy and discursive fashion, with many breaks and diversions, relates the story of the war between the Kauravas and Pândavas, two families of cousins living in the north-west of India or the Panjâb; in whose rivalries and contests the gods interpose with advice or active assistance, in a similar way to the Homeric deities in the war around Troy. And the aim of the whole is to describe how the devout god-fearing Pândavas triumph at last over their impious foes, and are received above into the habitations of the gods.

Of neither poem is it possible to determine with any certainty the exact date. Internal evidence seems to show that the Râmâyana, at least in its present form, is later than the Mahâbhârata. The numerous digressions of the latter work, the long and disconnected episodes which interrupt the progress of the narrative, forbid our assigning it, as it stands, to any single age. In all probability the composition or compilation of the poem extended over a considerable period of time, perhaps many centuries; and some of its elements or parts go back to a great antiquity.

Law-Books.—The last element in the moulding of Indian religious beliefs, to which it is necessary to refer here, is the legal and formal. The Hindu mind, over and above its essentially religious character, is also subtle and litigious, delighting in forms and rules, in generalisations and distinctions. From a very early age therefore there have been in existence in India elaborate codes of law, of marvellous intricacy and minuteness, providing rules of procedure for every conceivable occasion in public or private life, national individual and domestic. Law moreover and religion have always been so intimately and closely connected together in the life and thought of the Hindu, that it is impossible adequately to discuss the one without taking account of the other. The best-known and most widely esteemed of these Law-Books is that of Manu, which has been translated by the late G. Bühler in the *Sacred Books of the East*, with an elaborate and scholarly introduction and notes. Most of the *Sûtras* also, or rules bearing on public and private life, which pass under the names of other law-givers, have been translated and published in the same series, and are therefore readily accessible. Neither the date nor the age of Manu's work has been certainly determined. Professor Bühler would assign the authorship to the second or third century of our era.[1] This date does not imply of course that the book may not embody older material, or have suffered in the course of time many additions and interpolations. The laws of Manu begin, like the books of Moses, with the creation of the universe. They treat of civil and criminal law, of student and domestic life, of rites and sacrifices, of caste penance asceticism transmigration and other matters almost innumerable. And to the authority of Manu every orthodox Brâhman will at once submit himself. In the religious life of the Hindu there is no room left for private initiative or choice. Everything down to the minutest detail is regulated for him by rule and custom; to which he must conform on pain of loss of social position. The outward form and manner is all-important; into the inward spirit Hinduism did not and does not inquire. While therefore works like that of Manu have undoubtedly exercised a great influence in maintaining intact the fabric of ancient observance and ritual, they have done little or nothing towards retaining the ancient faith, without which the elaborate forms are empty of vitality and worth.

[1] *S. B. E.*, vol. xxv. pp. cvi. ff.

HINDUISM

HOW far the beliefs and observances of ancient Brâhmanism, of which a faithful picture has been preserved in the sacred books, ever became matters of actual practice beyond a very narrow circle, or filtered through to the common people, must remain uncertain. The influence which these have exercised on later cults, and on the developments of modern Hinduism, has been too varied and profound to allow of their being regarded as merely the possession of a few exclusive Brâhmans. On both sides, the literary and priestly as well as the popular and superstitious, the barriers were at least occasionally broken down. A proud philosophy and ritual so far unbent as for the sake of peace and its own predominance to adopt deities and countenance practices to which the lower orders tenaciously clung. The mass of the people, ignorant and without leisure for studying philosophical abstractions, allowed their own rude thought to be dominated by the higher conceptions of an intellectual aristocracy, and to be interpreted in accordance with their ideas. It would be of exceeding interest to be able to trace historically and consecutively this process of intermixture, of joint growth and decay, whereby a formal book-religion, living by rule and ordinance, adapted itself to the freedom and unconventionality of popular beliefs, and by yielding the letter and form vanquished in the spirit and in fact. This also would be the ideal and logical method by which to treat of the religious history of India,—to follow the course of faith and practice from the earliest times of which knowledge is attainable to the highly complex systems and forms in which these appear at the present day. Unfortunately in the case of the Hindu religions the necessary evidence and materials for such a consecutive narrative are almost altogether wanting. Rich as the indigenous Indian literature is in poetry and speculation and story, it fails in the more sober elements of historical or chronological records. Romance with imaginative and picturesque detail is to be found in abundance. The Hindu mind however seems to have refused or been unable to condescend to the unvarnished statement of plain facts. Contemporary accounts by the people themselves which should fill however imperfectly for the nations and country of India the place which is taken in our own past by the chronicles of Anglo-Saxon history, would be of inestimable value. But none such exist.[1] In the case of Indian history we are dependent almost entirely upon the records and writings of foreigners, which are rarely sympathetic, but on the contrary were composed in the interests of foreign dominion or state-craft,—Chinese, Greek, Muhammadan and Persian, Portuguese, etc.; with what help can be gained from coins monuments and tombs. All these convey little or no information with respect to religious practices and the currents of religious belief.[2]

It is therefore almost inevitable that the thread of a consecutive record should here be dropped; and the account of Hinduism, its religious and philosophical tenets and claims, be taken up as it were from the other end. That an attempt should be made to complete the survey of Indian creeds by briefly passing in review the

[1] It is altogether improbable that future discovery or research will ever supply the gap. Real historical works however appear to have been composed in Assam. See G. A. Grierson, in *Indian Antiquary*, vol. xxv. pp. 57 ff. The same is true of the local history of Kashmîr.

[2] As'oka's edicts may be said to form a welcome exception. While however they illustrate contemporary Buddhism, they throw no light on the conflicts or tendencies of native Hindu thought. They too are sectarian and confined to a single interest. Cp. *infra*, p. 229 ff.

present condition of the multiform Hindu faiths, their hold on the mind and heart of the people at the present day, and the future that seems to lie before them. Then only by the help of any reliable evidence or tradition that may be garnered, by cautious inference and analogy, may it be found possible successfully to grope our way backward, and to bridge over the interval between the visible present of our knowledge and experience, and the vivid picture of the past which the sacred literature unfolds. In some instances a fair amount of certainty may be attained, and the course may be indicated which religious development and variation have in all probability pursued. More often perhaps the clue breaks off in our hands. The past and the present refuse to come together naturally or easily. And there remain periods of time more or less prolonged, subjects involved in a greater or less obscurity, on which the last word has not been spoken, whether by the ancient literature and monuments or by the modern investigator. On these it is inevitable that we should wait with patience for further light.

Sectarian Religions.—The broad and somewhat vague term *Hinduism* is usually employed to cover all these later developments together with the existing forms of belief and worship in India, whose precise relationship as descendants or offshoots, or their measure of indebtedness to the ancient Brâhmanism it is thus frequently impossible to indicate. The internal connection moreover between the diverse creeds which pass under this name is often very slight,—a mere common name or ordinance, a tendency or a dislike, a sacred book and language. And therefore a definition of Hinduism, except in very general terms which call attention rather to that which strikes the eye than to its real nature or place in religious history, is scarcely to be framed. It will be found more satisfactory to follow a classification or method of sub-division of the nature here suggested. First and most prominent and important will come what may be termed the two official sects of modern Hinduism, *Vaishnavism* and *S′aivism*, to one or other of which every Hindu with few exceptions, who claims to be strict and intelligent in his religious observances, attaches himself. The adherents of the former recognise Vishnu as their supreme deity, and pay honour to him above all other divinities in one or other of his various forms. The S′aivites similarly assign to S′iva the position of pre-eminence. The worshippers of Vishnu are said to be on the whole more numerous throughout India; those of S′iva preponderate in the

South. Each of these again, especially Vaishnavism, has numerous sub-divisions, minor sects which acknowledge a human founder or leader, whose name they usually bear, and to whom in many cases divine or semi-divine honours are paid. Regarded as a whole they may be said to give expression in their practice and faith to the ritualistic and philosophical side of Modern Hinduism.

Popular Hinduism.—Wide-spread and very miscellaneous forms of religious belief are comprised under the name of *Popular Hinduism.* This is the religion of the village folk,—if indeed it can be called a religion, and not rather an assortment of ideas about the unseen, neither classified nor defined nor brought into agreement,—of the labouring agricultural population of India, who have neither time nor inclination for the abstractions and generalisations of philosophy, or for aught else but the demands and needs of daily food. The large majority of the inhabitants of India are resident in villages of but moderate size; and of those who thus spend their lives in the villages, by far the greater number while often apt disputants and natural philosophers are victims at heart of the terrors of popular superstitions. Translated into the terms and experience of ordinary life, this aspect or variety of Hinduism implies the worship of demons, of the spirits of the earth and air, of deified men and restless ghosts, of animals plants and stones, the worship of anything and everything in the heaven above the earth beneath or the waters under the earth. There is hardly a primitive belief existing in any part of the world but its representative may be found amongst the heterogeneous conceptions and faiths of the masses of India. And to the accepted and well-known objects of their reverence and fear they are always ready to make additions, and to enlarge their already comprehensive pantheon as authority or fancy may dictate.

Reforming Sects.—Lastly there will fall to be considered the Hindu reforming sects which have arisen within the present century under the influencc of Christian ideas and teaching. These are the *Bráhma-Samáj* and others of a similar nature which have essayed to purify Hinduism from within. Of none of them can the present position or prospects be said to be very bright. A notice however of their methods and creeds may perhaps open the way to a consideration of the relations of Christianity to these various forms of Hindu belief, and the place which it appears probable they will occupy in the future religious history of India.

Vaishnavism.—The leading conception of *Vaishnavism* is that of loyalty, devotion to a single supreme and personal deity. This idea is expressed by the Sanskrit term *bhakti*, a word which is sometimes rendered "faith." The translation however is inadequate and misleading. For *bhakti* is rather the clinging affection of the heart, and has no concern with the intelligence or the will, nor does it make any demand upon the moral consciousness. It is therefore more suitable on the whole to retain the technical word, for which no exact equivalent is to be found in English. Vaishnavism is the most spiritual of the many faiths of India, the least wedded to mere form and ceremony, and better worthy of the name of a religion than any other of the creeds or cults that have grown up on Indian soil. Its likeness in many respects to Christianity amidst the most striking differences will not escape notice. Of this system or creed the supreme divinity in the first instance is *Vishnu*, whose name is said to be derived from a root *vish*, meaning to "spread through," "pervade." *Vishnu* therefore is the all-pervader, the god who is present everywhere and in all things. In the Veda his chief characteristic is found in the three strides in which he compasses the three worlds.[1] He is there invoked, although with no great frequency, by the side of other well-known Vedic deities, especially Indra and his companions the Maruts; but superiority to these is never claimed for him. It is only in the later literature that he rises to the first rank, and that his chief mythological traits, including the so-called incarnations, are developed. In the great Hindu *Tri-múrti*, or Triad, he occupies the second place, and has then assigned to him the office of Preserver, as to Brahmâ that of Creator, and to S'iva of Destroyer. Equally with these also he is an emanation from the sole and supreme divine essence, brahmă, into which all will ultimately be re-absorbed. This triad of divinities is represented by the mystical sacred syllable *Om*,[2] which already in the Upanishads the object of profound reverence, and the theme of religious meditation, is later explained to typify the three supreme gods, *a*

[1] *Supra*, p. 48; Macdonell, *Vedic Mythology*, pp. 37 ff.

[2] *Supra*, p. 63. The origin of the syllable and of its sacred character are alike unknown. Sir Monier Williams suggests that the three sounds of which it is composed, *a u m*, are the initial letters of the members of an original triad, Agni Vâyu or Varuna and Mitra, or Fire Wind and the Sun; see *Brâhmanism and Hinduism*, p. 10. The syllable *Om* is equally sacred among the Buddhists, cp. *infra*, p. 336 ff.

being the symbol of Vishnu, *u* of S'iva, and *m* of Brahmâ. Subsequently however and in the estimation of those peculiarly devoted to his worship, Vishnu becomes the acknowledged lord of all. To him all the other gods are subordinate, and together with men and spirits they render him homage.

Theism of the Sectarian Religions.—This conception of a *personal* god, who stands alone without an equal or a rival, may be justly said to be the distinguishing feature of the later sectarian religions, as contrasted with ancient Brâhmanism or a mere philosophical or literary cult. They recognise a supreme Personal Deity. In practice, whatever may be said of their theory, the pantheistic idea of a featureless all-pervading intangible divine essence, whence everything proceeds and into which everything returns, passes out of sight and becomes if not forgotten yet practically unimportant; and a Divine Person, of whom personal attributes and actions are predicated presides over all, and is the source of all. It does not follow however that this conception is really later in point of time than that of *brahmă*, the indefinite and absolute unknown; although it presents itself before us at a later period in the history of Indian religious thought. Nor again is the inference altogether justified that the former more vivid and imaginative theory of the universe and its ruler was merely grafted into the stock of a barren and negative philosophy, and by its superior vitality drew into itself whatever of living force the other still retained. In all probability the two lines of thought, the material and philosophical and the spiritual and theistic, existed side by side; and the religious systems, as they are known and professed to-day, are the fruits of a compromise, in which the more human and sympathetic element has come naturally to predominate. But if either be the older, then it is certainly not the refined philosophy which must be concluded to antedate the personal conception and rule of the unseen world.

Vaishnavism therefore from this point of view may be considered to be a monotheistic religion, if the term be understood to mean a religion in which one god stands alone at the head, without excluding the possibility of the existence of other inferior deities. In the same sense and with the same limitations S'aivism also is monotheistic. In both systems however the pantheistic ideas, so congenial to the Indian mind, lie scarcely hidden beneath the surface. They co-exist with the other, apparently contradictory doctrines and beliefs occupying as it were different compartments of the mind. And a harmony between them is scarcely sought. The strictly monotheistic theory moreover allied itself in practice with an endless diversity, and permitted an unlimited multiplication of gods and goddesses of every rank and order, according to the will or fancy of their worshippers; so that the professors of a theoretical monotheism became practical polytheists.

Vishnu.—Vishnu himself, who is thus exalted to the supreme rank, is regarded as combining in his own person the qualities or characters of all three members of the Hindu Triad, that is of Brahmâ as Creator, and of S'iva as Destroyer, in addition to his peculiar province or office of Preserver. As lord of the universe and of the other gods he exercises every prerogative of power and uncontrolled dominion. He has his own especial heaven *Vaikuntha*,[1] where he dwells in eternal repose with his wife *Lakshmî* Good Fortune, or *S'rî* Prosperity. Lakshmî is said to have arisen from the foam of the ocean, and she is made the object of an independent and widely spread worship. By his followers Vishnu is reverenced under a thousand different names, expressive of various aspects of his

[1] "Not blunted," "not dulled," and so "ever fresh." Monier Williams.

nature and character, the mere repetition of which is an act of worship. And he is usually represented with a peculiarly auspicious mark on his breast called *S'rî-vatsa*, perhaps meaning "the darling of S'rî," in the form of a curl of hair, said to be white, and like a cruciform flower. In his hands he bears a conch-shell, which is blown as a signal for battle; a *c'akra* or discus, perhaps originally merely a sacred symbol like the Buddhist wheel of the law, but later a weapon of offence; a club; and a lotus. The swan or goose bears in relation to him a sacred character, and often appears in figure or sculpture by his side. He rides upon *Garuda*, the mythical eagle or vulture, king of birds and the destroyer of serpents; and the river Ganges issues from his feet. Those who put their trust in him, and worship him aright by the way of *bhakti*, he exalts to a place in his own heaven Vaikuntha. Vaishnavites bear on their forehead a kind of mark made with white or coloured earths, which varies slightly in its form in the different sects, but which is always shaped somewhat like a trident, intended to denote the impress of the foot or feet of the god,—an outward and visible sign of their profession and faith.

Avatâras of Vishnu.—The god who is thus exalted and reverenced is seldom if ever found entering into direct communication with his worshippers. He comes into contact with men only through his *avatâras* or "descents," when he "descends" from heaven to earth, and appears in bodily shape. These *avatâras* are sometimes termed incarnations, and have been erroneously described as offering a strict parallel to the Christian doctrine. The resemblance however is entirely verbal and superficial; and beyond the fact that in each religion the deity is understood to have presented himself in visible and tangible form there is no likeness between the two. The leading conception in the *avatâras* of Vishnu is that for a particular purpose some portion of the essence of the god "descended" and incorporated itself with the body of a man or animal, so that he or it became for the time being identified to a greater or less degree with the deity, and possessed of his attributes. The larger the portion of his essence that was received the more striking and important the avatâra, the more sacred and to be revered the creature or person into whom he entered. Such a person became to all intents and purposes a god. The *avatâras* of the god therefore admitted of degrees; and in fact as ordinarily related appear to have been designed to exhibit a gradation in importance, the earlier being partial and incomplete, while the later approach in succession more nearly to an ideal perfectness, which is yet to be reached in the last and greatest of the *avatâras*, still in the future. There is considerable analogy also between these descents of Vishnu, and the various appearances of the Buddha for the deliverance of mankind, as taught in the Buddhist religion.[1]

The number of these "descents" is differently stated by the different authorities. The most important are usually given as ten, and their date and order are traditionally fixed. Elsewhere however reference is made to twelve, twenty-two, or twenty-eight avatâras, and finally they are said to be innumerable. They have not indeed yet ceased, for at the present time in parts of India any man of peculiar sanctity or force of character is considered to be pervaded by a portion of Vishnu's essence, and to have a claim therefore to honour and worship as a manifestation of the god. These ten however hold so large a place in Indian religious thought, and have formed the basis and starting-point of so wide-spread a mythology and popular belief, that it is worth while briefly to enumerate them.[2]

[1] Cp. *infra*, p. 331 f.

[2] Cp. Monier Williams, *Brâhm. and Hind.*, p. 107 ff.; Frazer, *Literary History*, p. 339 f.

(1) The first is the *matsya*, or "fish" avatâra. Vishnu took the form of a fish in order to deliver Manu, the primæval man, a kind of Hindu Noah, in the time of the Deluge.[1] The fish drew Manu's ship to the northern mountain, where he descended in safety, and offered sacrifice to the gods.

(2) The *kûrma*, or "tortoise" avatâra. During the flood a number of valuable objects had been lost, including the moon, a beautiful nymph, the precious stone *kaustubha*, the cow of riches, and a deadly poison. The last when recovered was said to have been drunk by S'iva that he might save mankind. In order to rescue these Vishnu imparted of his essence to a huge tortoise, which then took its stand at the bottom of the ocean of milk that encircled the earth. On the back of the tortoise was placed a mountain, and around the mountain the serpent *Vâsuki* was coiled to serve as a rope. The opposite ends of the snake were then grasped by the gods and the demons, who by the aid of serpent and mountain churned the ocean, until one by one the lost treasures reappeared on the surface.

(3) The third avatâra is that of the "boar," *varâha*. The earth itself had been lost in the depths of the ocean, having been carried off by a

[1] *Supra*, p. 73 f.

demon. The boar, animated by the god, dived after it, fought the demon for a thousand years, and in triumph brought back the earth.

(4) The *narasimha*, or "man-lion" avatâra. The powerful tyrant, Hiranya-kas'ipu, had obtained from Brahmâ a promise that neither god nor man nor animal should be able to destroy him. Relying on this invulnerability he had usurped the dominion of the three worlds, and had even diverted to himself the sacrifices intended for the gods. Vishnu overcame and slew him by appearing in a shape that was neither god nor man nor animal. These four avatâras all occurred in the first, the *satya* age of the world.

(5) In the second or *tretâ* age of the world Vishnu entered into the form of a dwarf, *vâmana*, in order to destroy the demon Bali, who had attained to supreme dominion over the three worlds, and used his power to defy the gods and injure mankind. Presenting himself before the demon as a dwarf, Vishnu is said to have begged for the gift of as much land as he could cover in three steps. Bali granted his request; and the dwarf, at once expanding to a gigantic size, in two steps traversed heaven and earth, rescuing them from the sway of the demon; then stopped, and allowed the lower world to remain under Bali's control.

(6) The sixth avatâra is in the person of *Paras'u-Râma*, or *Râma with the Axe*, a great Brâhman hero, who twenty-one times destroyed the entire Kshatriya race, the royal and warrior caste, from the face of the earth. Later the virtue of the essence of Vishnu is said to have departed from him, and he was then overcome and slain by *Râma*, in whom the seventh and hitherto most important manifestation of the god took place.

(7) *Râma*, or *Râma-c'andra* as he is called to distinguish him from other *Râmas*, is the celebrated hero of the Râmâyana, the model son and husband, one of the most popular and widely worshipped of the gods of India at the present day. He was the son of Das'aratha, king of Ayodhyâ or Oudh, who reigned towards the end of the second age of the world. Banished from his father's kingdom through the jealousy of Kaikeyî, he went into exile in the forest country of the south. Thither his faithful wife *Sîtâ* followed him, and thence in the absence one day of Râma she was carried off by *Râvana*, the demon-king of Ceylon. With the aid of *Hanumân*, the "heavy" or "large-jawed" one, son of the wind and semi-divine chief or leader of the monkey race, Râma made a bridge of rocks to the island, which he then entered, and having slain Râvana recovered his wife, with whom he

was subsequently restored to his kingdom in Oudh. Both *Sîtâ* and *Hanumân* are widely reverenced as gods, the former being regarded as an incarnation of S'rî, the wife of Vishnu; and numerous shrines and images are erected in their honour. There is reason to believe that Râma was originally a lunar deity, god of the months and of agriculture. His reign, after his return to his kingdom, is described as the golden age of happiness and prosperity in India.

(8) The eighth avatâra took place at the end of the third, or *dvâpara*[1] age of the world, when *Krishna*, the "dark" or "swarthy" prince,

[1] There is some doubt as to the origin of the application of these terms, dvâpara and tretâ, to the third and second ages of the world respectively. One of the earliest references to them is found in the Aitareya Brâhmana:—"A man who sleeps is like the Kali age; a man who awakes is like the Dvâpara age; a man who rises is like the Tretâ age; a man who travels is like the Krita age." It seems clear that their use in this connection is derived from terms of play with dice. *Dvâpara* is a throw or cast of two, *tretâ* of three. *Krita*, which properly signifies "done," "accomplished," seems to denote the "perfect" throw. The *krita* age is otherwise called *satya*, true, good. The *kali* is the bad present age, the worst of the four. "In the kali age . . . the minds of men will be wholly occupied in acquiring wealth, and wealth will be spent solely on selfish gratifications. Women will follow their inclinations, and be ever fond of pleasure. Men will fix their desires upon riches even though dishonestly acquired. No man will part with the smallest fraction of the smallest coin, though entreated by a friend. . . . There will never be abundance in the kali age, and men will

was born near Delhi, imbued with the spirit and wisdom of the god. He is represented accordingly as brave and warlike, but at the same time crafty and false and habitually guilty of the grossest immorality. The son of Vasudeva and Devakî he became an object of hatred and fear to his uncle, king Kansa, to whom an oracle had declared that the eighth son of Devakî should put him to death, and who therefore schemed to anticipate the oracle by slaying K*ri*shna. In order to place the boy beyond the reach of his uncle he was transferred as soon as born to the care of a herdsman, who brought him up as his own son. Hence K*ri*shna is especially the god of shepherds, and of the lower castes in general. His youth was devoted to hunting and sports, varied by combats with robbers and demons. On arriving at manhood he fulfilled the prediction of the oracle, and became king of the Yâdavas in the stead of his uncle Kansa.

never enjoy pleasure and happiness. . . . The women will be fickle, short of stature, gluttonous ; they will have many children and little means. . . . They will be selfish, abject, and slatternly ; they will be scolds and liars. . . . Householders will neither sacrifice, nor practise becoming liberality. . . . Princes, instead of protecting, will plunder their subjects," etc. etc. *Vishnu Purâna*, vi. 1, see Frazer, p. 341 f. The kali age began 3102 B.C., and is to last altogether 432,000 years. At its close the world is to come to an end, and all things will be received back into the primæval essence or substance out of which they sprang.

After a prolonged reign he was himself slain, like Achilles, by a chance arrow in the heel. K*ri*shna is a prominent figure in the Mahâbhârata, the ancient epic of India, and the legends concerning him are the most varied and numerous that cluster round any single figure of the entire Hindu pantheon. He is said to have had 108,000 sons; and countless wives, of whom the chief was *Râdhâ*, one of the shepherdesses with whom he sported in his youthful days. She is sometimes said, like Sîtâ, to have been an avatâra of Lakshmî, the wife of Vishnu.

(9) The ninth avatâra is as *Buddha*, the "enlightened" one. The founder of Buddhism has thus been adopted by the Brâhmans into their religion, with the comprehensive tolerance or indifference which is one of the characteristics of the Hindu faith. In the same manner as many of them are prepared at the present day to adopt the Founder of Christianity, and to represent Him as a new avatâra of their god.

(10) The tenth "descent" of Vishnu is still in the future. He will appear as *Kalki*, the liberator, at the close of the present age when the world has become hopelessly corrupt, to destroy the wicked and to bring back the age of purity. Hinduism therefore, in theory at least, looks for a coming Deliverer.

If the foregoing list appear long, and the record in many respects childish, yet it must be borne in mind how large a part this theory and the details of the avatâras have played in the religious life and thought of India. They are as closely, probably more closely interwoven with the thought and mind of the people than the narratives of the gospels or the dramatic representations of Milton with the sentiments and presumptions of the population of Great Britain. It is impossible to understand present-day facts and beliefs unless account be taken of the mythology, and the more or less conscious prepossessions and ideas that form their background.

Vaishnavite Doctrines.—All sects and divisions of the Vaishnavites, of which there are many, hold in common certain fundamental beliefs and doctrines, which admit of being broadly and clearly stated; while the distinctions between the sects are often subtle and difficult to grasp. Their doctrine of a personal deity, to whom men owe and may refuse allegiance, involves them necessarily in a practical opposition to the philosophical dogma of *advaita*; although they may theoretically declare themselves Vedântists, and maintain in argument the distinctive tenets of this system. Manifestly however there can be no union or compromise between Vaishnavite belief on this point and the materialistic philosophy of the Sânkhya in its extreme and generally accepted form. Through all their teaching moreover there runs a strong vein of mysticism, which shows itself in an excess of refinement, and in the over-elaboration of theories and speculations which in the first instance have doubtless been inherited or adopted from ancient Brâhmanism. As an example might be cited the favourite doctrine of *bhakti*; which, simple and natural as it appears in a mere orderly statement, is in practice made the occasion for mystical developments and the theme of extravagant poetical raptures. This reliance upon a personal divinity, faith in and devotion to K*r*ishna, Râma, or some other manifestation of the supreme god, taught and enforced as the necessary condition of salvation, is the first distinctive mark of all Vaishnavite faiths.

Bhagavad-Gîtâ.—The element of mysticism is perhaps most apparent and pronounced in the *Bhagavad-gîtâ*, or "Song of the Blessed," an episode in the Mahâbhârata in which K*r*ishna, in the disguise of charioteer to Arjuna, the best and noblest of the Pândava brothers, expounds the mystery of his being and of the purpose and destiny of the universe. Arjuna is reluctant to fight against his cousins, seeing no gain either in victory or defeat; and K*ri*shna in a long philosophical discourse, which interrupts the action of the main poem, urges him to take up his arms, and play the part of a valiant hero. The two keynotes as it were of the poem may indeed be said to be "action" and "devotion." But the whole forms a strange mixture of dreamy speculation with practical injunctions to be up and doing, of elevated thought with uncontrolled imagination, of profound conceptions of duty and of God with scarcely intelligible fancies concerning the constitution and meaning of the universe; all wrapped in the garb and phraseology of a philosophy that seems to borrow its terms now from the Vedânta and now from the Sânkhya system. It would seem however that in most instances at least where Sânkhyan terminology is used, the author nevertheless intended to convey what are really Vedântic ideas. Neither age nor author of the *Bhagavad-gîtâ* are known. It clearly formed no part of the original poem of the Mahâbhârata, but has been inserted at what appeared to be an opportune moment for the delivery of philosophical views and directions. The work is certainly one of the most famous, if not the most famous product of Indian thought; and has been translated into all the chief languages of Europe.

The theme that action is better than inaction is developed in the following passages amongst many others[1]:—

> In this world there is a two-fold path—that of the Sânkhyas by devotion in the shape of (true) knowledge; and that of the Yogins by devotion in the shape of action. A man does not attain freedom from action merely by not engaging in action; nor does he attain perfection by mere renunciation. For nobody ever remains even for an instant without performing some action; since the qualities of nature constrain everybody, not having free-will (in the matter), to some action. . . . Do you perform prescribed action, for action is better than inaction, and the support of your body too cannot be accomplished with inaction.
>
> . . . .
>
> Renunciation and pursuit of action are both instruments of happiness. But of the two pursuit of action is superior to renunciation of action. . . . Children—not wise men—talk of sânkhya and yoga as distinct. One who pursues either well obtains the fruit of both.

All right action however must be based upon knowledge, the knowledge of the supreme, which is described or defined in similar language to that of the Upanishads:—

> I will declare that which is the object of knowledge, knowing which one reaches immortality; the highest Brahman, having no beginning nor end, which cannot be said to be existent or

[1] The translations are from *S. B. E.*, vol. viii. 2nd ed.

non-existent. . . . Possessed of the qualities of all the senses, (but) devoid of all senses, unattached, it supports all, is devoid of qualities and the enjoyer of qualities. It is within all things and without them; it is movable and also immovable; it is unknowable through (its) subtlety; it stands afar and near. . . . It is knowledge, the object of knowledge, that which is to be attained to by knowledge, and placed in the heart of all.

. . . .

Even if you are the most sinful of all sinful men, you will cross over all trespasses by means of the boat of knowledge alone.

The following description of the self offers parallels again with the Upanishads:—

He who thinks one to be the killer and he who thinks one to be killed, both know nothing. He kills not, is not killed. He is not born, nor does he ever die, nor having existed does he exist no more. Unborn, everlasting, unchangeable, and very ancient, he is not killed when the body is killed. O son of P*ri*thâ![1] how can that man who knows the self thus to be indestructible, everlasting, unborn, and imperishable, kill anyone or cause anyone to be killed? As a man, casting off old clothes, puts on others and new ones, so the embodied (self), casting off old bodies, goes to others and new ones. . . . It is everlasting, all-pervading, stable, firm, and eternal.

Devotion to K*ri*shna is the highest good:—

The devotee working with great efforts, and cleared of his sins, attains perfection after many births, and then reaches the supreme goal. The devotee is esteemed higher than the performers of penances, higher even than the men of knowledge, and the devotee is higher than the men of action; therefore,

---

[1] Arjuna.

O Arjuna, become a devotee. And even among all devotees, he who being full of faith worships me, with his inmost self intent on me, is esteemed by me to be the most devoted.

. . . .

Those who make vows to the gods go to the gods; those who make vows to the manes go to the manes; those who worship the Bhûtas[1] go to the Bhûtas; and those likewise who worship me go to me. Whoever with devotion offers me leaf, flower, fruit, water, that presented with devotion I accept from him whose self is pure. Whatever you do, O Son of Kuntî![2] whatever you eat, whatever sacrifice you make, whatever you give, whatever penance you perform, do that as offered to me. . . . Those who worship me with devotion (dwell) in me, and I too in them. Even if a very ill-conducted man worships me, not worshipping anyone else, he must certainly be deemed to be good, for he has well resolved. He soon becomes devout of heart, and obtains lasting tranquillity. . . . Coming to this transient unhappy world, worship me. (Place your) mind on me, become my devotee, my worshipper; reverence me, and thus making me your highest goal, and devoting your self to abstraction, you will certainly come to me.

The Guru.—A second distinctive feature of all Vaishnavite sects is their reverence for the religious teacher. The *guru* exercises an influence unquestioned and profound. All the sects, however far they may have travelled in doctrine and discipline, trace their origin to the labours and teaching of an individual founder, who is worshipped as a more or less complete incarnation of the god himself. These founders it is evident must generally have

[1] Spirits, or ghosts. [2] Arjuna.

been men of considerable ability, with a more than ordinary capacity for impressing their views on their contemporaries. In most instances they have transmitted their authority and sacred character to a line of successors, whose living personality often overshadows that of the founder himself. The power which these men possess over the faith and lives of their disciples is almost unbounded. Their persons are sacred; their word is law, inasmuch as it is regarded as inspired; and they are invested with a divine or semi-divine character, the deity himself in a greater or less degree having taken up his abode within them. It is their custom to make yearly or half-yearly progresses through the districts under their influence, when all the boys of a certain age are presented to them for confirmation.

Confirmation.—This practice of a kind of confirmation is a third characteristic possessed in common by all the divisions of Vaishnavism. They all recognise a rite or rites of initiation, in which the young Vaishnavite assumes the responsibilities and is invested with the privileges of full discipleship. The form of initiation sometimes consists merely in the communication of certain religious sentences or prayers, but is sometimes more elaborate. The age at which the initiation takes place, varies in the different sects; and in some instances different ceremonies are performed at an interval of time.[1]

Sectarian Marks.—All Vaishnavites moreover, to whatever denomination they belong, bear sectarian marks on the forehead, the sign and token of their devotion to the god. All regard as a sin the taking of life, even of the lowest animal or of an insect.[2] And all hope as a reward for their own works of merit to have a place given to them after death in *Vaikuntha*, the heaven of Vishnu, or in *Goloka*, the heavenly abode of K*ri*shna.

Râmânuja.—Perhaps the most celebrated and influential of Vaishnavite teachers was *Râmânuja*, a Brâhman born near Madras at the beginning

[1] For details see Monier Williams, *Brâhmanism and Hinduism*, pp. 117 ff.

[2] It has often been pointed out that this principle of the Vaishnavite religion has an intimate bearing on the credibility of the stories that have been told of frequent suicides in connection with the car and temple of Jagannâth in Orissa. Men will do strange things in the frenzy of excitement. And among the vast crowds that throng these festivals, fatal accidents must in earlier times have been very frequent; for in spite of all the care of a British trained and officered police they still occur. But self-destruction is absolutely opposed to the convictions and beliefs of the Vaishnavite worshipper, and it can never have been intentionally and deliberately compassed. That many have perished in the throng and under the wheels of the car is certain, on the testimony of eye-witnesses. They were not however victims of a desire for death from a religious motive.

of the eleventh century. He appears to have set himself against the hard and soulless doctrine of the Vedântic philosophers which identified everything with brahma; and to have maintained in opposition to the principle of advaita that the spirits of men have a separate and real existence, while he rejected at the same time the popular theory of mâyâ or illusion. His followers call themselves after his name Râmânujas, and are sub-divided into many minor sects, of which the chief are the *Vadagalais* in the north, and the *Tengalais* in the south. The latter have their own Veda, written in Tamil, which they regard as older and more authoritative than the Sanskrit text. The two sects are distinguished by a difference in the mode of making the frontal mark, as well as on various points of doctrine. All Râmânujas worship Râma as their principal divinity; and they are found in great numbers all over India, especially in the south.

The Tengalais and Vadagalais are the Calvinists and Arminians of India. The former hold what is called the "cat" rule or doctrine, *mârjâra-nyâya*, with regard to the relations of the human spirit to the divine. The spirit of man is entirely passive, and can do nothing to forward the work of its own redemption; as the kitten remains helpless and motionless, when carried about by the mother cat. The Vadagalais maintain by preference the *markata-nyâya*, or "monkey" doctrine, that the human spirit co-operates on its own behalf with the supreme spirit, as the baby monkey clings by its own effort to the coat of its mother. The Tengalais also teach that Lakshmî, the wife of Vishnu, is a created being and finite; the Vadagalais on the contrary regard her as uncreated and infinite. Among the former the shaving of the head of widows is said to be forbidden. Their system of marking the forehead is also more elaborate. Two side lines represent the two feet of Vishnu, and a central stroke prolonged down the nose is his wife Lakshmî and his lotus throne. The Vadagalais content themselves with a curved line like a U, which is the stamp of only one foot, adding the straight central line for Lakshmî, but omitting the lotus throne.[1]

^Anandatîrtha.—About the same time as Râmânuja, *Ânandatîrtha*, a Brâhman born on the Malabar coast of south India, enforced yet more strongly the essential distinctness of the individual soul. His teaching appears to have declared the existence of two eternal and

[1] Cp. *Brâhm. and Hind.*, p. 119 ff.; Hopkins, *Religions of India*, pp. 496 ff., 501.

separate principles, the soul or spirit of God, and the spirit or spirits of man. These last are unlimited in number, but all of the same kind. The two principles moreover although co-eternal are not co-equal, for the spirit of man is inferior to and dependent on the spirit of God. His followers, divided into minor parties or sub-sects, call themselves *Mâdhvas* after the surname of their founder, and bear on their foreheads a similar mark to that of the Vadagalais. They are almost entirely confined to the south of India, where however their numbers are very considerable.

C'aitanya.—The two remaining Vaishnavite sects of importance originated in the north of India, and at about the same time, the beginning of the sixteenth century. In both of them stress is laid upon the mystical and devotional, in preference to the philosophical aspect of faith. Theirs is a religion rather of the emotions than of the intelligence; and accordingly most of their converts were drawn from the lower classes. *C'aitanya*, the founder of the one, was a Bengal Brâhman born in or about the year 1485. He claimed to be an incarnation of K*r*ishna, became a *sannyâsî* or ascetic at an early age, and by his enthusiastic preaching of bhakti, personal devotion to the god, and especially by his doctrine of the equality of all men without regard to caste, attracted to himself large numbers of disciples. His teaching spread chiefly in Bengal and Orissa, where his followers are numerous at the present time. They still affect to disregard caste, but in practice its rules are observed except at the great festivals, when food offered to the god is distributed and eaten by all in common. C'aitanya himself is said to have been translated to Vaikuntha without dying at the age of forty-two; and to him, as well as to his immediate successors, the members of the sect pay divine honours.

Vallabha.—The second northern sect is that of the *Vallabhâc'âryans*, founded by *Vallabha*, a Brâhman born on the borders of Nepâl towards the close of the fifteenth century. He appears to have been a man of considerable intelligence and force of character, who opposed himself to the ascetic tendencies and practices which have found so congenial a soil in many parts of India. According to Vallabha's teaching, the child Kr*i*shna is especially to be worshipped by the way of devotion and self-surrender.[1] Human

[1] An example of the form of vow that is taken is given by Monier Williams:—"I here dedicate to the holy Kr*i*shna my bodily organs, my life, my inmost soul and its faculties, with my wife, my house, my children, with all the wealth I may acquire here or hereafter, and my own self. O Kr*i*shna, I am thy servant." *Brâhm. and Hind.*, p. 117; cp. Barth, p. 233 ff.

love in all its forms is sacred and a type of the divine. Naturally this last doctrine was open to misconstruction, and liable to be corrupted. In reality also the followers of Vallabha have become the Epicureans of India, and have sunk generally to a very low level of morality. They are to be found mainly in Bombay and on the west coast. The lineal descendants of the founder bear the title of Mahârâjas, are often men of wealth and influence, and are worshipped as gods, as living incarnations of K*ri*shna himself.

Nârâyana.—A reforming movement within the sect was initiated at the beginning of the present century by *Swâmi-Nârâyana*, a high-caste Brâhman of Oudh. Early in life he took up his residence in Ahmadâbâd in Gujarât, and there preached doctrines of self-denial and a lofty morality with so great success that he was persecuted, compelled to leave the city, and subsequently arrested and imprisoned. After his release he gathered round him many followers, who have on the whole maintained his doctrine and discipline to the present day. There are said to be now about a thousand celibate priests, who are called "*sâdhus*," saints or holy men, and more than two hundred thousand laity, "*grihasthas*" or householders. They possess a sacred book, the work of Swâmi-Nârâyana, which is a collection of moral precepts and directions for daily life.[1]

Kabîr.—With Vaishnavite sects must also be classed the movement that originated in the Panjâb with the famous teacher *Kabîr* at the beginning of the sixteenth century. *Kabîr* is said to have been a pupil of Râmânanda, a disciple of Râmânuja, and was apparently a Musalmân by birth. Early in life however he came under the influence of all that was best in the philosophic and tolerant creed of Hinduism. Whether he ever really adopted and professed the Vaishnavite faith must be looked upon as uncertain. But in his teaching he essayed to combine the pure elevated monotheism of Islâm with a liberalism and breadth of view that has its nearest parallel perhaps in the Buddhist creed. Eclecticism has always found a congenial home on Indian ground. And Kabîr, while he strenuously rejected and denounced idolatry and the various superstitions that had been engrafted on the Vaishnavite faith, taught that the essence of all religion was devotion to the one God, to whom Hindu and Muhammadan alike paid homage, though under different names. Withal however he seems never to have entirely escaped

[1] *Brâhm. and Hind.*, pp. 148 ff.

from pantheistic tendencies, and in his reported sayings there are found expressions and sentiments which recall the philosophy of the Vedânta. The chief value of his teaching undoubtedly consisted in the high morality which he inculcated:—

> No act of devotion can equal truth; no crime is so heinous as falsehood; in the heart where truth abides, there is my abode.
>
> Put a check upon the tongue; speak not much. Associate with the wise. Investigate the words of the teacher.
>
> When the master is blind, what is to become of the scholar? When the blind leads the blind both will fall into the well.
>
> That a drop falls into the ocean all can perceive; but that the drop and the ocean are one, few can comprehend.[1]

The direct followers of Kabîr call themselves *Kabîr-panthîs,* and are found in considerable numbers in the north of India. A few also exist in the south. Their religious centre is Benares, to which city they come together at the festivals. They are said to be divided at the present time into twelve principal sub-sects.

Nânak and the Sikhs.—The most celebrated disciple of Kabîr was *Nânak,* the founder of the Sikhs or "disciples" in the Panjâb. Born near Lahore in the year 1469 he inherited the views

[1] Quoted with other examples of the traditional sayings of Kabîr in Monier Williams, *Brâhm. and Hind.*, p. 160.

and principles of his predecessor; but appears to have combined with them a larger measure of the mystical and pantheistic ideas of true Hinduism, and to have laid greater stress on the duty of implicit obedience to the living voice of the *Guru* or teacher. Nânak himself was looked upon as inspired by, or according to the Hindu conception as a manifestation of the deity. He further transmitted this authority to a line of successors, nine in number, each of whom was nominated by the preceding Guru, and to each of whom the same reverence was paid. These with Nânak form the ten chief Gurus of the Sikh religion. Their sacred book is the *Adi-Granth*, or "First Book," a collection of the sayings of Nânak, Kabîr, and the first three Gurus, with additions from various sources. It has been translated into English and published by Dr. E. Trumpp in the year 1877.[1] The fourth Guru, *Râm-dâs*, founded in 1574 Amritsar, the sacred city of the Sikhs and the head-quarters of their religion. There in the "Golden Temple" the great copy of the Granth is preserved, and an almost idolatrous regard is paid to it. The tenth Guru *Govind* refused to appoint a successor, declaring that henceforth

[1] A new edition of the Sikh Scriptures with translation is promised by Mr. M. Macaulifie, of the Indian Civil Service.

the Granth was to be the real guru of the people.

By Govind also was effected the transformation of the Sikhs from a body of religious sectarians, of loftier views and more upright practices than their neighbours, and united solely by a common faith and a common reverence for their founder and the Guru as his living representative, into a warlike and fanatical nation, who defended and propagated their faith by the sword. They adopted the name of the Khâlsâ, the portion or community of God; and their subsequent history belongs rather to the political than to the religious history of India. They are said however to be more and more falling back into Hindu usages and idolatry. The impulse of the reforming movement which Kabîr and his successors originated and guided has long since spent its force. And unless some new impulse to a higher and purer faith is brought to bear on them which shall regenerate the spirit of the people, they seem destined to be re-absorbed into the great mass of Hinduism that surrounds them on every side.

S'iva.—Of *S'aivism* it is not necessary, perhaps not possible, to say as much as with respect to Vaishnavism. It is an eminently less respectable and influential cult, and appears to be declining in popularity all over India. *S'aivism* is that form or variety of Hinduism in which the first place as an object of worship is taken by the deity euphemistically termed *S'iva,* the auspicious or fortunate god. The name is not found in the Vedic hymns, but comes early and increasingly into prominence in the later literature. As the third member of the Hindu Tri-mûrti, he is the great Destroyer. By his worshippers however he is elevated to a position of superiority to either Brahmâ or Vishnu, and is regarded as combining in his own person besides the attributes proper to himself those also of Creator and Preserver. It seems probable that the rapid advance of S'iva in popularity and influence, which the references in the books appear to indicate, is to be explained by the fact that he was originally a malevolent deity, a god of storms like his prototype Rudra, the "roarer," in the Veda, to whom indeed the same epithet *s'iva* is actually applied. Like Vishnu, S'iva has his own heaven *Kailâsa,* which is placed in the Himâlaya Mountains; and thither he bears his faithful disciples. There he dwells with his wife *Pârvatî* and his sons *Skanda* the god of war, and *Ganes'a* the god of wisdom, both of whom are widely known and honoured divinities. He is distinguished by a thousand and eight names, which describe his different attributes; and is represented with five faces, or with one face bearing three eyes, his body smeared with ashes, and in his hands various instruments of war or revelry, as a trident a cord an axe and a small drum. He rides upon the sacred bull *Nandi.* S'iva is the peculiar god of ascetics; as well as, in another aspect of his being and character, of all learning, or again of fasting and self-gratification. But especially he presides over all the acts and processes of nature. In his temples there is often placed a mere stone, sometimes entirely rough, which receives worship as the symbol of the god, and to which offerings are made usually consisting of water and Bilva leaves. The bull is sacred to S'iva, probably as being the type of reproductive energy; and a stone image of a bull is often found in connection with shrines dedicated to his worship.

Although the name of the supreme god thus makes its appearance in Hindu literature later than that of Vishnu, the germs of the S'aivite form of faith must be sought further back than any historical records will take us. As a religion it is at least as old, probably older than Vaishnavism. Certainly the earliest examples in India of religious symbols on coins are S'aivite and Buddhist, on the coins of the Indo-Scythian kings about the beginning of the Christian era; and from these the peculiar signs or emblems of the great rival sect are entirely absent.

S'aivism.—As a religious creed *S'aivism* might perhaps be best described as a combination of ancient free speculation, chiefly Sânkhyan or dualistic and materialistic, with the lower forms of nature and animal worship, which are to be met with everywhere among primitive and even more advanced peoples; a combination in which the latter element has had a larger share than the former in determining the final shape which the resultant faith and practice should assume. And thus if Vaishnavism in its better moods represents the most spiritual side of Hindu religion, S'aivism on the other hand in many of its forms descends to the lowest depths of a debasing and sensual idolatry. While therefore it is true that in India as elsewhere many individuals are better than their creed, it is not easy to discover in the S'aivite faith any features that invite commendation.

S'âktism.—By the side of S'aivism and not independent of its forms of belief and ritual is the wide-spread worship of *S'akti*, force or energy. Regarded as the power that pervades all nature and maintains it in being, *S'akti* is personified as a goddess, the wife of the god, and the agent as it were by which he carries out his will. Or to use the language of philosophy, the god himself may be said to be the efficient cause of all things, his *s'akti* the instrumental or effecting cause, and the *prakriti* the material cause.[1] The power or energy therefore of every god was conceived as in a sense resident in his wife, Sarasvatî for example being the *s'akti* of Brahmâ, Lakshmî of Vishnu, and Durgâ of S'iva. But the worship of the S'akti early became an entirely distinct cult, with temples and a literature of its own. This worship of the female principle in nature, which is intimately connected with dualistic conceptions of the origin of the universe, is met with in other branches of Hinduism; but amongst the *S'âktas*, or those especially devoted to this cult, it has been most completely developed, and provided with an organisation and ritual.

Goddess Worship.—The central and most important divinity in this form of worship is the wife of S'iva, who as *Devî* or *Mahâdevî*, "the great goddess," has largely usurped the place and functions of her lord, and become the head of a wide-spread, many-sided, and altogether disreputable cult, which possesses great influence

[1] Barth, p. 199.

especially among the lower classes. It is in the temples of Mahâdevî that bloody sacrifices have been, and to a certain extent are still offered in India. Human sacrifice, if ever it existed in the land,[1] existed in connection with or was adopted into her worship. She is the cruel deity who delights in blood, and who unless she is propitiated and her desires gratified will bring disease and death on mankind.[2] As *Kâlî*, the black goddess, her name is immortalised in Calcutta, Kâlî-kata, perhaps meaning Kâlî's burning or burying-ground. Mahâdevî stands at the head of a variety of female powers, the *Mahâmâtris* or "great mothers," the *Yoginîs* or "sorceresses," etc., whose number is unlimited. Of these the most important are the Mahâmâtris, who are usually represented as the wives of the gods, but exercise an independent sway and demand an independent homage. In general

[1] I venture to think that this still remains an open question. The passages quoted from the books, so far from regarding the practice as usual and familiar, appear to me to treat it as something altogether legendary and outside the range of their experience,—to be undertaken perhaps at the divine command, but otherwise inadmissible. It does not of course follow that such sacrifices were unknown to the rude and savage religions, whose thoughts and ways have found no record in the sacred literature.

[2] Cp. *Brâhm. and Hind.*, p. 189 f., and the passages there quoted from the Tantras.

they are to be considered as either benevolent or malignant, corresponding to the two aspects, *Gaurî* or "white," and *Kâlî* or "black," of Mahâdevî herself. The former preside over creation reproduction and life, the latter over destruction and death; and the latter are by far the more numerous. To this last class belong the goddesses who bring small-pox and fever, who inflict pain and cause disaster, and whose wrath it is incumbent upon men to avert by sacrifice.

Sects.—The *S'âktas*, or worshippers of the *S'akti*, are divided at the present time into two principal sects, with various sub-divisions scarcely to be distinguished except by the adherents themselves. These are the followers of the right-hand, the *Dakshinamârgîs* or *Dakshinâc'âryas*, who carry out in general the rules and public ceremonies of Hinduism, but add to them animal sacrifice in honour of Kâlî or some other form of the great goddess; and the *Vâmamârgîs* or *Vâmâc'âryas*, the followers of the left-hand, who practise all manner of secret observances and magic, in order to secure for themselves supernatural powers. The former, the adherents of the right-hand, are numerous and widely spread throughout India. The latter are believed to be scarcely inferior in number. It is however almost impossible to arrive at an accurate estimate of their diffusion and influence. For except in rare cases no one will openly avow himself an adherent of the left-hand with its mysterious rites of sorcery and sensual indulgence.

Very numerous also in the south of India is the Sâkta sect, termed *Lingavats*, or *Lingâyits*, from their worship of the *linga*, or phallus. Their founder is said to have been a Brâhman named Basava, who lived in the Dekhan about the beginning of the twelfth century. He gained for himself a large following by preaching against caste, the pretensions of the Brâhmans, and the entire order and ritual of the orthodox religions. The *Jangamas*, or "itinerant" monks, who penetrate to the furthest parts of India, belong to this sect. Mingled with their active repudiation of distinctively Hindu practices, and with ideas that appear to us sensual and degrading, there is a spirit of mysticism and devotion, that has found expression in hymns that have gained considerable popularity. The members of the sect bear upon the neck a cord on which is hung a small silver or metal box containing the linga symbol. They also bury instead of burning their dead. But in other respects, especially in the observance of caste distinctions, they are said to be largely returning to the customs and habits of ordinary Hindus.

Popular Beliefs.—It must however be borne in mind that these elaborate and as it were scientific systems of religion have by no means penetrated to the lowest strata of the life of India, or are in any degree co-extensive with all that bears the name of Hinduism. They are largely confined to the upper and intellectual portion of the population, a small minority, constituting perhaps one-tenth of the whole. The vast majority of the people of India are the unlettered inhabitants of the villages.[1] And no survey of Indian religious thought can justly lay claim to completeness which fails to take account of village habits and beliefs. The agricultural inhabitants of the villages, low-caste and non-caste, as a rule know nothing and care nothing for philosophic theories or systems of religious doctrine. Their religion is summed up in the desire to propitiate malevolent deities who might wish to do them harm, and to extort

[1] In the Indian census of 1891 there are enumerated 227 towns with a population of 20,000 and upward, containing 4·84 per cent. of the entire population of the country; as compared with 182 towns and 53 per cent. in England. The difference is very striking. Altogether 2035 places were returned in the census as "towns," including a considerable number where the population was less than 5000. But the total for all these was only 9·48 of the whole. See J. A. Baines, *General Report of the Census of India*, 1891, p. 42 ff.

gifts and benefits from divinities whose disposition is neutral or disposed to bless. Nor is it less true in India than in other countries where similar beliefs hold sway, that the malicious and hurtful deities receive by far the largest amount of attention. Hence the worship of the great majority of the people of India may be rightly described as demonolatry. Life on its religious side is in their case a prolonged attempt to avert the anger of evil spirits. Sir Monier Williams writes of this class that from birth to death they are "victims of a form of disease which is best expressed by the term *demonophobia.* They are haunted and oppressed by a perpetual dread of demons. They are firmly convinced that evil spirits of all kinds, from malignant fiends to merely mischievous imps and elves, are ever on the watch to harm harass and torment them, to cause plague sickness famine and disaster, to impede injure and mar every good work."[1] In some villages in the south of India no hut is permitted to have its door facing towards the south, lest it should facilitate the entrance of a demon. Every tree, every rock, every stream, the very winds themselves have their appropriate devil; whose evil designs must if possible be turned aside by

[1] *Bráhmanism and Hinduism*, p. 210 f.

offerings. Moreover every village has its own tutelary deities, who watch over it and the fields of the peasants. Every house has its household gods. And the ill-omened ranks are being continually recruited by men and women who, if they have been in any way remarkable during life, are after death apt to become unquiet ghosts to the disturbance of their former neighbours. Nor is this worship confined to the dead. It is extended also to the living. The lower classes have long been accustomed to worship the Brâhmans as little gods. And they readily offer a similar homage to any placed in authority over them, especially if they are the representatives of a power felt, but unseen and mysterious.[1]

Popular Deities.—To enumerate these various divine and superhuman beings, who are active for evil or for good, would be impossible. They are countless in number, and occupy every

[1] Perhaps this worship does not always mean so much as to us it appears to do. There can be no doubt however that in many homes in India at the present day adoration is regularly paid to the Empress of India, and her picture is habitually worshipped. The same thing took place at the time of the Jubilee celebrations of 1887, when a statue of the Queen was erected in one of the public thoroughfares of Madras, and not a few natives were reported to have been seen "doing *pûjâ*," or performing worship before it.

position in the scale, from deities whose rights and dignity are almost equal to those of the great gods to spirits who rank in capacity scarcely higher than men, but are untrammelled by limitations of time and space. One of the most popular is *Hanumân*, the monkey-god, the ally of Râma in his assault on the kingdom of Râvana; he is the leader and lord of the monkey tribes. In the North *Bhairava*, the "terrible," or *Bhairon*, is an impersonation of S'iva, whose form and worship are worthy of his name. To him a certain class of Yogîs, or ascetics, especially devote themselves, and chant hymns in his praise. S'iva's wife also, Devî, appears as *Bhairavî*. Another supposed incarnation of the same god is *Khandoba* or *Khandoji*, widely reverenced among the Marâthâs, and usually represented on horseback with a dog at his side; whose worship is infamous from the custom, still prevalent, of marrying young girls to the god, and so giving them over to a life of shame. The elephant-headed *Ganes'a*, the lord of good-fortune and of learning, is everywhere honoured. While of the village tutelary deities of the South perhaps the best known is *Ayenâr*, who goes by the name of "father Ayenâr," and is said to have been the son both of Vishnu and S'iva. For his use the villagers place models of horses in clay or terracotta in their fields, that mounted upon them he and his followers may chase away the evil demons from the crops.[1]

Animal Worship.—Many if not all animals are worshipped, from the sacred bull and monkey and snake down to creatures that hold a very low place in the scale of being. To those that are useful regard is paid for the sake of their usefulness. Those that are cruel or malicious are propitiated to induce them to refrain from doing harm. The goose is sacred to Brahmâ, the eagle and monkey and serpent to Vishnu, the bull to S′iva, the tiger to Durgâ the dread wife of S′iva, the rat to Ganes′a, the parrot to Kâma-deva or the god of love. Horses, crows, cats, and crocodiles all possess a divine or semi-divine character in different parts of India, and religious rites are observed in their honour.[2] In connection with some of these, especially the serpent tribe, an elaborate mythology exists.

[1] Cp. for the north of India W. Crooke, *Popular Religion and Folk-Lore of Northern India*, new edition, London, 1896; two most interesting volumes, stored with curious information. For the south the works quoted of Professor Monier Williams; or *Popular Hinduism*, Madras, 1887, with the authors to whom reference is there made.

[2] It is said that on one occasion in Bengal a hundred thousand rupees (£6250) were expended by a wealthy Râjah on the marriage ceremonies of a pair of monkeys.

Worship of Plants, Streams, etc.—Certain species of trees or plants moreover are especially sacred, and before them homage is regularly offered. The deification of the Soma, the intoxicating plant of the Veda, was most complete; and the same sacred character is attributed to many even of the commonest products of the soil. The *Tulasî* or *Tulsi*, the holy Basil, is believed to be possessed either by Lakshmî or Sitâ, and a specimen of it may be found growing in the court-yard of most Indian houses. The women of the household pass daily round the Tulasî plant, and before it make their prayers with offerings of rice and flowers. Often they know and perform no other worship than this. The Pîpal tree, *Ficus Religiosa*, is peculiarly holy, and no Hindu it is asserted will tell a lie under its branches. The banyan the mango and the wood-apple all share to a greater or less extent in this sacred character. A kind of grass, the *Kus'a* grass, and the sacred lotus are both symbolical of extreme sanctity, although worship may not actually be paid to them. Fire is regarded as holy, not only by the Brâhmans and Parsîs, but by many also of the wild and uncivilised tribes. All running water is holy; especially the water of certain rivers as the Ganges, the Narbada, the Indus, and the

Godaveri. To wash in the Ganges is a certain means of purification from all sin. To die on its banks is to go straight to the heaven of the gods. And water from the Ganges is carried all over India for the benefit of those who cannot themselves visit the stream. The sun, moon, planets, and all the heavenly bodies receive constant worship. And thus the list of objects to be reverenced or that are reverenced in some parts of the country might be prolonged to any extent. Mountains rocks and stones, the tools which a man uses in his trade, the fire that warms him, the books out of which the school-boy learns his lessons, the pots with which the wife cooks the dinner, all have a part in this strange and elaborate deification, and become the objects of a worship that is by no means confined to the lowest and most ignorant strata of the population. The rites also in which this multifarious worship finds expression are as various as are the demons or deities to whom it is addressed. No doubt the spread of Western culture and education is doing much, in the centres of population at least, to weaken the hold of these and similar customs. It will however be a long time before they altogether vanish before the advance of science and in the light of truth.

Hindu Religiousness.—In the presence then of this multiplicity of gods or superhuman powers, the life of the ordinary Hindu might be expected to be greatly taken up with endeavours to satisfy the claims of his many deities by means of offerings and religious ceremonies. And this is more or less true of all classes of society. The time and attention of the orthodox Hindu is largely occupied with a constant round of religious observances, performed either by himself or vicariously through a Brâhman, to meet his obligations to one or other of these gods, or to avert the consequences of the wrath of some demon. Not the simplest act of life, a rising up or a lying down, much less a great event such as a birth marriage or death, a festival anniversary or holy-day, may pass strictly speaking without the discharge of its appropriate rite of worship or purification. Undoubtedly to those who have come much under Western influences, the stringency of this religious discipline is in practice greatly relaxed; although such men remain true Hindus in name and external form. As compared however with the mass of the population they are still the comparatively rare exceptions. The ascendency of the Brâhman and of his rules for life and conduct may be breaking down under the solvent forces of education, civilisation and Christianity. It is not however yet abolished; and its strongest weapon, social ostracism, is hardly touched.

^Ac′âra.—For the Hindu all the concerns of daily life, great and small, are regulated by *ác′âra*, custom, which is only another name for religious observance handed down from his forefathers, to disregard or neglect which is to break caste, with all its tremendous consequences of proscription and persecution. He is also by nature very religious and patient of detail; and finds a satisfaction in the forms and minutiæ decreed by tradition, which to the impatient onlooker from the West is often simply unintelligible. To him nothing is secular, in the sense that it is unshared in by the supernatural powers. When it is remembered also that according to the faith which he has been taught to cherish it is to him an ever-present and very real possibility that the animal or insect he meets, even the blade of grass at his feet, may be the outward form in which dwells the spirit of his deceased ancestor; that in harmony with the universally held doctrine of metempsychosis, there is no hard and fast line or insurmountable barrier between gods and demons, between demons and men, between men and animals, between animals and plants, but that the same individual soul may inhabit the body now of a man, now of an animal, or again may live as a demon, a god, or a mere vegetable,—wonder ceases at the reverence with which the Hindus regard every form and manifestation of life, or the vivid imagination with which they people with spirits every nook corner and cranny of the universe visible and invisible. It would be unjust of course to say that to every Hindu religion is simply a matter of outward observance and ceremony. The reform movements that have sprung up from within, and have achieved a wide if temporary success, bear witness to the contrary. Of the great majority of the people however it remains true that religion to them has nothing to do with the heart or the spiritual life. Nor is it a question of the intelligent acceptance of well-understood formulæ or creeds. It is a round of mere external performances, unrivalled in any country for their minute and exacting character, in the regular and precise execution of which consists the whole duty of man.

Summary of Reform Movements.—On a review therefore of the whole course of Indian religious history it has been seen to be marked by constant efforts at reform, which have derived their inspiration now from within and now from without. There has been continual degeneracy, interrupted by spasmodic revivals more or less influential and far-reaching. The earliest of these, of which we have any knowledge, has found expression in the older and purer of the Upanishads, in a genuine and thoughtful attempt to penetrate behind and above the crude nature worship of the Vedic hymns or the dead formalism of the Brâhmanic ritual, and to reach a more philosophic soul-satisfying creed. Buddhism in its turn, impelled largely by the upanishad spirit, represented the feeling of weariness with the lifeless ceremonies of Brâhmanism, of revolt against its priestly arrogance, and of distrust of speculations which tended more and more to reduce man to ineffectiveness, to mere passive acquiescence in a Power that he had no choice but to obey. The reform or compromise again out of which Vaishnavism and the other sectarian religions arose, gave expression to the protest of the human heart against creeds and material systems, which left no place for personal communion with a living god; and their founders and successive teachers or regenerators sought to direct their fellow-countrymen back from the degenerate practices of idol worship to a supposed primitive and more excellent faith. Lastly came the reform movement that led to the formation of the Sikh nation in the north-west of India and the Panjâb, which presents itself as in many respects the most striking instance of the law of revolt and recoil, which seems to have beset the Hindu peoples with fatal persistency. Here however the initial impulse came from without. Kabîr and his successors endeavoured to combine the strict monotheism of Islâm and its abhorrence of idolatry with whatever was best or most deeply rooted in the creed and affections of the Hindu. In each case the reforming movement has appeared to run its course, gradually to exhaust itself and die away, leaving the great mass of orthodox belief and observance comparatively untouched, and the fabric of Brâhmanism at least in externals in no degree less powerful and imposing. Buddhism and the religions of Vishnu and S'iva form no real exceptions. Undoubtedly Brâhmanism has received from Buddhism, to which it so largely gave; but Buddhism has disappeared from India, leaving its rival in possession of the field. Vaishnavism and S'aivism again have been adopted into, and form outwardly the larger part of the religious system that represents ancient Brâhmanism. But the Hindu system as it exists to-day does not depend for its support and continued life on any of these. Notwithstanding all the profound modifications of thought and practice through which it has passed, the substance of modern Hinduism, that which holds the fabric together, its strength and stay, is not belief in Vishnu or S'iva or any other personal divinity, but the customs and laws which have been handed down from Brâhman ancestors and formulated by Brâhmanic authority.

MODERN RELIGIOUS REFORM

THERE have been in India a considerable number of minor movements of a more limited range and influence, which it is impracticable here to trace. In no country has the play of religious thought been less restrained, or its expression more varied. The latest attempt however at reform from within, in the direction of the establishment of a pure theistic worship, has arisen within the present century; and of this great hopes were entertained at one time by many who believed that the people would and could work out their own spiritual regeneration in their own way. The originator and founder of the movement was Râmmohun Roy, a Brâhman born in the year 1774 at Râdhâ-nagar, in the district of Mushidâbâd in Bengal.[1] Precisely as Kabîr had attempted to form a composite creed out of the best

[1] The date and name of the village are given by Monier Williams, *Brâhm. and Hind.*, p. 478. Others place his birth two years earlier, and in the district of Bardwân, further south; see Barth, p. 291.

elements of Muhammadanism and Hinduism, so Râmmohun Roy aimed at setting up a new eclectic system, on the professed basis indeed of a primitive and expurgated Brâhmanism, but which really combined and intermingled Hindu and Christian beliefs and modes of worship. His indebtedness to Christianity and to Christian books was freely acknowledged by Râmmohun Roy and his successors; but they all repudiated the name of Christian and formally rejected many of the distinctively Christian doctrines.

Râmmohun Roy.—The history of the founder himself may be briefly summarised. His life is illustrative of a spiritual and mental eagerness and unrest not at all uncommon in the country of his birth. Brought up as a Vaishnavite he studied when quite a lad Muhammadan books and especially the Qurân, with a view probably to worldly advancement. At the age of sixteen he wrote a pamphlet against idolatry, and in consequence of the hostile feeling aroused was compelled for a time to leave his father's house. Some years were spent in travel in India and Tibet, making inquiry into the different systems of religion, and acquainting himself with Arabic Persian Pâli and even Greek and Hebrew, in order that he might be able to read the various sacred books in their original languages. To these after a time he added English; and entered into the service of the Government, acting as Dîwân in several districts of Bengal. During all this period he was engaged in religious controversy, publishing treatises against what he held to be the errors of Hinduism, and translations into the vernacular of the Upanishads and other Sanskrit works. The position which Râmmohun Roy then took up, and which he consistently maintained to the end, was the one so familiar since his day, that the superstitious and idolatrous practices of Hinduism are a later accretion; that all therefore that is necessary for the renovation and purification of the Hindu religion is to return to the teaching of the earlier sacred books and especially the Upanishads; and that these if rightly interpreted will be found to inculcate, so he asserted, a pure and strict monotheism.

Founding of Brâhma-Samâj.—In or about the year 1814 having removed to Calcutta, Râmmohun Roy established there with the help of other native gentlemen like-minded with himself an association for the promotion of spiritual religion. Meetings were regularly held, at which passages from the Veda were read, hymns were sung, and addresses delivered. A few years later, in the beginning of 1830, the first building set apart for this new worship was opened in Calcutta. This was the earliest theistic church of India, which has been the parent of many others, scattered here and there in the great towns to which the movement has spread. Râmmohun Roy gave to his society the name of *Brâhma-Sabhâ*, or *Brâhma-Samâj*,[1] the company of believers in Brahma, or God; and by the latter name it has become generally known. He thus employed the ancient Hindu or Vedic term to designate the one God, whom he regarded as the true and only object of faith; and claimed to have initiated or established a pure monotheistic worship, in which Hindus, Muhammadans, Christians, Buddhists, Jews or any other race or creed might join on the simple basis of belief in the one supreme God. Before the year closed he left India for England on a mission from the ex-Emperor of Delhi. On his arrival he was presented at the court of King William the Fourth, and remained in the country during all the Reform agitation of 1831–32, in which he took a deep interest. The following year he visited Paris, and returned in the autumn to Bristol. There, having been

[1] *Brâhma-Samâj* is Sanskrit. The usual Bengali form is *Brâhmo-Samâj*.

taken ill with fever, he died on September 27th, 1833. His body was buried with all due Brâhmanical rites in a private garden, but was subsequently removed to the Arno's Vale cemetery, where a tombstone stands to his memory.

Relation to Christianity.—It has often been asserted that Râmmohun Roy was in reality a Christian. Undoubtedly it is true that he believed the moral teaching of the New Testament to be far superior to that found in any other sacred book; that he associated much with Christian missionaries, and was always ready to aid them in their work; that he denounced caste, though never himself ceasing to observe its rules and restrictions; and that he abandoned much of the peculiar teaching of Hinduism. On the other hand many of the essential and characteristic doctrines of Christianity he refused to accept. Of the doctrine of the Trinity he declared that it was equivalent to polytheism; and a belief in the Divinity of Christ was with equal decision rejected. With all his enlightened views he never entirely broke with the old faith, wore to the last the thread of the twice-born, and remained a true if reformed Brâhman. Of the many noble sons however whom India has sent forth in the long course of her history

Râmmohun Roy was assuredly one of the noblest and greatest, whether regard be had to the powers of his mind or the sincerity of his heart.

Debendra-nâth Tâgore.—The successor of Râmmohun Roy in the leadership of the theistic church was a Brâhman, Debendra-nâth Tâgore, a man of a liberal spirit, but as strongly attached as his predecessor to the name and forms of ancient Brâhmanism. He drew up a theistic creed or declaration, by which every member of the church was expected to bind himself, avowing his intention to worship only one God, to shun all sin, especially the sin of idolatry, and to do good works. The attention of Debendra-nâth was given mainly to the organisation and consolidation of the new society; and he endeavoured, while providing for the future, to break as little as possible with the past. In 1847 the number of members was reported to be 767.

Keshab Chandar Sen.—There was growing up however within the church itself a spirit of unrest, and of dissatisfaction with the strongly conservative tendencies of the leaders and older men. In the new party which aimed at more radical changes in faith and worship the most influential representative of advanced views was Keshab Chandar Sen, a member of the *Vaidya* or medical caste, who at the age of twenty had joined the theistic church in 1858. In his eyes the reforms already carried out appeared partial and incomplete. He consistently urged the breaking with all Hindu usages, especially the abolition of caste distinctions, of ancestor worship and other practices never by the older members entirely dropped, and the disuse of the sacred thread. His zeal and ability speedily won for him an acknowledged leadership among the younger adherents of the church; and in 1865 he and those who sympathized with him in these views seceded, and formed a new society called the *Brâhma-Samâj* of India, the members of which professed to have entirely surrendered Brâhmanism and Brâhmanical observances. The original church adopted the name of the *Adi Brâhma-Samâj*, or First Brâhma Samâj, and sought to maintain a position of compromise, holding an eclectic creed without forsaking many of the distinctive practices of Hinduism. The new Samâj was more independent of traditions and old associations than that from which it seceded, less artificial in its creed, and more profoundly influenced by the spirit and ethics of Christianity. Its leader never attempted to conceal his admiration for Jesus Christ as a man, nor the obligation under which he lay to the moral teaching of the New Testament. And in this respect his followers have been true to his example. Like his predecessor Râmmohun Roy however he refused to go further in the acceptance of Christian doctrine, denying for example the Divinity of Christ, and while he freely used Christian terms interpreting them always in an Indian and almost pantheistic sense. The earliest confession of faith drawn up by him for the use of the members of the Brâhma-Samâj includes belief in one God, as Creator, Preserver, and Lord of all, who is infinite in power and wisdom; in the immortality of the soul; and in the equality and brotherhood of all men. It expressly rejects the Hindu doctrine of transmigration, prescribes certain duties to be performed, and urges the pursuit of holiness of life:—

God Himself never becomes man by putting on a human body. His divinity dwells in every man, and is displayed more vividly in some; as in Moses, Jesus Christ, Muhammad, Nânak, C'aitanya, and other great Teachers, who appeared at special times, and conferred vast benefits on the world. They are entitled to universal gratitude and love.

. . . .

Duties are of four kinds: (1) Duties *towards God*—such as belief in Him, love, worship, and service; (2) Duties *towards self*—such as preservation of bodily health, acquisition of knowledge, sanctification of soul; (3) Duties *towards others*—such as veracity, justice, gratitude, the promotion of the welfare of all mankind; (4) Duties *towards animals* and inferior creatures —such as kind treatment.[1]

In the year 1870 Keshab Chandar Sen visited England, was received by the Queen, spoke at various large meetings in London and the provinces, and preached in Unitarian and other Nonconformist places of worship. The numerous sects into which the Christian world appeared to be divided caused him perplexity. He regarded them as presenting each some aspect of the Christ. But nowhere did he find "the genuine and full Christ as He was and as He is":—

When the Roman Catholic, the Protestant, the Unitarian, the Trinitarian, the Broad Church, the Low Church, the High Church, all come round me, and offer me their respective Christs, I desire to say to one and all,—"Think you that I have no Christ within me? Though an Indian, I can still humbly say, Thank God that I have my Christ."[2]

Some of his last public words before leaving England well describe his attitude to Christianity:—

The result of my visit to England is that as I came here an Indian, I go back a confirmed Indian. I came here a Theist, I return a confirmed Theist. I have not accepted a single new

[1] Monier Williams, *Brâhm. and Hind.*, pp. 503–504, where the complete creed is given.

[2] *Brâhm. and Hind.*, p. 506.

doctrine that God had not put into my mind before; I have not accepted new dogmas and doctrines, but I have tried as far as possible to imbibe the blessed influence of Christian lives.[1]

After his return to India his energies were devoted to the service of the Brâhma-Samâj, to the promotion of measures of social reform, and to the propagation of the theistic faith. In connection with this work he was accustomed to deliver annual public addresses or manifestoes, in which much that was personal was mingled with expositions of doctrine and earnest appeals on behalf of purity and truth. In the most famous of these, spoken in the Town Hall, Calcutta, in the spring of 1879 before a great audience which included Europeans as well as native Indians, he announced as his subject,—"India asks, Who is Christ?" and after declaring "I am not a Christian," proceeded to call upon his hearers to accept Christ as the true Asiatic Saint, the greatest Yogî that the world had known, and avowed his belief that Christianity was destined to be the future religion of India:—

Behold Christ cometh to us as an Asiatic in race, as a Hindu in faith, as a kinsman and a brother, and He demands your heart's affection. The devout Christ, like your Yogis and Rishis, lived a life of sweet devotion, and loved to dwell always

[1] *Religious Reform*, p. 33.

in the Supreme Spirit. In accepting Him you accept the spirit of a devout Yogi and a loving Bhakta,—the fulfilment of your national scriptures and prophets.

. . . .

Gentlemen, you cannot deny that your hearts have been touched, conquered, and subjugated by a higher power. That power, need I tell you? is Christ. It is Christ who rules British India, and not the British Government. England has sent out a tremendous moral force in the life and character of that mighty prophet to conquer and hold this vast empire. None but Jesus, none but Jesus, none but Jesus ever deserved this bright, this precious diadem India, and Jesus shall have it.[1]

A further and last illustration of Keshab Chandar Sen's indebtedness to Christian inspiration and Christian books may be given from a confession of faith, which as "apostle of the Church of the New Dispensation" he issued a few years later, in 1883. The source and model from which were derived both thought and language it is not difficult to recognise:—

Keshab Chandar Sen, a servant of God, called to be an apostle of the Church of the New Dispensation, which is in the holy city of Calcutta, the metropolis of Âryâvarta,

To all the great nations in the world, and to the chief religious sects in the East and the West,

To the followers of Moses, of Jesus, of Buddha, of Confucius, of Zoroaster, of Mahomet, of Nânak, and the various branches of the Hindu Church,

Grace be to you, and peace everlasting.

Whereas sectarian discord and strife, schisms and enmities prevail in our Father's family, causing much bitterness and

---

[1] *Rel. Reform*, p. 39; *Brâhm. and Hind.*, p. 516.

unhappiness, impurity and unrighteousness, and even war, carnage, and bloodshed,

. . . .

It has pleased the Holy God to send unto the world a message of peace and love, of harmony and reconciliation.

This New Dispensation hath He in boundless mercy vouchsafed to us in the East, and we have been commanded to bear witness unto it among the nations of the earth.

Thus saith the Lord,—Sectarianism is an abomination unto Me, and unbrotherliness I will not tolerate.

I desire love and unity, and My children shall be of one heart, even as I am one.

At sundry times have I spoken through My prophets, and through My many and various dispensations; there is unity in them.

. . . .

Blessed are the peace-makers, who reconcile differences and establish peace, good-will, and brotherhood in the name of the Father.

These words hath the Lord our God spoken unto us, and His new Gospel He hath revealed unto us,—a gospel of exceeding joy.

And these blessed tidings the Loving Father hath charged me and my brother apostles to declare unto all the nations of the world, that being of one blood they may also be of one faith and rejoice in one Lord.

Gather ye the wisdom of the East and the West, and accept and assimilate the examples of the saints of all ages.

Above all, love one another, and merge all differences in universal brotherhood.

Let Asia, Europe, Africa, and America, with diverse instruments praise the New Dispensation, and sing the Fatherhood of God and the Brotherhood of Man.[1]

---

[1] Quoted by Sir Monier Williams from the "Times of India," for Jan. 12th. 1883; see *Brâhm. and Hind.*, pp. 517–518.

Succession.—Early in the year 1884 Keshab Chandar Sen died, and his body was burnt with simple rites on the banks of the Ganges. The leadership of the movement has devolved on P. C. Mozumdar, a man of ability, and thoroughly imbued with the liberal views of his predecessors; but little or no advance appears to have been made either in numbers or influence.[1]

Reformed Worship.—The services conducted in the halls or churches of the Brâhma-Samâj are more or less close imitations of Christian worship. Hymns are sung, prayers offered, passages read from sacred books, as the Vedas Qurân New Testament Zend-Avesta and perhaps others, and a sermon preached. In particular the *Mandir*, or place of worship which Keshab Chandar Sen himself built, is described as outwardly like a Gothic church with spire complete, and in its internal arrangements similar to a plain Nonconformist chapel. They have a rite answering to Baptism, another to Confirmation, and a third to the Sacrament of the Lord's Supper. It is

[1] Mr. Mozumdar's authority is not recognised by all members of the New Dispensation Church, still less by all branches of the Brâhma-Samâj. Within the former there are at least three divisions, each with its own literary organ and place of worship; that of which Mr. Mozumdar is the head is the largest and most influential. See Note at the end of this chapter.

also reported,—although the statement appears almost incredible,—that in addition to these services regular dances are held, and even in some places and on certain occasions jugglery performances. In the churches the women do not sit with the men, but have a separate gallery provided for them, screened off from the rest of the congregation.

Related Societies.—Kindred societies to the Brâhma-Samâj of Calcutta have been established in most of the principal cities of India, especially Bombay and Madras. The members of these societies all hold theistic views, profess the most unbounded admiration for the character and person of Christ,[1] and have nominally at

[1] An illustration of this is found in a recent article by a writer of the Brâhma-Samâj:—"Jesus Christ seems to us to be as the loftiest Himâlaya of the spiritual world, and during these many centuries people have been struggling hard to climb to the top of the holy mountain by various ways, but still they are far from the goal. . . . Among these seekers of Christ the Brahma-Samaj is one. The torch with which it humbly goes forth on the holy pilgrimage is the word of Christ, that no one can reveal the Son except the Father. . . . Our attitude to him crucified has been one of sincere loyalty, faith, reverence and obedience. His words make our guide, which we interpret according to the light that has been vouchsafed unto us, and we have now landed in a place where knowledge and faith, letter and spirit, history and inner light, the past and the future, the East and the West harmonise." Quoted in *Harvest Field*, 1898, p. 342.

least rejected the distinctive usages of Hinduism, and especially the observance of caste. The mantle however of the genius and enthusiasm of Keshab Chandar Sen does not seem to have fallen on any of his successors. There is little or no connection between the associations of the different towns. They neither form nor have attempted to form a united church, but are split up into various sections, numerically and individually weak. They have moreover never gained or sought to gain a footing in the villages, and a society or church that in India ignores the villages is self-condemned to a very limited influence or success. Their leaders themselves ascribe their comparative powerlessness to-day to the lack of union among the churches, and the decay of the "missionary" spirit.[1] The membership of all the societies of the Brâhma-Samâj, numbered at the last census, was returned at a little over three thousand.

^Arya-Samâj.—A somewhat similar association, which doubtless owes its origin to similar influences, is that of the *^Arya-Samâj*, the society of pure Vedic Hindus, founded by Dayânanda Sarasvatî about the middle of the present

[1] See for example extracts quoted in *Church Missionary Intelligencer*, 1897, pp. 602-603.

century. The principle which he proclaimed was that of a return to the simple teaching of the Vedas, in which he professed to find an exact theism. The adherents of the Arya-Samâj are strict Hindus, rejecting all Christian doctrines, but claiming to have purified their religion from later additions and idolatrous practices, which form no part of the true worship as inculcated in the Vedas. The number of members is given as forty thousand.

Numbers and Prospects.—Thus the Reformed Theistic Church of India cannot count altogether fifty thousand adherents, or scarcely one in every six thousand of the population. Moreover their most eminent men themselves being witness, the spiritual life and force within them is abated. And thus within a century of its birth the last and in many respects the most promising attempt at a moral rehabilitation and purification of Hinduism from within seems to have entered on a period of decadence. What the future may have in store for the Brâhma-Samâj, should some new leader arise with the ability and enthusiasm of Keshab Chandar Sen, it is impossible to foresee. But the failure of the latest effort after compromise and reform has served to re-emphasize the incapacity of the Hindu faith to meet the needs of the human heart, or to bear the searchlight of truth.

NOTE:—The most active and important of the Reformed churches at the present time is the *Sâdhârana Brâhma-Samâj*, or "Catholic" Brâhma-Samâj. This Society took its rise during the life-time of Keshab Chandar Sen from the dissatisfaction felt by many of his followers at his inconsistent conduct in relation to the marriage of his daughter, and his claim to a personal inspiration. There is a membership of 500 at the Calcutta church, with small branches in several of the mofussil towns; and an annual report is published after the model of the Christian Missionary Societies. Their weekly organ is "The Indian Messenger," the ablest and most enlightened of the papers that are published in the interests of the Brâhma-Samâj. Altogether six principal Reformed churches now exist in Calcutta, with as many smaller halls or preaching-places.

BUDDHISM

LITERATURE. GENERAL.—Sir Monier Monier-Williams, *Buddhism*, London, 1889; T. W. Rhys Davids, *Buddhism*, London, n.d.; and Hibbert Lectures on the *Origin and Growth of Religion*, London, 1881.

SPECIAL.—H. Kern, *Manual of Indian Buddhism*, Strassburg, 1896; R. Spence Hardy, *Manual of Buddhism*, second edition, London, 1880; R. S. Copleston, *Buddhism in Magadha and Ceylon*, London, 1892; W. W. Rockhill, *Life of the Buddha*, London, 1884; L. A. Waddell, *Buddhism of Tibet*, London, 1895; J. Edkins, *Chinese Buddhism*, second edition, London, 1893; G. A. Cobbold, *Religion in Japan*, London, 1894; W. R. Winston, *Four Years in Upper Burma*, London, 1892.

TRANSLATIONS.—H. C. Warren, *Buddhism in Translations*, Cambridge, Massachusetts, 1896; T. W. Rhys Davids and H. Oldenburg, *Vinaya Texts*, three vols., Oxford, 1881–85; E. B. Cowell, F. Max Müller, and J. Takakusu, *Buddhist Mahâyâna Texts*, Oxford, 1894.

BUDDHISM

THE religious system which takes its name from *Buddha*, or more correctly *the Buddha*,[1] is at once distinguished from the Indian faiths which have already been considered in that, like Muhammadanism or Christianity, it traces its origin historically to the work and teaching of an individual founder. The person and life of that founder have been enveloped in a cloud of romance and fable, through which it is not always easy to discern the simple truth. The main outlines of his life however as derived from the records of the sacred books and from the accounts of disciples and pilgrims may be determined with a fair degree of certainty.

Complex Character.—Greater difficulty besets the question of doctrine. How far the details

[1] The word is of course a title or descriptive epithet, not a proper name; and signifies the "wise" or "enlightened" one. A list of earlier Buddhas, who preceded the Buddha of history, is given in Monier Williams' *Buddhism*, p. 135 f., or Warren, *Buddhism in Translations*, p. 32.

of this are due to the Buddha himself, or to what precise extent the original form of his teaching has become distorted supplemented or enlarged in later times, must remain for the present at least open to question. That in India Buddhism arose as a protest against the unfruitful doctrines of a philosophical Brâhmanism, especially the way of salvation by works, *karma-kânda*; and that this was the secret of its early and wide-spread success, can hardly be doubted. While however it was thus direct and simple in its beginnings, in the many countries where it has found a home, in Ceylon and Burma, in China Korea and Japan, in Tibet and the central table-land of Asia, Buddhism is as many-sided as Hinduism itself, and has scarcely any more right to be regarded as a single or consistent form of religious faith. Philosophically it is mere pessimism; conscious existence in any form is an evil; from this therefore the wise man will make good his escape at the earliest possible opportunity. Morally it has made perhaps the nearest approach to the Christian standard that the world has known; by its sacred books it inculcates, if its adherents do not always practise, a lofty morality and philanthropy. Theologically it is atheistic. Doctrinally it is a combination of idealism and superstition, often in their most extravagant forms, with far-sighted strivings after truth. In practical life it occupies every extreme, from the hard tyranny of an ignorant and greedy priesthood to the light-hearted fatalism which eats and drinks and enjoys itself. Modern Buddhism has thus travelled far from the simplicity of its early faith. And the attempt to return, made by some of its leaders and adherents to-day, cannot but command sympathy, in so far as it is an endeavour to substitute nobler ideals for that which had descended to the level of the commonplace and unworthy.

Expulsion from India.—From its birthplace and ancient home the religion of the Buddha has been entirely driven. There are now no Buddhists proper in India. That it went forth after a long and keen struggle for existence can scarcely be doubted; and it has left its mark upon Brâhmanism and Brâhmanical practice scarcely less deeply than Hindu philosophy and thought through its founder and early adherents have entered into it. The circumstances however and precise date of its departure remain in obscurity. There is no proof of a violent conflict between the established religion of the Brâhmans and the Buddhist heresies. Such a conflict is in itself improbable, and all the available evidence tends to show that the two religions lived at peace. On the contrary the Muhammadan invasions of the eleventh and following centuries were attended by persecutions and bloodshed on a large scale, and carried the fire and sword of religious fanaticism through the whole north of India. More pliant Brâhmanism bent to the storm and survived, to place itself at the service of the conqueror and to win its greater victories in the arts of peace. Buddhism, perhaps already decadent, could neither compromise nor resist, and was forced to retire from the field, leaving behind it only striking monuments of its former greatness. Thus while the Buddhist faith is predominant in the countries already named, and wields a measure of influence elsewhere, in its native country its tenets and teaching are represented only by the independent but closely related sect of the Jainas, who with a comparatively small following have similar doctrines and constitution. The number of real Buddhists existing at the present time it is not easy to determine, the uncertain factor in the account being China. Its place is probably fifth in order of the great religions, with less than a hundred million adherents.[1]

Life of the Buddha.—The precise date of the birth of the future Buddha has been much disputed, and it is scarcely to be expected that complete certainty on the point will ever now be attained.[2]

[1] See *supra*, p. 15 ff.

[2] Early Buddhist chronology is admittedly uncertain and obscure. But the limits of uncertainty have been much diminished by the very thorough discussion which the subject has received. The great antiquity claimed by Buddhist tradition for the life and work of Gautama has never been accepted by European scholars. On the other hand the extreme scepticism, which transferred his entire existence to the region of fable, has been abandoned. Three dates form land-marks in the early religious history of India, and have been determined from external considerations beyond the reach of reasonable doubt. These are the reign of the great Buddhist king As'oka, whose grandfather C'andragupta is identified with the Sandrokottos of the Greek historians, contemporary with Seleucus I. Nicator who died in the year 280 B.C.; and the visits to India of the Chinese monks and pilgrims Fâ-Hian and Hiuen-Tsiang. As'oka's reign is assigned by Max Müller to the years 259–222 B.C.; others place it slightly earlier. The Chinese pilgrims are *circa* 400 A.D. and 630 A.D. respectively. To these fixed dates may be added as a fourth the period of the life and travels of I-Tsing in the last quarter of the seventh century.[1] From these data, combined with the records of the native Buddhist chronicles, Max Müller finds that the death of the Buddha took place 477 B.C.; and to this conclusion the late Prof. Georg Bühler gave his support. Since therefore

[1] Cp. I-Tsing's *Record of the Buddhist Religion*, translated by J. Takakusu, Oxford, 1896, pp. xxv.–xxxviii.

The most probable view places his birth about the middle or end of the sixth century before Christ. The details also of his life have been so overlaid with romance, and so encrusted with legend and fable, that it is difficult if not impossible to distinguish in all cases the false from the true. Dismissing the miraculous element, there is not much that is really known concerning him. His father was named S'uddhodana, a prince of the royal family of the S'âkyas, a Râjput clan, holding sway in the part of India which is now the kingdom of Oudh together with the adjoining districts of Nepâl. There in the Lumbini Grove by the town of Kapilavastu, the ruins of which lie hidden in the dense *tarai* region beyond the British border about thirty miles north-west of the modern village or station of Uska Bazar, Gautama Buddha was born.[1] The name which

all accounts agree that he lived to the age of eighty, it would follow that he was born in or about the year 557 B.C. T. W. Rhys Davids, *Buddhism*, p. 213, concludes "that the Buddha died within a few years of 412 B.C.," and this date is accepted by Monier Williams. Others, as Westergaard and Kern, bring the time of his death down to a considerably later period, *circa* 370 B.C. The subject is discussed by Prof. Max Müller, *S. B. E.*, vol. x[2]., p. xliii. ff., with a chronological table, and at greater length in *History of Sanskrit Literature*, 2nd ed., pp. 262 ff., 299; Kern, p. 101 ff.; Barth, p. 105 ff.

[1] On the recent discovery, which has excited so much

he received is perhaps derived from that of the ancient *ri*shi Gotama, to whom are ascribed

interest, of the true site according to ancient belief of Kapilavastu, see articles by Vincent A. Smith in *Journ. Royal Asiat. Soc.*, 1897, pp. 615 ff., 644 ff.; and a letter from G. Bühler, which originally appeared in the *Athenæum*, *ib.* p. 429 ff. The city itself was destroyed, according to the tradition, during the life-time of the Buddha; but the spot was visited by king As'oka, and by both Fâ-Hian and Hiuen-Tsiang. "The identification of Kapilavastu was determined by the discovery in March 1895 of the As'oka pillar at Niglîva, and the associated *stûpa* of Konâgamana, or Kanaka Muni Buddha. Niglîva is a small Nepalese village in the Tarâi, or lowlands below the hills . . . about thirty-eight miles north-west of the Uskâ Bazar Station on the Bengal and North-Western Railway, and about twelve miles from the Chilliâ Police Station in the Basti District."[1] The Chinese pilgrims indicate that Kapilavastu is distant only a few miles from Niglîva; and the ruins of the city were actually so found, overgrown with jungle, with an inscribed pillar of As'oka half buried in the ground. The inscription or edict is thus translated by G. Bühler:— "King Piyadasi, (*i.e.* As'oka), beloved of the gods, having been anointed twenty years, himself came and worshipped, saying, 'Here Buddha Shakyamuni was born' . . . and he caused a stone pillar to be erected, which declares, 'Here the worshipful one was born.'"[2] See also an article on *Kapilavastu in the Buddhist Books* by T. Watters in the same Journal for 1898, p. 533 ff.; and notes and descriptions of discoveries by V. A. Smith, *ib.* p. 573 ff. "The Niglîva pillar with the inscription recording As'oka's visit to the *stûpa* of Kanakamuni lies . . . just outside the southern limit

[1] *Loc. cit.*, p. 616. "Thirty-eight miles" admittedly, I believe, by an error overstates the distance.

[2] *Ibid.*, p. 429.

some of the hymns of the Rig-Veda; it would therefore signify "related to" or "descended from" Gotama. He is also called *S'âkyamuni* "the sage of the S'âkyas," and *Siddhârtha* "he who has accomplished his aim." The dream of his mother Mâyâ or Mahâ-Mâyâ is well known, in which she beheld the future Buddha descending from heaven, and entering her womb in the form of a white elephant. Hence to a Buddhist the elephant is the most sacred of all animals. She herself died within seven days of his birth, and was transported to the heaven of S'akra or Indra, whither her son later ascended in order in person to instruct her in his law. Over his birth the gods themselves presided, and his coming was heralded by favourable omens and portents. In particular it was prophesied concerning the son who was to be born, that he would become either a Universal Monarch or a Buddha. Mighty earthquakes

of the ruins of Kapilavastu, which extend for several miles east and west. The western end of the ruins of the city rests on the left or eastern bank of the Bângangâ river, a considerable stream which descends from the hills and joins the Râpti in the Bastî District. The breadth of the city of Kapilavastu north and south was much less than its length east and west. The position of Kapilavastu may be defined as approximately in latitude 27° 37′ N. and longitude 83° 8′ E."[1]

[1] *J. R. A. S.*, 1898, p. 580.

and miracles of healing took place; flowers bloomed and gentle rains fell although out of season; heavenly music was heard, delicious scents filled the air, and the very water of the ocean lost its saltness and became sweet and refreshing. On his birth the boy was received by four Brahma angels; and proclaimed at once with a loud voice his own greatness.[1] At the same moment his future wife was born, and also the sacred Bo-Tree, under which he was destined to attain Buddhahood.

A further and more definite prophecy was uttered by a gifted ascetic to whom the child was brought, that at the age of thirty-five he would surely become a Buddha; and again to the father the announcement was made that in due time the "four signs" would appear to his son, which would lead him to retire from the world and enter upon the course ordained for him:—

> Then said the king, "What shall my son see to make him retire from the world?"
>
> "The four signs."
>
> "What four?"
>
> "A decrepit old man, a diseased man, a dead man, and a monk."

---

[1] In two of his previous existences also the Buddha is said to have uttered words immediately after his birth. See *Jâtaka*, i. 53, quoted in Warren, p. 47.

"From this time forth," said the king, "let no such persons be allowed to come near my son. It will never do for my son to become a Buddha. What I would wish to see is my son exercising sovereign rule and authority over the four great continents and the two thousand attendant isles, and walking through the heavens surrounded by a retinue thirty-six leagues in circumference." And when he had so spoken he placed guards for a distance of a quarter of a league in each of the four directions, in order that none of these four kinds of men might come within sight of his son.[1]

The prince also marries, and in due course has a son born to him. In spite however of all precautions, and of the delights and distractions by which he is surrounded, the four signs successively appear before him by the intervention and contrivance of the gods themselves. He accordingly determines to renounce the world; but before carrying out his purpose visits once more his wife and child as they lie asleep, only abstaining from waking them lest their entreaties and caresses should interfere to turn him from his settled resolve. At this time, the hour of the "Great Renunciation," he is said to have been twenty-nine years old.

His departure from the city was accompanied by miraculous signs, in the same manner as when he had been born. The gods themselves stifled the sound of his horse's neighing, lest the warders and city should be aroused, and pre-

[1] *Jâtaka*, i. 57; Warren, p. 53.

vented its hoofs from noisily touching the ground; while the heavy outer gates opened to him of their own accord. *Mâra* too, the prince of evil, endeavoured but without success to win him to return. Then began the so-called "Great Struggle," lasting according to the tradition for six years. After visiting Râjagṛiha,[1] the future Buddha proceeded to Uruvelâ, where in company with five ascetics he entered upon a course of austerities, which were by him carried to such an extreme that he fell down senseless and was believed to be dead:—

Then certain of the deities said, "The monk Gotama is dead;" but others said, "This is a practice of the saints." Then those who thought he was dead went to king Suddhodana, and announced to him that his son was dead.

"Did he die after becoming a Buddha, or before?" asked the king.

"He was unable to become a Buddha, but in making the Struggle he fell to the ground and died."

When the king heard this he refused to credit it, saying, "I do not believe it. Death cannot come to my son before he attains to enlightenment."

. . . .

---

[1] Râjagṛiha, the capital of Magadha, is represented by the modern village of Râjgir, about twenty-five miles south-south-east of Patna. The name means the king's house or palace. The ruins of the old town lie directly south of Râjgir, and cover an area of about sixteen square miles. Three of the five surrounding hills are now occupied by Jaina temples. See *Gazetteer of India, s.v.*; Monier Williams, pp. 403–406.

But the future Buddha recovering his consciousness and standing up, the deities went a second time to the king, and told him that his son was well again.

Said the king, "I knew that my son could not have died."

Now the six years which the Great Being thus spent in austerities were like time spent in endeavouring to tie the air into knots. And coming to the decision, "These austerities are not the way to enlightenment," he went begging through villages and market-towns for ordinary material food, and lived upon it. And his thirty-two physical characteristics as a great being again appeared, and the colour of his body became like unto gold.[1]

Attainment of Buddhahood.—On his abandonment of the practice of austerities, the five ascetics his companions left him; and alone under the sacred Bo-Tree,[2] having bathed and fortified himself with food, seated on the eastern side of the tree upon a seat or throne of grass, he gave himself up to the attainment of supreme wisdom. Here he was again assailed by Mâra with all his host, at whose approach the gods fled away defeated and terrified, and the future

[1] *Jâtaka*, i. 67; Warren, p. 70 f.

[2] The Bodhi or Bo-Tree, the "tree of Knowledge," is the pîpal, the *As'vattha*, or *Ficus Religiosa*, a tree as holy to Buddhists as to Hindus. Each of the Buddhas has his own sacred tree, under which he attains Buddhahood. There seems no reason to doubt that the very old pîpal existing a few years ago at Buddha-Gayâ was a descendant of the original Bo-Tree. It was firmly believed by all Buddhists to be the identical tree. See Monier Williams, pp. 392–94; *Gazetteer of India*, *s.v.* Buddh Gayâ.

Buddha was left without companion or help. Mâra and his forces direct against him in succession whirlwinds and storms of miraculous violence, with showers of rocks, weapons, live coals, etc., but these are all changed to flowers when they reach the Buddha, and fall at his feet. Finally Mâra hurls his mighty discus, which could "cut through solid stone pillars as if they had been the tips of bamboo shoots." The result is however equally disappointing, and the forces of evil are compelled to retire discomfited; while the gods reassured chant hymns of victory.

It was before the sun had set that the Great Being thus vanquished the army of Mâra. And then, while the Bo-Tree in homage rained red coral-like sprigs upon his priestly robes, he acquired in the first watch of the night the knowledge of previous existences; in the middle watch of the night the divine eye; and in the last watch of the night his intellect fathomed Dependent Origination.[1]

Up to this time Gautama had been merely a *Bodhisattva,* one who is destined to gain supreme wisdom. Henceforth he is *Buddha*, the "enlightened one."

Different traditions exist with regard to the events of the time immediately succeeding the Buddha's attainment of omniscience. According

[1] *Jâtaka*, i. 75; Warren, p. 82.

to one account he remained fasting for seven weeks, "enjoying the bliss of emancipation," and meditating on the truths he had discovered. Others describe him as spending seven days in succession under the Bo-Tree; the "Goat-Herd's Banyan," where Mâra with the help of his three daughters, Thirst Craving and Lust, endeavoured without success to incite him to evil thoughts, and to abandon his purpose of preaching the law; the Muc'alinda tree, from beneath which Muc'alinda the king of the serpents came forth, and spread his hood above the Buddha to protect him from the clouds and rain; and the Râjâyatana tree, whence he returns to the banyan. At the Râjâyatana tree two merchants approached and offered him food, which he accepted, eating out of a bowl presented to him at the moment by the four divinities that guard the four quarters of the globe. The two merchants made reverent obeisance to him, and professed themselves his followers. Thus they became the earliest lay-disciples.

Early Converts.—The first converts to enter the order of monks that the Buddha established were the five ascetics, with whom he had previously lived practising austerities. These he sought out in the Deer-Park, *Isipatana*, at Benares; and proclaimed to them the new doctrine, "setting in motion the wheel of the law," and by this his first sermon founding "the highest kingdom of Truth."[1] Thenceforth he devoted himself to itinerating from place to place, and preaching to all whom he encountered. These journeyings were confined mainly to the kingdom of Magadha, and especially the country around Râjagriha and S'râvastî,[2] but are traditionally said to have extended also far into the North-West of India and the Panjâb. Of the early converts two of the most notable were Sâriputta and Moggallâna, both of whom received the truth from the lips of a certain monk Assaji, a disciple of the Buddha, who declared to them the substance of his doctrine. Thereupon they made their way to the Buddha himself, professed the faith, and were admitted by him into the Order.[3] Both are recorded to have died before their Master. Other celebrated names among the early followers of the Buddha are those of 'Ananda,

[1] *Mahâvagga*, i. 6. 30.

[2] The site of S'râvastî has been identified with extensive ruins, covering several miles of country, which have been discovered in Nepâl beyond the British boundary, on the right bank of the Râptî river, about a hundred miles north-west of Kapilavastu. See Vincent A. Smith in *J. R. A. S.*, 1898, p. 520 ff. ; *ib.*, 1900, p. 1 ff.

[3] *Mahâv.*, i. 23, 24.

his cousin and favourite disciple and attendant: Kâs'yapa, the President of the first great Council, held immediately after his death; and Upâli, who responded at this Council concerning the Vinaya rules, while 'Ananda declared the Dharma. These and many others the Buddha ordained, and sent forth as missionaries to proclaim his doctrine. The last of his immediate converts was Subhadda, who came to him on the day before his death, seeking instruction and the resolution of his doubts. He was taught the noble eight-fold path, and admitted a member of the order of monks.[1]

Death of the Buddha.—Forty-five years were thus spent in teaching and preaching, during which time Gautama Buddha appears never to have had a settled dwelling-place. At the close of this period, when the appointed time drew near for his passing away, or for the attainment of *parinirvâna*,[2] he came attended by

[1] *Mahâ-Parinibbâna Sutta*, v. 52–69.

[2] The authoritative account of the death of the Buddha, which though embellished with extravagant details appears in essentials to have preserved a true tradition, is contained in the *Mahâ-Parinibbâna Sutta*, or "Book of the Great Decease," translated by T. W. Rhys Davids, *S. B. E.*, vol. xi. The relevant portions are in Warren, pp. 95–110. The translator assigns the composition of the work to a date at least 100 years after the Buddha's death, about the end of the fourth or

ʻAnanda to the s'âla-tree grove at Kus'anagara.[1] There he invited the assembled monks to question him if they had any doubt in their minds or difficulty unsolved. They remained silent, and their Master delivered to them his last charges:—

Now the Blessed One addressed the venerable ʻAnanda, and said:—It may be, ʻAnanda, that in some of you the thought may arise, "The word of the Master is ended, we have no teacher more!" But it is not thus, ʻAnanda, that you should regard it. The Doctrine and Discipline which I have set forth and laid down for you all, let these, after I am gone, be the Teacher to you.

. . . .

Then the Blessed One addressed the brethren, and said:—It may be, brethren, that there may be doubt or misgiving in the mind of some brother as to the Buddha or the Doctrine or the Order or the Path or the course of conduct. Enquire, brethren, freely. Do not have to reproach yourselves afterwards with the thought, "Our Teacher was face to face with us, and we could not bring ourselves to enquire of the Blessed One when we were face to face with him."

---

beginning of the third century B.C.; *loc. cit.*, pp. xvii., xix. It may be doubted whether this is not an excessive estimate of its antiquity. *Parinibbâna* is the Pâli form of the Sanskrit *parinirvâna*, further or final nirvâna.

[1] The scene of the Buddha's death has not been identified. Sir A. Cunningham placed it at Kasiâ in the North-West Provinces, about 40 miles east of Gorakhpur. Recent investigations and discoveries appear to have made the identification improbable if not impossible. According to Fâ-Hian, chh. xxiii., xxiv., it was 25 *yojanas* east of Kapilavastu.

And when he had thus spoken the brethren were silent.

And again a second and a third time the Blessed One addressed the brethren in the same words; and a second and a third time the brethren were silent.

Then the Blessed One addressed the brethren, and said:— It may be, brethren, that you put no questions out of respect for the Teacher. Let one friend communicate to another.

And when he had thus spoken the brethren were silent.

And the venerable Ânanda said to the Blessed One:— "How wonderful a thing is it, Reverend Sir, and how marvellous! Verily, I believe that in this whole assembly of the brethren there is not one brother who has any doubt or misgiving as to the Buddha or the Doctrine or the Order or the Path or the course of conduct."

"With you, Ânanda, it is a matter of faith, when you say that; but with the Tathâgata, Ânanda, it is a matter of knowledge that in this whole assembly of the brethren there is not one brother who has any doubt or misgiving as to the Buddha or the Doctrine or the Order or the Path or the course of conduct. For even the most backward, Ânanda, of all these five hundred brethren has become converted, and is no longer liable to be born in a state of suffering, and is assured of final salvation."

Then the Blessed One addressed the brethren, and said:— "Behold now, brethren, I take my leave of you; all the constituents of being are transitory; work out your salvation with diligence."

This was the last word of the Tathâgata.[1]

According to the very curious tradition, which can hardly be a mere invention, death was due to over-indulgence in "dried boar's flesh." This was served to the Buddha and his disciples

[1] *Mahâ-Parin. Sutta*, vi. 1, 5–10; *S. B. E.*, xi. p. 112 ff.; Warren, p. 107 ff.

together; but he refused to allow the others to partake lest injury should thereby be caused to them, and gave orders that the remainder of the meat should be buried in the ground.[1]

Funeral Pyre and Relics.—The text proceeds to describe the effect produced by his death on the deities as well as on the physical universe, together with the sorrow of his disciples and of the men of Kus'anagara. Under the direction of 'Ananda the body was borne to a spot outside of the city on the east, and there placed on a "funeral pile of all kinds of perfumes." The chiefs of the city in vain endeavoured to set fire to it. After however the corpse had been reverentially saluted by Mahâ Kâs'yapa with five hundred brethren, who arrived late at the spot, and passed thrice round the pyre, it spontaneously began to burn; and when the flames had done their work, they were again miraculously extinguished. The bones and relics that remained were gathered together, divided into eight portions by the Brâhman Drona, and distributed to as many claimants. Over each portion, and over the vessel in which the relics had been collected, a *dâgaba* was erected and homage paid. These buildings remained for many years centres of pilgrimage, and

[1] *Mahâ-Parin. Sutta*, iv. 17 ff.

were visited amongst others by the Chinese monks, who came to India in search of copies of the Law.

Council at Râjagriha.—The accepted tradition goes on to relate that the details of the Law, as far at least as the main outlines of the system and the regulations for the monastic life were concerned, were determined at a great Council held at Râjagriha immediately after the Buddha's death. In the eleventh book of the *C'ullavagga* is found the canonical record of the Council, certain preliminary sections of which coincide verbally with parts of the *Mahâparin. Sutta*, betraying a common origin.[1] In the latter work however no mention is made of a general Council, to the holding of which in the former the same recorded incidents are immediately preliminary. It appears therefore to be a legitimate inference that at least in its present form this part of the C'ullavagga is later than the Parin. Sutta, and may only doubtfully be relied upon as an authority for the facts.[2] The historical framework as it were of the Council itself does not however vary in the different accounts that have been preserved. At the instance and under the presidency of Mahâ Kâs'yapa, five hundred monks came together at Râjagriha, where

[1] *C. V.*, xi. 1 = *P. S.* vi. 36–41.

[2] Cp. *S. B. E.*, xi. p. x. ff.

they spent the rainy season, and in response to the questions of the president Upâli and 'Ananda rehearsed respectively the Vinaya and Dharma. Thus was established a fixed and authorised version of the sayings of the Master immediately after his decease.[1]

Apart from the general uncertainty attaching to tradition there seems no reason to doubt that a gathering of this kind of the early and most respected disciples of Gautama was really held, and in some sort determined a received text of the Buddhist Scriptures. It is noteworthy however that no precise date is given for the Council, beyond the vague indication that it took place shortly after his death. And no reference is made to the Abhidharma, the third division which with the Vinaya and the Dharma completes the Buddhist Canon.

Council at Vais'âlî.—A hundred years later a second general Council met at Vais'âlî to pronounce upon the lawfulness or otherwise of certain relaxations of strict rule and discipline, which had been adopted by a party among the monks. The account of this second Council is

[1] Compare the curious and naïve account in *C. V.* xi. 11 of the monk Purâna, who refused to accept the text adopted by the members of the Council, preferring his own recollection of the Buddha's words.

contained in the twelfth, or last book of the C'ullavagga. Of the "ten points" concerned, the most important were the prohibitions against receiving gifts of money or using unfermented spirits,[1] and the right of an assembly of monks to perform official acts even though they were not unanimous. The questions raised were purely disciplinary, restrictions of the habits and freedom of members of the Order, and did not concern the laity or the outside world. To all ten points a formal and careful consideration was given, and the opinions of the most respected and influential monks obtained thereon; with the result that the orthodox view which forbade these licences was affirmed, and the more lax party censured. Sinhalese chronicles add that after the decision had been given, a second or supplementary Council was summoned, and attended by no fewer than ten thousand dissentient monks. To this Council was given the name of *Mahâsangîti*, or "Great Council"; and here, as at Râjag*ri*ha, the Vinaya and Dharma were rehearsed, no mention being made of the Abhidharma.

If the name *Mahâsangîti* is to be taken

[1] These are explained to be "spirits which have left the condition of not being spirits, and yet have not acquired intoxicating properties." *C'ullav.*, xii. 1. 10, 2. 8.

seriously, it would seem to imply that the unorthodox were numerically stronger than their opponents. The tradition of the Northern school however gives a different explanation of the term. The earlier orthodox assembly is altogether ignored ; and it is asserted that the Council was called Mahâsangîti, because attended by both monks and laymen. The date there assigned to it is a hundred and ten years after the death of the Buddha. In neither tradition is any direct mention made of the place at which this Council was held.

Whether the Council at Vais'âlî is to be regarded as a historical fact, or whether the accounts that have been preserved are only confused echoes of earlier and later gatherings for the settlement of disputed points, that in southern tradition have crystallized into one, must be allowed to be uncertain. In either case the period of one hundred or one hundred and ten years from the parinirvâna is to be considered a round number. It is probable enough that attempts would be made to reconcile or put down practices regarded as abhorrent to the strict rule of earlier Buddhism. But how far these attempts were seriously meant, or to what extent they secured their object, it is impossible to determine. The conflicting accounts of tradition would appear to conceal or gloss over a very limited success. All that can with confidence be asserted is that a schism in thought and feeling if not in name had already begun.

Council at Pâtaliputra.—Of the third great Council held at Pâtaliputra, or Patna, under the presidency of king As′oka, about a century after that of Vais′âlî, no mention is made in the canonical books; and by the Northern school it is passed over in complete silence. The extant narratives of the Council therefore are derived entirely from Southern tradition, and as far as details are concerned appear to be less trustworthy from a historical point of view than even those of the earlier Councils. The assembly at Patna was at least in no sense oecumenical, since the party whose broader laxer views had given rise to the contentions at Vais′âlî held aloof, and attendance was confined to the *Sthaviras*, or elders, who adhered to the older and stricter form of doctrine, which later developed or hardened into the *hînayâna* system.

According to the received account the holding of this later Council was foretold by the monks at Vais′âlî, who indicated that after one hundred and eighteen years, in the time of a great Buddhist king As′oka reigning at Pâtaliputra, there would arise a renowned leader within the Order, by name Tissa Moggaliputta, who would be instrumental in the uprooting and destruction of all false doctrine. In due time at his instance the monks to the number of a thousand, or as otherwise stated sixty thousand, were convoked in council, and condemnation passed on all innovations and heresies. Thus the aim of the conservative and orthodox party was completely attained, and their views ratified by royal authority.

Significance of the Patna Council. — These accounts are clearly one-sided, and would seem to have been written in the interests of a particular school, who regarded themselves and desired to be regarded by others as the true representatives of primitive orthodox Buddhism. That a Council was actually held at Patna, and in the reign of As′oka, appears indisputable. Its doctrinal importance however is small. The real significance of the assembly lies in its connection with the Buddhist king, the greatest of Indian sovereigns previous to the days of the Moghul Emperors; and in the fact that it proved to be the starting-point of a large and comprehensive scheme of missionary enterprise under royal patronage, which was personally conducted in Ceylon if the tradition may be trusted by the son of the king.

As'oka.—The limits of the Empire of As'oka, in which Buddhism became the religion of the State, it is not possible to fix with absolute precision. He certainly however reigned over the greater part of the country lying between the Himâlaya and the Vindya Mountains on the north and south, the Indus and the Bay of Bengal on the west and east; and there is reason to believe that his authority extended considerably to the west and south of these boundaries. He is said to have succeeded his father Bindusâra on the throne three or four years before the formal inauguration of his reign. This last event is referred to as his *Abhisheka*, or "anointing"[1]; and the Council at Patna is placed eighteen years later. The date also of his conversion to Buddhism is uncertain. It cannot have been long subsequent to, even if it did not precede the *Abhisheka*. The king then became a most generous patron of the Order, supporting according to the tradition 64,000 monks. Later in life, after the death of his first wife he appears to have been himself received as a member of the Order. Subsequently he married again, and his death is

[1] According to the Ceylon chronicle, the Mahâvamsa, this event took place 218 years after the Parinirvâna, and in As'oka's fourth year; therefore in 259 B.C.

placed *circa* 225 B.C. after a reign of thirty-seven years.

Edicts.—Apart from the traditions contained in the native chronicles, direct evidence of As'oka himself has been preserved in the numerous edicts which he caused to be engraved on rocks and pillars throughout his great empire. Of these memorials of his thoughts and will the king is said to have erected 84,000, and more than forty have been discovered at widely distant places from north of Peshawar to within a few miles of the coast-line in Orissa, and south in Kâthiâwâr and the Central Provinces. They are dated in some cases by the years of the king's reign, and appear to have been issued at intervals until within a short time of his death. Moreover the same edict is found repeated in different places, and it is then a fair inference that these were promulgated or engraved at or about the same period. The subjects with which the edicts are concerned are usually quite general. They enjoin virtue and gentleness, kind treatment of men and animals; urge upon all the duty of moral behaviour and toleration of other religions, the adherents of which are to be won by persuasion not by violence; appoint overseers or censors of public morals, and missionaries to propagate the true faith in foreign countries; and finally contrast the peace and prosperity of the present reign with the ignorance and unrest of former times. Only one edict is formally addressed to the Order of the monks, and makes explicit mention of the Buddha and the Law. Since the same edict gives the names of certain religious books which the king desires should be read by both monks and nuns, it follows that there was already in existence as early as As'oka's time something of the nature of a recognised body of canonical writings. The titles given are however, with one exception, very doubtfully identified with any extant works. Apart from this edict, which is usually considered to be the latest of the series, the phraseology and distinctive terms of the Buddhist books are conspicuous by their absence.[1]

[1] The Edicts of As'oka are of greater importance from the point of view of history and palæography, than from that of religion. Fourteen rock inscriptions are known, seventeen in caves, and nine inscribed pillars including the two recently discovered in the Tarai (*supra*, p. 209). The chronological order in which these edicts were issued is quite uncertain, the only guide being the occasional dating by the year of the king's reign. It is generally assumed however that the pillar edicts, and those distinctively Buddhist in tone, are later than the rest; and that where several occur on one and the same stone, the order in which they are engraved corresponds to the order of promulgation. The following are the fourteen rock inscriptions; they are usually quoted or

Council of Kanishka.—The fourth great Buddhist Council met after an interval of

referred to by the name of the place where they are found :—

At Shâhbâzgarhî and Mansera or Mansahra in the extreme north of the Panjâb. These are engraved in a northern character, the so-called Kharoshthî, Bactrian or Bactro-Pali, "ass' lips," which is written from right to left, and has been derived from a late form of a north-eastern Semitic alphabet. The remaining inscriptions are in the character known as Brâhmî, the Southern or Indian Pali, sometimes Maurya from its use by the Maurya kings. The latter form of script appears to have been employed all over India; while the Kharoshthî entered the country later, and was always confined to the North-West and the Panjâb. This Brâhmî alphabet also has its origin in an ancient north Semitic form of alphabet.[1]

At Khâlsi, on the Jumna, about twenty miles north-west of the hill-station of Mussooree.

Girnâr, in Kâthiâwâr.

At Dhauli and Jaugada, in the east-coast districts of Cuttack and Ganjam respectively. Two inscriptions are found at each place.

On the Khandgiri Hill, near Dhauli.

At Bairâth in Râjputâna, about forty miles north-east of Jaipur. Two inscriptions.

Rûpnâth, thirty-five miles north of Jabalpur.

Sahasarâm, or Sâsscrâm, in the Shâhâbâd District, seventy miles east-south-east of Benares.

---

1 The standard authority on the ancient Indian writing is G. Bühler's *Indische Palæographie*, published at Strassburg in 1896, with elaborate tables of the various alphabetic forms. The results which Dr. Bühler has reached are not I believe seriously controverted. A convenient English summary will be found in No. III. of the same author's Indian Studies, *On the Origin of the Indian Brâhma Alphabet*, Vienna, 1895; 2nd ed., Strassburg, 1898.

three hundred years under the Indo-Scythian king Kanishka, whose name and influence for Northern Buddhism are as significant as those of As'oka for the South. The period between the two reigns is filled in for the North by vague traditions, which admit of only the most general conclusion on the tendency and movement of religious thought. It was clearly however a time of great activity and success, both in the propagation of the faith and the discussion and formulating of doctrine. Apparently a crisis was reached in the reign of Kanishka, and the Council with which his name is inseparably connected was summoned in order to effect a settlement, and to lay down rules for future guidance.

The date of Kanishka's birth is said by the native authorities to have been four hundred

Deotek, in the Central Provinces, fifty miles south-east of Nâgpur.

At Shâhbâzgarhî, Khâlsi, and Girnâr, the series of fourteen edicts is complete, but the texts are not in all cases precisely identical. They are dated between the eleventh and fourteenth years of the king's reign. It does not however necessarily follow that all were engraved at the same time. The second Bairâth inscription, without date, is that referred to above as couched in Buddhist phraseology. It is now in the Calcutta Museum. The mention of "Antiochus king of the Yâvanas" and other Greek kings occurs in the last edict but one of the Girnâr stone, and the corresponding texts.

years after the death of the Buddha. Other accounts give the same date for his accession to the throne. The last-named date is of especial importance as being the initial year of the S'aka or Indo-Scythian era, widely employed throughout India in the early centuries. Modern research has placed the beginning of his reign and of this era in the year 78 A.D., thus supplying another fixed point for Indian chronology. The kingdom of Kanishka with its centre in Kashmîr extended on the west as far as Kâbul, northwards beyond the Himâlayas into modern Turkestan, and on the east and south over parts of the North-West Provinces and Sindh. The precise date of the Council cannot be fixed, but it must have met towards the close of the century. According to Hiuen-Tsiang the king himself convoked the assembly, desiring to obtain an authoritative settlement of disputes and exposition of the sacred writings. The monks to the number of five hundred under the presidency of Vasumitra came together at Jâlandhara, an ancient city which is still of some importance, lying in the district of the same name that borders on Kashmîr on the south. Others say that the Council was held in a monastery in Kashmîr itself.

Of the details of the proceedings of the Council nothing is known. It is in itself probable enough that the motive of the gathering was to compose differences within the Order; and the same inference may be drawn from the traditional accounts of the conclusions that were reached. Since however the monks of Ceylon and of the South generally took no share in the Council, its debates and decisions concerned Northern Buddhism alone. Equally therefore with As′oka's, although in an opposite sense, the assembly at Jâlandhara was sectarian. Three great commentaries, each consisting of one hundred thousand *s′lokas* or verses, were composed or put together in Sanskrit, attached to the three recognised canonical books. These formed the foundation of the later extended Canon of the Northern Buddhists. The Council further accorded its official recognition to eighteen principal sects, who differing in minor points of doctrine and observance were yet allowed to hold in all essentials the true faith. Finally the assembly made provision for the writing down and preservation of the sacred books.

SACRED BOOKS

BUDDHIST Canon.—The sacred canonical works of the Buddhists of the Southern school, including Ceylon Burma and Siam, consist of three collections termed *pitakas*, or baskets, the complete Canon receiving the name of *Tripitaka*, or triple basket. This title does not however find recognition within the books themselves; but is first met with in the Ceylon chronicles, where it is apparently adopted as a convenient name to designate the canonical in distinction from later uncanonical works which deal with similar subjects, or from the commentaries on the sacred text. These sacred books are written in *Pâli*, a language closely allied to if not a mere dialect of Sanskrit, and in the character of each of the countries in which the Buddhist faith prevails. This practice, as far as the form of the writing is concerned, is in accordance with the directions said to have been given by the Buddha himself, that in every land his teaching should be circulated in the vernacular of the people.[1] The original home of the Pâli, whence it was carried to Ceylon especially, remains uncertain. The language is at any rate distinct from Mâgadhî, the dialect of Magadha or the sacred land of Buddhism, although it is said to contain "Mâgadhisms," idioms or terms adopted from that dialect. On the strength mainly of resemblances in the Khandgiri inscription, H. Oldenburg and others have identified Pâli with the original dialect of Kalinga, the strip of country lying on the east coast between Cuttack and Madras.[2] In later times the vocabulary of the language became largely intermixed with Sinhalese words. Pâli is now little understood or studied even by the Buddhist priests themselves, except under the inspiration and direction of Western scholars, and is entirely an unknown tongue to the common people. In this respect a striking contrast therefore is presented to the zeal with which the Brâhmans have always prosecuted the study of Sanskrit.

[1] *C'ullav.*, v. 33. 1. "You are not, O monks, to put the word of the Buddhas into (Sanskrit) verse. Whosoever does so shall be guilty of an offence. I allow you, O monks, to learn the word of the Buddhas each in his own dialect." *S. B. E.*, xx. p. 151.

[2] Cp. Kern, p. 7 f., notes and references; E. Müller, Pref. to Pâli Grammar.

Tripitaka.—The Pâli *Tripitaka* then which forms the Canon of the Buddhists of the South is divided into three parts, namely (1) the *Vinaya* or discipline Pitaka, treating of the rules and regulations for the life and behaviour of the Buddhist monks, together with professedly historical details of the time and circumstances under which each rule was promulgated; (2) the *Sûtra* Pitaka, the Pitaka of doctrine or discourse, containing the statement of Buddhist faith and theology, accompanied by philosophical theories and speculations, all in the form of sermons put into the mouth of the Buddha himself; (3) the *Abhidharma* Pitaka, the Pitaka of metaphysics, supplementary treatises dealing with controverted points of doctrine and practice, enlarging upon and making additions to the earlier Pitakas. Of this last the subject-matter is not really different from that of the Sûtra Pitaka, and it is neither more nor less metaphysical in its nature and stand-point. Moreover it bears upon its face that it is later in composition and date than either of the other two. All three Pitakas are characterised by what appears to an Occidental student to be wearisome repetition, phrases and even paragraphs frequently recurring with slight variation.[1] The first Pitaka has been printed and edited in full by Dr. H. Oldenburg, and the greater part is available in the translations of the Sacred Books of the East.[2] The complete Tripitaka also, with the exception of a few minor treatises, has recently been issued under the inspiration and at the cost of the king of Siam in thirty-nine volumes, printed in the Siamese character.

Vinaya Pitaka.—The Vinaya Pitaka is composed of four or five books or divisions, of which the first is termed the *Sutta-Vibhanga*, and deals with offences against the monastic Order. It is sub-divided into *Pârâjika*, or offences which are followed by excommunication; and *Pâc'ittiya*, or offences needing expiation and forgiveness. There follow the *Mahâvagga* and *C'ullavagga*, or great and little sections, collectively named *Khandhakas*, containing elaborate directions for the regulating of the lives of the monks and nuns. Lastly the *Parivâra-pâtha*, a dependent or supplementary text or treatise, of

[1] Prof. T. W. Rhys Davids' comparative estimate of the length of the Pâli Scriptures gives the result that apart from the repetitions "the Buddhist Bible is probably even shorter than ours." Including these it is stated to contain nearly twice as many words as the Old and New Testaments together, and in translation to be about four times as long. *Buddhism*, p. 19 f. note; cp. *id.*, *S. B. E.*, vol. xxxv. p. xxxvii.

[2] *S. B. E.*, vols. xiii., xvii., xx.

later date and less importance than the others. The Sûtra, or in Pâli Sutta-Pitaka, consists of five *Nikâyas*, or collections, the last of which is again sub-divided into fifteen treatises. The *Dhammapada*, verses or sentences of the law, the second of these treatises, is perhaps the best known of Buddhist sacred texts, and has been often translated.[1] The third Pitaka is divided into seven books, treating of very various subjects, among which the causes and nature of existence hold a considerable place.[2]

[1] *E.g.* by Professor Max Müller, *S. B. E.*, vol. x., 2nd edition, 1898. The meaning of the name, and the precise significance attached to it by the native commentators themselves, is curiously uncertain. It has been rendered Path of the Law, or of Virtue, Foundation of the Law, Footsteps or Vestiges of Religion, or more freely Religious Sentences. See Max Müller, *l.c.* pp. x., liii. ff.

[2] The following is a complete list of the Pâli canonical Scriptures, in three pitakas:—

Vinaya-Pitaka:—

1. Sutta-Vibhanga { Pârâjika. / Pâc'ittiya.
2. Mahâvagga.
3. C'ullavagga.
4. Parivâra-pâtha.

Sutta-Pitaka:—

1. Dîgha-nikâya, a collection of thirty-four "long" suttas, or verses.
2. Majjhima-nikâya, one hundred and fifty-two "middle" suttas.
3. Samyutta-nikâya, a collection of "joined" suttas.

Formation and Growth of Canon.—With regard to the date of these writings Buddhist tradition

4. Anguttara-nikâya, a miscellaneous collection.
5. Khuddaka-nikâya, or collection of short treatises, subdivided into:—(1) Khuddaka-pâtha; (2) Dhammapada; (3) Udâna, eighty-two suttas of praise, with explanations of historical circumstance; (4) Itivuttaka, a hundred and ten stories or reports of sayings of the Buddha; (5) Sutta-nipâta, a collection of seventy-one brief philosophical and ethical tracts: translated by V. Fausböll in *S. B. E.*, vol. x.; (6) Vimâna-vatthu, stories of the celestial mansions; (7) Peta-vatthu, stories of pretas, or disembodied spirits; (8) Thera-gâthâ, songs of monks; (9) Therî-gâthâ, songs of nuns; (10) Jâtaka, five hundred and fifty birth-stories of the Buddha: rendered into English by T. W. Rhys Davids; a new translation is in course of publication in seven or eight volumes at the Cambridge University Press under the superintendence of E. B. Cowell; (11) Niddesa, commentary on part of the Sutta-nipâta, ascribed to Sâriputta; (12) Patisambhidâ-magga, the road to insight or discernment; (13) Apadâna, legends of saints; (14) Buddha-vamsa, history of twenty-five Buddhas, including Gautama; (15) C'ariyâ-pitaka, basket of conduct, on the virtues and merit of the Buddha in former births.

Abhidhamma-Pitaka:—

1. Dhamma-sangani, conditions of life in various worlds.
2. Vibhanga, eighteen tracts on various subjects.
3. Kathâ-vatthu-pakarana, a thousand suttas on points open to discussion.
4. Puggala-pannatti, regulations touching personal character and behaviour.

ascribes the completion of the Sacred Canon to the second great Council, which met at Vais'âlî a century after the death of Gautama Buddha.[1] The last two divisions of the C'ullavagga are occupied with an account of this and of the earlier Council at Râjag*ri*ha under the presidency of Kâs'yapa, with especial reference to the determination of the form and contents of the Scriptures. Accordingly the Vinaya is recounted by Upâli, the Dharma by ^Ananda. If this tradition therefore may be accepted, there was recognised within a very short time of Gautama's death a sort of primitive Canon, consisting of only two parts, the discipline and the doctrine, both of which were equally believed to be the exact utterances of the Master himself; and these were set by his immediate disciples in a kind of framework of the time and circumstances under which they had been delivered.

5. Dhâtu-kathâ, account of the elements or primary substances.
6. Yamaka, pairs, that is contrasts or oppositions.
7. Patthâna-pakarana, book of causes or origins, that is the causes of existence.

It will be noticed that many of the titles refer rather to the form than the contents of the treatises. The Siamese edition contains the complete text of the Tripitaka except Nos. 6–10, 13–15 inclusive of the Khuddaka-nikâya. See Warren, p. xviii. note. Cp. Max Müller, *Sel. Essays*, vol. ii. p. 177 ff.

[1] *Sup.* p. 223 ff.; on the date, cp. *S. B. E.*, x². p. xliii. ff.

Subsequently the doctrine or law was divided into two, the Dharma proper and the Abhidharma, and large additions were made.[1]

That a real historical growth underlies this traditional account is very probable. Little reliance can of course be placed upon the details of the narrative. But the broad fact of the early existence of a two-fold collection of sacred texts, which was subsequently enlarged or developed into the Tripitaka or Triple Basket, appears both natural and one likely to be preserved in tradition. The subjects proper to Abhidharma were more or less fully treated of under the head of Dharma. Only later, at a date impossible to determine, was a separation effected, one however which was never logically or completely carried out in the sense that law or doctrine and philosophy or speculation stood finally and always apart. This third division received the name of the Abhidharma Pitaka, and was placed on an equality with the other two.

In the earlier books of the C'ullavagga and in other parts of the Vinaya Pitaka no mention is made of the heretical views or lax practices which, according to the twelfth book, became the immediate cause of the summoning of the

[1] Cp. *S. B. E.*, x². p. xl. ff.

Vais'âlî Council, and which were there formally condemned. The same statement is true of the subject-matter of the eleventh book, the Council at Râjag*r*iha. It would appear to follow that these two concluding books or divisions of the C'ullavagga are a later addition,[1] and that whatever the date of their compilation the rest of the Vinaya Pitaka, with the exception of the undoubtedly more recent Parivâra-pâtha, must be regarded as in the main of earlier origin. Further within the Sutta-Vibhanga itself three successive strata at least of teaching and comment may be distinguished. There can be traced first an inner or primitive kernel, which consists of a number of rules laid down for the use of the Buddhist monks at their semi-monthly assemblies at new and full moon. These rules concerned the confession of and purification from sin, and in substance at least are not improbably to be ascribed to Gautama himself. At the meetings the offences were recited in order with the regulations bearing upon them, and appeal was then made to the assembled monks to voluntarily

[1] A curious confirmation of this inference is that if these books are taken away the C'ullavagga would be really, as its name imports, a "little" section, as compared with the Mahâvagga. The former contains in its present form twelve Khandhakas or divisions, against the ten of the latter. But the Mahâvagga has slightly the advantage in actual length.

confess their wrong-doing, if guilty. Silence was held to be an assertion of innocence. Comments upon and explanations of these rules were subsequently framed, which were recited together with them, and came to form part of the same collection. Finally new additions were made, further explanations offered, and the usual historical framework invented, which detailed for each rule or precept the circumstances under which it was first promulgated by the Buddha. The result was the Sutta-Vibhanga as it now exists with its two-fold classification of offences.

Pâtimokkha.—This nucleus of rules however is extant as a separate work called the *Pâtimokkha*, or in Sanskrit *Pratimoksha*, meaning "release" or "deliverance," that is from the guilt of offences.[1] This work is justly regarded as in substance the oldest Buddhist law-book in existence, and if any of the laws and regulations of the Order are to be traced back to Gautama Buddha himself, about which more scepticism has been expressed than is perhaps justified, they are to be found here. It is not easy

[1] The precise significance of the term again is doubtful, or at least is disputed. See *S. B. E.*, xiii. p. xxvii. f.; Kern, p. 74 n. The latter scholar denies that the word can convey the meaning above given, and would substitute the idea of a protective charm, "something serving as a (spiritual) cuirass."

however to account for the further fact that although the Pâtimokkha is thus embodied in the Sutta-Vibhanga, it is not in its separate form considered by the Buddhists to be a canonical work.[1]

The Mahâvagga and the C'ullavagga appear to have been gradually built up on much the same plan as the Sutta-Vibhanga. A nucleus of dogmatic rule and instruction intended for the Order has received enlargement with details

[1] The Pâtimokkha has been translated by Profs. T. W. Rhys Davids and H. Oldenburg in *S. B. E.*, vol. xiii. The directions for its recitation are given *Mahâv.* ii. 4 :—

At that time the monks, considering that the Pâtimokkha recitation had been instituted by the Blessed One, recited the Pâtimokkha every day.

They told this thing to the Blessed One.

'The Pâtimokkha, O monks, is not to be recited every day. He who recites it (every day) commits a serious offence. I ordain, O monks, to recite the Pâtimokkha on the Uposatha day' (*i.e.* at the fast-day service).

At that time the monks, considering that it had been prescribed by the Blessed One to recite the Pâtimokkha on the Uposatha day, recited the Pâtimokkha three times each half-month, on the fourteenth, fifteenth, and eighth day of each half-month.

They told this thing to the Blessed One.

'The Pâtimokkha, O monks, is not to be recited three times each half-month. He who recites it (three times) commits a serious offence. I prescribe, O monks, that you recite the Pâtimokkha once each half-month, on the fourteenth or on the fifteenth day.'

historical and explanatory. The component parts are not however in this case so readily discernible; nor has any portion of the Khandhakas, with slight exceptions, been preserved as a separate work. Beyond the fact therefore that the last two chapters of the C'ullavagga are of later origin, little or nothing can with any confidence be affirmed concerning their date or age. The Parivâra-pâtha however, which consists largely of repetitions of laws and teaching found in the earlier books, undoubtedly belongs to a considerably later period, and has been supposed to have come into existence in Ceylon.

Dhammapada.—Upon the time and place of origin of the remaining pitakas it is even more difficult to form a reliable judgement. With regard to the Dhammapada especially, the most interesting and important part of the Sutta-Pitaka, a knowledge of its age and history would throw welcome light upon the development of the ethics of Buddhism. None of these works contain within themselves materials for definite conclusions as to the time of their composition; nor is any external standard of comparison at present available which would enable them to be ranked in chronological order. Buddhist tradition ascribes to all a monotonous and uniform antiquity. A further fact that must be taken into account in estimating the age of these works is that parts of the pitakas were early translated into the languages of other Eastern countries into which Buddhism penetrated. Of the Dhammapada, for example, four Chinese renderings or versions are extant, and one in the language of Tibet.[1]

This law-book is on the whole the best worth reading, as it has been usually considered the most typical of Buddhist writings. The extracts that follow will illustrate briefly its style and the character of its teaching. The entire work is deserving of study:

Hatred does not cease by hatred at any time; hatred ceases by love, this is an old rule.[2]

If you see a man who shows you what is to be avoided, who administers reproofs, and is intelligent, follow that wise man as you would one who tells of hidden treasures; it will be better, not worse, for him who follows him.

. . . .

Do not have evil-doers for friends, do not have low people for friends; have virtuous people for friends, have for friends the best of men.[3]

If one man conquer in battle a thousand times a thousand men, and if another conquer himself, he is the greatest of conquerors.

---

[1] *S. B. E.*, x^2. p. lviii. ff.

[2] *Dhammap.*, i. 5; the translations are by F. Max Müller.

[3] *Ib.* vi. 76, 78.

One's own self conquered is better than all other people; not even a god, a Gandharva, not Mâra with Brahman could change into defeat the victory of a man who has vanquished himself, and always lives under restraint.[1]

A man should hasten towards the good, and should keep his thought away from evil; if a man does what is good slothfully, his mind delights in evil.

. . . .

Let no man think lightly of evil, saying in his heart, It will not come nigh unto me. Even by the falling of water-drops a water-pot is filled; the fool becomes full of evil, even if he gather it little by little.

Let no man think lightly of good, saying in his heart, It will not come nigh unto me. Even by the falling of water-drops a water-pot is filled; the wise man becomes full of good, even if he gather it little by little.[2]

Many men whose shoulders are covered with the yellow gown are ill-conditioned and unrestrained; such evil-doers by their evil deeds go to hell.

. . . .

As a grass-blade, if badly grasped, cuts the arm, badly practised asceticism leads to hell.[3]

It is good to tame the mind, which is difficult to hold in and flighty, rushing wherever it listeth; a tamed mind brings happiness.

Let the wise man guard his thoughts, for they are difficult to perceive, very artful, and they rush wherever they list; thoughts well guarded bring happiness.[4]

Look upon the world as you would on a bubble, look upon it as you would on a mirage; the king of death does not see him who thus looks down upon the world.[5]

A man is not just if he carries a matter by violence; no, he who distinguishes both right and wrong, who is learned and

---

[1] *Dhammap.*, viii. 103 ff. [2] *Ib.* ix. 116, 121 f.
[3] *Ib.* xxii. 307, 311. [4] *Ib.* iii. 35, 36. [5] *Ib.* xiii. 170.

guides others, not by violence but by the same law, being a guardian of the law and intelligent, he is called just.

A man is not learned because he talks much; he who is patient, free from hatred and fear, he is called learned.

A man is not a supporter of the law because he talks much; even if a man has learnt little, but sees the law bodily, he is a supporter of the law, a man who never neglects the law.

A man is not an elder because his head is grey; his age may be ripe, but he is called 'Old-in-vain.'

He in whom there is truth, virtue, pity, restraint, moderation, he who is free from impurity and is wise, he is called an elder.[1]

A man does not become a Brâhmana by his platted hair, by his family, or by birth; in whom there is truth and righteousness, he is blessed, he is a Brâhmana.

What is the use of platted hair, O fool! what of the raiment of goat-skins? Within thee there is ravening, but the outside thou makest clean.

The man who wears dirty raiment, who is emaciated and covered with veins, who meditates alone in the forest, him I call indeed a Brâhmana.

I do not call a man a Brâhmana because of his origin or of his mother. He is indeed arrogant and he is wealthy; but the poor, who is free from all attachments, him I call indeed a Brâhmana.

. . . .

Him I call indeed a Brâhmana who calls nothing his own, whether it be before, behind, or between, who is poor, and free from the love of the world.

Him I call indeed a Brâhmana, the manly, the noble, the hero, the great sage, the conqueror, the indifferent, the accomplished, the awakened.

Him I call indeed a Brâhmana who knows his former abodes, who sees heaven and hell, has reached the end of births, is

---

[1] *Dhammap.*, xix. 256 ff.

perfect in knowledge, a sage, and whose perfections are all perfect.[1]

Mahinda and the Canon in Ceylon.—The completed Canon of the three Pitakas was according to the tradition carried with him into Ceylon by *Mahendra*, or in Pâli *Mahinda*, the son of King As'oka, when he journeyed thither after the great church Council held at Patna. The authority for this third Council it must be remembered is not canonical, no mention being made of the Patna assembly in the Tripitaka. If this account were historically reliable and accurate in detail, then the Southern or Pâli Canon of Buddhist Scriptures was closed not later than the middle of the third century before Christ. On other grounds however this conclusion is improbable. This mission of Mahinda to Ceylon in order to preach the doctrines of the Buddha is said to have been undertaken in consequence of a decision of the Council to send teachers into all the surrounding countries. He is regarded as the apostle and founder of Ceylon Buddhism. In addition to the Tripitaka certain Pâli commentaries on the

[1] *Ib.* xxvi. 393 ff., 421 ff.; the whole chapter is interesting, giving the Buddhist conception of a perfect man. Compare the character of the *Muni*, or sage, in *Sutta-Nipâta*, i. 12, *S. B. E.*, x[2]. second part, p. 33 ff.

sacred text were brought from Magadha at the same time, which Mahinda himself after his arrival in Ceylon translated into Sinhalese. These renderings were subsequently known to Buddhaghosha, the great Buddhist scholar and commentator, at the beginning of the fifth century A.D.; and by him, after the loss of the originals, retranslated into Pâli.

Writing of the Sacred Books.—Further the entire Canon is traditionally recorded to have been for the first time committed to writing in Ceylon during the reign of the Buddhist king Vattagâmani, whose date is given 88–76 B.C. Portions may have been thus written down at an earlier period; for the art of writing had long been known and practised in India. It was however employed mainly if not exclusively for brief edicts, letters, deeds of sale or gift, where either a temporary object alone was sought, or absolute permanence was necessary for a state or private record. For longer treatises and the ordinary purposes of literature the memory was considered a safer and more convenient repository than leaves or stones. And in the absence of more appropriate materials for writing those who took this view were undoubtedly right. The impulse to a widely spread use of the art of writing is usually given by the invention or introduction of a cheap and suitable material, such as was the papyrus in Egypt and the Western world, or the stiff clay of Babylonia. It is therefore inherently probable that a longer or shorter period of oral transmission preceded the writing down of the sacred books. Such a mode of transmission does not in the East in any way imply great dislocation or corruptness of the text, such as would be suffered at the hands of copyists through a moderately long series of manuscripts.

Commentaries.—In addition to the canonical books there exists a large number of commentaries and works on grammar history and other subjects, written in Pâli and Sinhalese, the trustworthiness of which it is often difficult to estimate. These are of much importance for the right understanding of the interpretation which the Ceylon Buddhists themselves put upon the sacred text. The commentaries on parts of the Tripitaka were termed *Atthakathâ*, and a semi-authoritative or canonical character was ascribed to them on the ground of their assumed introduction into the island by Mahendra together with the Pitakas themselves. Of the writers of commentaries the most renowned was Buddhaghosha, who has often been called the second founder of Buddhism in

Ceylon. The name by which he is known, the "sound" or "voice of the Buddha," is perhaps in reality only an honorary epithet. He is said to have been a Brâhman convert to Buddhism, who settled in Anurâdhapura during the reign of King Mahânâma, A.D. 410–432.[1] There he heard the assembled monks in the Mahâvihâra monastery reciting the Atthakathâ, and sought permission to translate these commentaries into Pâli. Having given satisfactory proof of his capacity, he was allowed access to the entire collection, and produced a complete rendering of all the commentaries from the Sinhalese. His Pâli commentary upon the Dhammapada is still extant. Buddhaghosha is also credited with the authorship of many independent works, of which the most important is the *Visuddhi-magga*, the "way of purity," a kind of systematic treatise or compendium of Buddhist doctrine. This treatise was so highly esteemed that later writers composed commentaries upon it.[2] In all probability Buddhaghosha gave a direction and tone

[1] For a discussion of the date of Buddhaghosha, see Max Müller in *S. B. E.*, x^2. p. xxii. ff.; and cp. Copleston, *Buddhism*, chap. xxiv.

[2] The text of the *Visuddhi-magga* was prepared for the press by the late Mr. H. C. Warren, of Cambridge, Massachusetts, and his translation was nearly complete at the time of his death. It is to be hoped that both may be published.

to the religion of Ceylon, the strength of which it is impossible now to estimate.

Milinda-panha.—Another famous work was the *Milinda-panha*, or Questions of King Milinda. It contains a series of dialogues between the king and Nâgasena, a Buddhist sage, wherein the former propounds a series of philosophical and metaphysical questions, which are more or less successfully answered by the monk.[1] Milinda, or in Greek Menander, was a well-known Indo-Scythian king who reigned in the latter half of the second century before Christ. The work in question bears internal evidence of having originated in the north or north-west of India, and its composition is usually assigned to the early part of the first century of our era. It is based upon the Pitakas, and presupposes the same characteristics of life and currents of thought as are there found. The *Milinda-panha* is quoted by Buddhaghosha, and must therefore have been carried to Ceylon and translated into Pâli at a comparatively early period.

Ceylon Chronicles.—The two most important works for the ecclesiastical history of Ceylon and of Southern Buddhism generally are the *Dîpavamsa*, or Chronicle of the Island, and the

[1] Translated by Rhys Davids in *S. B. E.*, vols. xxxv., xxxvi.

Mahâvamsa, or Great Chronicle. These two compilations, which are supposed to have been put together about the beginning and middle of the fifth century A.D. respectively, deal with the history of Buddhism from its origin, and present many variations in detail from the accounts preserved in the Tripitaka. The ancient portion of the *Mahâvamsa* includes only one-third of the whole, and breaks off with the thirty-seventh chapter. The work however has been continued by a later author or authors, who have carried the history down to the middle of the eighteenth century. The Mahâvamsa in its present form thus consists of one hundred chapters. The whole with the Dîpavamsa has preserved a most extensive and interesting store of history and tradition, the parts of which are necessarily of very different value.[1]

Northern Canon.—The Canonical books of the Southern Buddhists are recognised generally speaking by the adherents of the Northern school in China Japan and Tibet, but occupy an entirely subordinate position. The *Mahâ-*

[1] The earlier part of the *Mahâvamsa* was translated into English by the late George Turnour, and published in 1837; the latter by L. C. Wijesinha, a native Sinhalese scholar, at Colombo in 1889. An edition of the Dîpavamsa, text and translation, appeared under the editorship of H. Oldenburg in 1879.

yânists accept the Tripitaka, but add to it other works on mythology and metaphysics, which are either written in Sanskrit or more usually are translations or adaptations from the Sanskrit, and to which they attach a greater importance. The Tibetan Canon in particular is most extensive and elaborate. In the belief and regard of the Buddhists of China and Japan the foremost place is taken by three works, which are all of a more popular and mythological character than the authoritative books of the South. These are the Greater and the Less *Sukhâvatî-vyûha*, or "description of Paradise," and the *Amitâyur-dhyâna-sûtra*, or "treatise on meditation on Amitâyus" or Amitâbha, the Buddha of boundless splendour or light. The subject of the three writings is very similar. They all describe with an Oriental wealth of imagery the joys of Sukhâvatî, the heaven of Amitâbha; of whom the greater Sukhâvatî-vyûha proceeds to narrate the history, beginning with his appearance in the world as a *Bhikshu*, named Dharmâkara. His home is in the west, which is therefore sacred to him:—

This is the quarter where that Blessed Amitâbha, the Tathâgata, holy and fully enlightened, dwells, remains, supports himself, and teaches the Law, whose spotless and pure name, famed in every quarter of the whole world with its ten quarters, the blessed Buddhas, equal to (the grains of) the sand of the river Gangâ, speaking and answering again and again without stopping, extol, praise, and eulogize.[1]

In the smaller Sukhâvatî-vyûha, meditation upon Amitâyus with repetition of his name and prayer appears to be regarded as sufficient for salvation; while the larger book demands in addition works of merit.[2] According to the tradition, this was one of the last works composed by the Buddha after his return from the Trayastrims'a heaven in the eightieth year of his age.

The *Amitâyur-dhyâna-sûtra* begins with the

[1] *Sukh.-vyûha*, 39; *S. B. E.*, xlix. 2nd. pt. p. 59.

[2] The Sanskrit text of the Greater and the Less Sukhâvatî-vyûha was published by Max Müller in 1883, in *Anecdota Oxoniensia*, Aryan Series, vol. i. pt. ii.; and translations of the same in *S. B. E.*, vol. xlix. The popularity of the larger work may be inferred from the fact that no fewer than twelve translations are said to have been made into Chinese, of which five are still extant, differing considerably from one another and from the Sanskrit original. The most important and best is that by Sanghavarman, dated 252 A.D. The smaller Sukhâvatî-vyûha was three times translated. A complete edition of the Chinese Tripitaka is now in course of publication through the efforts and at the expense of Chinese native scholars, and more than 3000 volumes have already appeared. The Sukhâvatî-vyûha was known in Japan at least as early as 640 A.D., or within a century of the introduction of Buddhism into the island; and was there studied in the original Sanskrit as well as in Chinese translations. See the Introductions to the works above cited.

story of Ajâtas'atru, the prince who dethroned his father Bimbisâra, king of Magadha, and shut up his mother Vaidehî in strict confinement, because she brought nourishment to her husband in prison. To her the Buddha reveals himself, and instructs her how to obtain the heaven of Amitâbha, which he describes. The Buddha Amitâbha then appears in dazzling splendour, and worships the Buddha (*i.e.* Gautama). And the latter explains to ^Ananda and Vaidehî the methods of meditating upon Amitâbha, and the character and virtues of those who will be born into that blessed country, where he abides.[1]

A work held in the highest esteem by one sect at least of the Buddhists in Japan is the *Vajrac'c'hedikâ*, or Diamond - Cutter, which in strong contrast to the three treatises already referred to, devotes itself to the exposition of the Indian doctrine of *mâyâ.* All phenomenal things including the self are unreal; only mind has a true existence; and the objects of sense are all of them an illusion. This metaphysical teaching is placed in the mouth of the Buddha

[1] The Sanskrit text of the Amitâyur-dhyâna-sûtra has not, I believe, been published. A translation by Mr. J. Takakusu from a Chinese version is contained in *S. B. E.*, vol. xlix.; where the date of the Chinese rendering is given as 424 A.D.

himself. And the book has by the leaders of Buddhist thought in Japan been accepted as in substance a fair statement of their doctrine and views.[1] The same work under the same name is found among the sacred books of the Tibetan Buddhists.

Tibetan Canon.—This Tibetan Canon is in mere bulk unequalled by the sacred scriptures of any other nation. Few or none of the books however are original. The Canon consists of a number of works brought into the country by Indian monks, and translated into Tibetan from the Sanskrit; some also derived from the Chinese, and a few in all probability direct

[1] See a long quotation in *S. B. E.*, xlix. 2nd pt. p. xvi. ff. from a Buddhist manifesto presented in 1893 to the Chicago Congress of Religions:—"In contradistinction to the fallacious phenomena, there is the true essence of mind. Underlying the phenomena of mind, there is an unchanging principle which we call the essence of mind; the fire caused by fagots dies when the fagots are gone, but the essence of fire is never destroyed. The essence of mind is the entity without ideas and without phenomena, and is always the same. It pervades all things, and is pure and unchanging," etc. (*l.c.* p. xviii.). The Sanskrit text of the Vajrac'c'hedikâ was published by Max Müller in 1881 in *Anecd. Oxon.*, Aryan Series, vol. i. pt. i.; and a translation in *S. B. E.*, vol. xlix. The work has been six times translated into Chinese; amongst others by Hiuen-Tsiang and by I-Tsing in the middle and end respectively of the seventh century. Versions also exist in Tibetan Mongolian and Mandshu.

from the Pâli.[1] The dates of these translations range generally from the eighth to the thirteenth centuries of our era. Old books and manuscripts, of which a large number exist in the monasteries of Tibet, are held in almost superstitious reverence, and at the hands of the common people receive actual worship. There are two great divisions of the canonical books:—the Canon proper, termed the *Kāh-gyur*, or Translated Commandment, because derived from the Sanskrit; and the Commentaries, or *Tan-gyur*. The former is of stupendous length, comprising one thousand and eighty-three distinct works, distributed in 100 or 108 volumes. These volumes are printed from wooden blocks, the art of printing having been introduced from China about 200 years ago, on native paper made from the inner bark of a shrub; and consist each of about 1000 pages. A complete edition is therefore of considerable bulk and weight; but most of the monasteries of Tibet and Sikhim are said to possess copies. There are only two places in Tibet where the work of printing is carried on; the earlier edition

[1] Dr. Bendall has recently reported the finding of Pâli manuscripts in the capital of Nepâl; a proof that Hînayâna literature was known to some extent at least in the north, *J. R. A. S.*, 1899, p. 422.

in 100 volumes at Narthang in the western part of the country, the later in 108 at Derge in the east. There is also a Pekin edition, a copy of which is in the Academy of Sciences at St. Petersburg. The whole was translated into Mongolian about the beginning of the fourteenth century.

The Kâh-gyur is divided like the Pâli Tripitaka into three parts, namely (1) *Dul-va* or Discipline, which is said to have been compiled by Upâli; (2) *Dô*, the Sûtra or Sermon section, which is further sub-divided into five sections, of which the last, the *Tantra*, is especially romantic and mystical, and has nothing answering to it in the Pâli scriptures; and (3) *Ch'os-non-pa*, or metaphysics, the book of "Transcendental Wisdom," a collection of speculative teaching said to have been revealed by the Buddha shortly before his death. This third portion of the Kâh-gyur is contained in 21 volumes, which are not however all independent. Another division of the scriptures, which appears to be current in Nepâl, is into nine *dharmas*, or laws.[1] The *Tan-gyur*, or Commentary, is divided into sûtra and tantra

[1] See complete lists and brief abstracts of the contents of the several books in Waddell, pp. 159–64; Max Müller, *Selected Essays* vol. ii. pp. 170 ff., 183 f.

sections, and occupies 225 volumes, which deal with mystic and magical ritual and ceremonies, with literature science philosophy and mythology. A few of the treatises have been examined and translated. But the contents of the whole, as might be expected, are not accurately known.[1] Large numbers of Tibetan books have been brought to Europe, and are to be found in the libraries of London Oxford Paris and St. Petersburg.

[1] Waddell, p. 164 f.

HISTORY AND DEVELOPMENTS

HISTORICAL Growth of Buddhism: Ceylon and Burma.—It was thus at a comparatively early period in its history and career that Buddhism spread to Ceylon. On all grounds the inference appears to be justified that in this island and in its Pâli scriptures the teaching of the founder has been most faithfully preserved, and developed in most sympathetic harmony with his spirit. From Ceylon according to the received view Buddhism was introduced into Burma at an uncertain but early date; and the recognition of the Pâli Canon and books in that country is a sufficient proof of a close historical connection with the southern island. It has however been justly pointed out that the presence in Burma of ancient Sanskrit inscriptions written in a North Indian character, bearing date in the early centuries of the Christian era, and which make reference to temples and statues of the Buddha, together with certain features that Burmese Buddhism shares rather with the Mahâyâna than with the Hînayâna school of thought, is evidence that immigrants from Bengal and the Ganges Delta must have passed before this time by land through Manipur and reached upper Burma, bringing with them their language and their religion.[1] Not improbably these visitors from North India did actually anticipate in point of time the Ceylon preachers. The Buddhism of Burma is therefore certainly composite, and its character is perhaps best explained in the light of a fusion of northern and southern elements, which met and exercised a mutual influence in the valley of the Irawadi; but of which the latter proved itself the more powerful, and gave a prevailing tone to the whole. Missionaries from Ceylon also carried the Buddhist faith throughout the Malay Peninsula Sumatra and Java, and probably to other islands of the Eastern Archipelago.

Kashmîr and Nepâl.—The attempt however to trace the spread of Buddhism to other countries than its original home is beset with all the difficulties and uncertainties that surround the chronology of ancient India and the East in general. The dates furnished by tradition or the native records can in most

[1] See for instance a note by R. C. Temple in *Indian Antiquary*, vol. xxiv. p. 275.

instances hardly be relied upon as more than approximate. The faith is said to have reached Kashmîr within half a century of the death of Gautama Buddha, being preached by the great monk and evangelist Madhyântika, a disciple of ^Ananda. Nepâl has been Buddhist from the earliest times; but the Buddhism of its inhabitants has always been of a lax and accommodating order. Only some four centuries ago apparently did the religion penetrate from Nepâl into Bhutân and Sikhim.

China Japan and Tibet.—China received the faith direct from India in the year 62 of our era. Thence it was carried to Korea in 372 A.D., and in 552 A.D. to Japan. These last two countries have always been religiously dependent upon China, as far as Buddhism was concerned; and in Japan in particular the sacred books were studied in Chinese more than in their original tongue. Buddhism was introduced into Tibet from North India during the years 638–40 A.D. at the instance of king *Sron Tsan Gampo,* who had married Buddhist wives from Nepâl and China. Little progress however was made until about a century later, when at the invitation of another king named *Thi-Sron Detsan,* a great conqueror and Buddhist, the Indian monk and saint *Padma-Sambhava* arrived in

Tibet, and became there the real founder of Lâmaism, the form which the religion of the Buddha has assumed in that country. Popular tradition and belief has credited Padma-Sambhava with the most extensive miraculous powers. His name is as much revered as that of the Buddha himself, and throughout Tibet he receives divine honours. This Lâmaist form of the Buddhist religion is known also in the western parts of China, and is in almost exclusive possession of Mongolia, where it appears to have been introduced about the close of the sixteenth century. The majority of the inhabitants of Manchuria are nominal adherents of the same faith.[1]

Egypt and Russia.—In the north-west of India and beyond the border, the rule of the Græco-Scythian kings, with the comparative security which it afforded, would facilitate the spread in that direction of the religious movement of Buddhism. Buddhist missionaries are said to have penetrated as far as Egypt, whence according to the Mahâvamsa thousands of *Bhikkhus* or monks came to the Patna Council. The Tartar Lords of the Golden Horde, who with their hosts overran the east of Europe in the thirteenth century, and to whom the early

[1] Waddell, *Buddhism in Tibet*, ch. iii.

Christians paid tribute, were Buddhists. And in European Russia there exists a small colony of Kalmuks settled on the lower Volga, according to the latest census about 160,000 in number, who profess the Buddhist, or rather the Lâmaist faith. These are the remnant of a great nation who migrated into Russia in the seventeenth century, but the majority of whom returned in 1771 to Zungaria, their ancient home in the south-west of Mongolia, between the Altai and the Tian-Shan Mountains.[1]

Chinese Buddhist Monks.—The communication of religious literature and thought between India and China was for a number of years maintained by the means of Buddhist monks from China, who at great risk and with great expenditure of time and effort made their way to India, and visited the sacred places of Buddhism. Some of these travellers have left memorable records of their experiences and of the religious condition of the lands which they visited. The three of greatest importance, whose works have been preserved, were, in the order named, Fâ-Hian, Hiuen-Tsiang, and I-Tsing. These monks, whose enthusiastic and

[1] Cp. A. H. Keane in *C. M. S. Intelligencer*, 1894, p. 730, or *Atlas*, p. 10; Waddell, p. 42.

self-denying zeal on behalf of their faith has rarely been surpassed, travelled with the intention not only of seeing the sacred places and most flourishing centres of Buddhism, but of securing copies of the sacred books for translation into Chinese. The determination of the exact routes which they followed presents often great difficulties, and in parts at least the subject needs entire re-consideration in the light of the recent discoveries in Nepâl and the North-West. Their journeyings involved an absence from their own country of many years; and the narratives of their experiences which they furnish have proved to be the most valuable material for forming a true conception of the position which Buddhism held in India in their day. They also supply us with welcome fixed dates in Indian chronology. All three works have appeared in English translations.[1]

Fâ-Hian.—The earliest of the three was Fâ-Hian, a native of the province of Shân-si in

[1] *Record of Buddhistic Kingdoms,* being an account by the Chinese monk Fâ-Hien of his Travels in India and Ceylon in search of the Buddhist Books of Discipline, translated by J. Legge, Oxford, 1886; *Si-yu-ki,* or Buddhist Records of the Western World, translated from the Chinese of Hiuen-Tsiang by S. Beal, 2 vols., Boston, 1885; *Record of the Buddhist Religion as practised in India and the Malay Archipelago,* by I-Tsing, translated by J. Takakusu, Oxford, 1896.

North China, who undertook a journey to India and Ceylon at the beginning of the fifth century of our era for the purpose of obtaining copies of the Vinaya Pitaka, parts or the whole of which he is said after his return to have published in a Chinese rendering. His visit to Ceylon coincided in time with that of Buddhaghosha. The account which he wrote of his journey is entitled "A Record of Buddhistic Kingdoms," but in the Japanese recension "Narrative of the Travels of Fâ-Hian." Setting out with four companions over-land in or about the year 400 A.D., he made his way westwards across Central Asia slowly and with many halts to Khotan, where he found a strong Buddhist community, and where he remained three months. Thence his route is difficult to follow in detail, but the party crossed the "Snow Mountains," and found themselves in North India, where at a place named To-leih, or To-li, doubtfully identified with Dardistân or the country of the Dards on the upper Indus in the extreme north-west of India,[1] they saw a miraculous wooden image of Maitreya, the future Buddha. The same image was also

[1] Cunningham, *Ancient Geography*, p. 82 f.; Legge, p. 24, note 2, where the latitude and longitude are apparently wrongly printed; and also note on Sketch-Map, p. xvii.

visited and seen later by Hiuen-Tsiang. Turning eastward Fâ-Hian passed through the Panjâb and parts of the North-West Provinces, finding everywhere a flourishing Buddhism and relics of the Buddha. Thence he came down to Mathura or Muttra and a place near Kanauj, at which Gautama descended after preaching the law to his mother in the Trayastrims'a heaven. The miraculous appearances attending his descent are all duly detailed. Still further south-east and south was S'râvastî, which is described as almost deserted, and Fâ-Hian recounts the legends and miracles of its history. Westward from S'râvastî they came to the birthplace of Kas'yapa Buddha, and thence again south-east and south to Kapilavastu, in which "there was neither king nor people"; the site was abandoned, and the Chinese traveller found only a few monks and some poor families. From Kapilavastu his route led him to Kus'anagara, Vais'âlî, and Pâtaliputra or Patna, the capital of king As'oka. This city he describes with its monasteries. After a brief round of visits to Râjag*ri*ha, Buddha-Gayâ, and Benares, he returned to Patna and settled there for three years, studying Sanskrit and the Buddhist law, and copying manuscripts of the sacred texts. From Patna he travelled down the river to the kingdom of Tâmraliptî, the modern Tamlûk in the district of Midnapur, where he spent two years, and from which place he took ship to Ceylon.[1] The date of his arrival in the island must have been about the year 411 during the time of the king Mahânâma, who reigned 410–32 A.D. He describes the wonders of Ceylon, its relics including the Buddha's tooth, with the religious ceremonies and monasteries of the island. After a stay here of two years he sailed by way of Java for China, where he arrived safely with his books after many perils by sea, upon which he cannot look back without emotion. According to his own statement his travels thus covered altogether a period of fifteen years. He is recorded to have died at the age of eighty-eight in the Chinese monastery of Sin.

Hiuen-Tsiang.—After the lapse of rather more than two centuries Fâ-Hian was followed by another Chinese monk,[2] Hiuen-Tsiang, whose

[1] The modern town is sixty miles from the sea. But at the time of Fâ-Hian's visit Tâmra-liptî was a seaport, and so it was found to be by Hiuen-Tsiang two centuries later. I-Tsing also embarked from and returned to Tâmra-liptî. The fact illustrates the rapid growth of the land in and about the delta of the Hûglî river. See Hunter, *Gazetteer, s.v.* Tamlûk.

[2] Other Buddhist pilgrims had visited India in the interval, and Indian monks had made their way to China and spent

travels extended over sixteen years from 629 to 645 A.D., and who is said after his return to have produced a Chinese rendering of no less than seventy-five Buddhist works which he had brought back with him. In his journey from China Hiuen-Tsiang followed the same general course as Fâ-Hian, but travelled much more widely in India itself. He did not moreover visit Ceylon; and returned to his own country by land through the northern part of Tibet. His account of his life there and experiences forms the most vivid and complete picture of ancient India in existence. The religious condition of things did not greatly differ from what the earlier pilgrim had found it to be. Everywhere with few exceptions Buddhism was flourishing, but the Mahâyâna school and teaching had gained considerable ground at the expense of the Hînayâna. The most striking feature however of the religious life of the country was the revival of Brâhmanism, which even in Buddha-Gayâ, the great centre of Buddhist faith and pilgrimage, had to a considerable extent supplanted its rival. To this day the place is sacred to both Hindus and Buddhists, and the

many years there. No records however of their work or journeyings have been preserved beyond brief notices by later writers.

pilgrims of both faiths resort thither.[1] At Kanauj a great Buddhist sovereign Harsha-vardhana S'îlâditya[2] was in power, and at his capital Hiuen-Tsiang found as many as a hundred monasteries with 10,000 monks. Under his presidency a numerously attended Council assembled at Prayâga, or Allahâbâd, in the year 643 A.D., at which the Chinese traveller was present, when discussions were held between Buddhists and Brâhmans, and between members of the different sects of the two religions. Eighteen kings are said to have attended the Council with 500,000 monks and laymen. The proceedings lasted three days, on the first of which with much pomp and ceremony the statue of Buddha was erected, on the second that of the Sun, and on the third that of S'iva. Other indications show that the king was not always the convinced and enthusiastic Buddhist that Hiuen-Tsiang represents him to be. For on a copper-plate grant from Mâdhuban he calls himself a S'aivite. Every five years on the plain near Allahâbâd a festival took place, accompanied with much feasting and distribution of treasure and gifts to Buddhists and Brâhmans

[1] Cp. Monier Williams, *Buddhism*, p. 398 f.

[2] Monier Williams calls him the fourth great Buddhist king of India, *l.c.* p. 167.

alike, and closing with a ceremony in which the king, to imitate the Great Renunciation, stripped himself of his robes, and went forth in a beggar's rags. Hiuen-Tsiang describes also the important and flourishing Buddhist university at Nâlanda, the modern Barâgâon near Gayâ, with its numerous monasteries and temples maintained at the king's cost, and its thousands of monks belonging to the eighteen principal Buddhist sects, constantly engaged in the study of the sacred writings and commentaries.

I-Tsing.—I-Tsing, the third and last of the great Buddhist scholars and pilgrims from China, followed not long after Hiuen-Tsiang, perhaps inspired by his example, in the latter half of the seventh century. His journeyings were prolonged for twenty-five years; and his principal work is an account of Buddhist manners customs and belief in the lands in which he travelled. In the year 671 at the age of thirty-six he started for India from Chang-an, the then capital of China, in the province of Shen-si, and with only one companion sailed for the South from Kwang-Tung. The place where he first landed is called Bhoja, or S'rîbhoja, and is supposed to be the same as Sumatra. Thence after a stay of a few months I-Tsing took ship for Tâmra-liptî, where he arrived two years after leaving Chang-an. Through many difficulties and dangers he made his way to Nâlanda and there remained for ten years, devoting the time to study and the collection of Sanskrit books. During the twenty-five years that he spent abroad he is said to have travelled in more than thirty different countries, and to have brought or sent home to China 400 Buddhist texts. Of these after his return, with the help of native Indian scholars who accompanied him to China, he published translations in 230 volumes of 56 separate works. His own treatise shows acquaintance with the earlier accounts of Hiuen-Tsiang; and he seems to have been present in Chang-an in 664 at the time of the death of the latter. I-Tsing himself died after an adventurous and laborious life in his 79th year, A.D. 713. Although he did not travel in India itself so extensively as his predecessors, yet his industry in collecting information and the care with which he records his observations render his work of especial interest and value both from a historical and religious point of view. Of the four chief *nikâyas* or schools of Buddhist thought and practice which he found existing in India, his account applies especially to the *Mûlasarvâstivâdins*, or "those who affirm the principle of the reality of all existence."

DOCTRINES AND SECTS

THE doctrine or truth which formed the basis of the Buddha's teaching, and which he claimed to have received under the Bo-Tree as a flash of spiritual and intellectual enlightenment, is comparatively simple. Richly diverse and complex as were the developments of the faith and ritual of Buddhism in the countries to which it spread, the original form in which it was proclaimed by Gautama himself, as recorded in the sacred books, is characterized by an absence of ornament or elaboration, which is all in favour of its genuineness. These fundamental truths were set forth in the first sermon which Gautama preached after his attainment of perfect wisdom to the five monks or ascetics with whom he had formerly in vain practised austerities. In themselves they are not difficult to state or to understand. They represent however a philosophy or a moral system, rather than a religion. And their precise significance in relation to other and earlier creeds, together with the construction placed upon them by his contemporaries; how much is really original, and how much is due to later building upon a foundation already laid, but which is now obscured beyond recovery, are subjects upon which much has been written, but which can hardly be said even yet to have been relieved of all difficulty and confusion.

^Aryasatyâni.—The teaching of the Buddha then starts from the principle, so familiar to Indian thought, that all existence is and must be encompassed with misery. It is not only the conditions of existence that are out of joint; existence itself is an evil, and necessarily involves suffering for the creature that exists. Life in itself is not and cannot be other than a source of pain and unhappiness. This was the first and fundamental truth which the Buddha proclaimed. And although the form in which it was clothed might be new, the doctrine itself was old on the soil of India, and is recognised as a truism by all the foremost of her philosophers. The teaching is conveyed after the usual manner in formulas or aphorisms, which are known as the four *^Aryasatyâni*, or Noble Truths, and which may be briefly summarised as follows:—All existence involves suffering; suffering is caused by desire, especially the desire for continuance of existence; the suppression of desire therefore will lead to the extinction of suffering. These are the first three Noble Truths. The fourth and last is the doctrine or path by which this deliverance may be effected; the Noble Eight-fold Path, sometimes called the Middle Path because it avoids the two extremes of bodily indulgence and self-mortification or asceticism.[1] The elements or grades of the Path are defined to be right belief, right resolve, right speech, right conduct, right occupation, right effort, right contemplation, right concentration.[2] This primary teaching of the Buddha on

[1] The four catch-words as it were of the Âryasatyâni are *duhkha*, pain; *samudâya*, cause; *nirodha*, suppression; *mârga*, way or path.

[2] *Mahâv.*, i. 6. 17 ff., translated in *S. B. E.*, xiii. p. 94 ff. The subject is often referred to and the terms repeated in the Buddhist books. See especially the Sutta of the "Foundation of the Kingdom of Righteousness," *S. B. E.*, xi. p. 146 ff., and "Exposition of the Path leading to the Cessation of Misery," translated from *Mahâ-satipatthâna-Sutta*, 107. 35, in Warren, p. 372 ff., where the meaning of the terms used is explained in detail. It is not easy to find English equivalents, precise and sufficient, for the half-technical Pâli words. The rendering adopted is practically that of Warren, *l.c.* Monier Williams gives "right belief or views, right resolve, right speech, right work, right livelihood, right exercise or training, right mindfulness, right mental concentration" (*Buddhism*, p. 44). Rhys Davids and Oldenburg in *S. B. E.*, *l.c.*, have "right belief, right aspiration, right speech, right conduct, right means of livelihood, right endeavour, right memory, right meditation":—

the four Noble Truths and the Middle Path is referred to as the setting in motion of the Wheel of the Law, or the founding of the Kingdom of Truth.[1] According to some authorities these four doctrines or truths, or at least the terms in which they are expressed, are

"This, O monks, is the Noble Truth of Suffering: Birth is suffering; decay is suffering; illness is suffering; death is suffering. Presence of objects we hate is suffering; separation from objects we love is suffering; not to obtain what we desire is suffering. Briefly, the five-fold clinging to existence is suffering.

This, O monks, is the Noble Truth of the Cause of suffering: Thirst, that leads to re-birth, accompanied by pleasure and lust, finding its delight here and there. (This thirst is three-fold), namely, thirst for pleasure, thirst for existence, thirst for prosperity.

This, O monks, is the Noble Truth of the Cessation of suffering: (it ceases with) the complete cessation of this thirst, —a cessation which consists in the absence of every passion,—with the abandoning of this thirst, with the doing away of it, with the deliverance from it, with the destruction of desire.

This, O monks, is the Noble Truth of the Path which leads to the cessation of suffering: that holy eight-fold Path, that is to say, Right Belief, etc.

. . . .

And as the Blessed One had founded the Kingdom of Truth (by propounding the four Noble Truths), the earth-inhabiting devas shouted: 'Truly the Blessed One has founded at Benares in the deer-park Isipatana, the highest Kingdom of Truth, which may be opposed neither by a Samana nor by a Brâhmana, neither by a deva, nor by Mâra, nor by Brahma, nor by any being in the world.'"

[1] *Mahâv.*, i. 6. 30; *Dhamma-c'akka-ppavattana-sutta*, 25 ff.

derived from Indian medical science, being merely transferred from the region of matter and physics to that of the spirit.[1]

Nidânas.—The second fundamental doctrine or principle is of great interest as an early attempt to find an explanation of the origin of evil. This is the theory of the twelve *Nidânas*, or causes, a chain of cause and effect, said to have been discovered or thought out by Gautama in the period immediately following his attainment of Buddhahood. The links of causation begin with ignorance, which therefore is the primary root of all evil—

> "On ignorance depends *karma*; on *karma* depends consciousness; on consciousness depend name and form; on name and form depend the six organs of sense; on the six organs of sense depends contact; on contact depends sensation; on sensation depends desire; on desire depends attachment; on attachment depends existence; on existence depends birth; on birth depend old age and death, sorrow, lamentation, misery, grief, and despair." [2]

---

[1] Kern, p. 46 f.

[2] *Mahâv.*, i. 1. 2; cp. Warren, p. 83 ff.; Barth, *Religions of India*, p. 110 f. The Sanskrit terms are *avidyâ*, ignorance; *samskârâs*, constituents of being, everything that goes to make up the universe and its content, a word which Warren rather paraphrases than translates by *karma*, and Kern renders by "impressions," while Rhys Davids and Oldenburg prefer to retain the Pâli expression; *S. B. E.*, xiii. p. 75 f. There is no real English equivalent, simply because the idea conveyed finds

These terms, it will be noticed, express *states*, not substances or things. The interpretation of them presents many difficulties; and in fact the series has been very variously explained. As thus formulated there appears to be in the whole little logical sequence or obvious meaning. The successive *Nidânas* moreover are not always given in the same order; nor are the Sanskrit or Pâli words themselves absolutely free from ambiguity. Nevertheless the statement or theory appears to represent a genuine attempt to explain the anomalies of existence, and to solve the mystery of suffering. The same theory is known by the name of "Dependent Origination," because the elements of being arise out of and are dependent upon one another, and can only come into existence in succession. Elsewhere it is spoken of as "The Middle Doctrine," lying between the two extremes of belief in being, τὸ ὄν, and nihilism or belief in not being, τὸ μὴ ὄν.[1]

no place in Western philosophy. The remaining terms of the series are *vijnâna*, consciousness; *nâmarûpa*, name and form; *shadâyatana*, the six senses, or rather the organs in which they reside; *spars'a*, touch or contact; *vedanâ*, feeling; *trishnâ*, desire, literally thirst; *upâdâna*, exertion, attachment; *bhava*, becoming, being; *jâti*, birth; *jarâmaranam*, old age and death. Cp. Monier Williams, p. 102 f.

[1] Cp. *e.g. Visuddhi-Magga*, xvii., quoted in Warren, p. 168 ff.;

Origin of Theory of Nidânas.—On the meaning and explanation of this curious string of causes and effects various theories have been propounded, none of them entirely satisfactory. There is sufficient in common with the articles and technical terms of the Sânkhya philosophy to warrant the conclusion that elements are to be found in each which have been derived from one and the same ultimate source. Direct dependence however of the one upon the other is not probable. It has been suggested that in reality the Nidânas contain a philosophical theory of life, in which the history of the human being is traced in metaphysical terms from birth to death. An obvious objection to this explanation, which has often been pointed out, is that

Mahâ-Nidâna-Sutta, *ibid.* 202 ff.; *Samyutta-Nikâya*, xxii. 90. 16:—

"The world for the most part, O Kaccâna, holds either to a belief in being or to a belief in non-being. But for one who in the light of the highest knowledge, O Kaccâna, considers how the world ceases, belief in the non-being of the world passes away. And for one who in the light of the highest knowledge, O Kaccâna, considers how the world ceases, belief in the being of the world passes away.

. . . .

That things have being, O Kaccâna, constitutes one extreme of doctrine; that things have no being is the other extreme. These extremes, O Kaccâna, have been avoided by the Tathâgata, and it is a middle doctrine he teaches:—

On ignorance depends *karma*," etc. Warren, p. 165 f.

assuming a philosophical or biological origin of the formula there are two life-histories, not one, comprised within its limits. The first begins with ignorance, and through the *samskârâs* and consciousness reaches its full development in name and form. The second returns again to birth, which is explained as originating in desire or longing, and leads on in due course to old age and death. It seems not improbable that this is, in part at least, the true interpretation of the repetitions and incoherencies of the Chain of Causation in its present form, that it endeavours to combine two or perhaps more ancient formulæ or hypotheses concerning human life, working them up together and seeking to fit them the one into the other. Later and more ripened conceptions were imposed upon earlier; and the whole, which was really the product of a subsequent age, was put into the mouth of the Buddha himself. How far this was really the case it is impossible now to determine. But that the theory in the form in which it has come down to us ever sufficed for the text of an attractive public discourse, such as Gautama is represented as delivering, appears incredible.[1]

Others have found in the Buddhist doctrine of causation an adaptation of an ancient cos-

[1] Cp. Warren, *Buddhism in Translations*, p. 115.

mology, supposing that a creation myth is here translated into philosophical terms, and applied to the unravelling of the mysteries of human life. Dr. Waddell has figured a large diagram or picture of the Wheel of Life from the Ajanta caves in the north-east of the State of Haidarâbâd, on which the twelve Nidânas are represented in succession around the rim of the wheel,—"a complete authentic account of human life from the absolute stand-point of the earliest Buddhist philosophy." The figure of a wheel without beginning or end expresses the perpetual round or recurrence of life. At the centre are the three vices, passion or lust, hatred, and folly, to denote the forces that control and perpetuate life. Between the rim and the nave are represented scenes of blessedness or woe from the various heavens, worlds, and hells. The wheel is grasped by a demon or monster, who is emblematic of the evil craving for existence. While outside stands the Buddha, to show that he has escaped from the vicious circle, and is no more subject to re-birth.[1]

Buddhist Confession of Faith.—By the side of

[1] *Buddhism of Tibet*, p. 107 ff.; cp. Kern, p. 47. The traditional explanation of the picture was given to Dr. Waddell by the Lâmas themselves. On the caves at Ajanta see Hunter, *Gazetteer of India*, *s.v.*, and the references there given.

this explanation or theory of the origin of being, and in a great measure independent of it, was the celebrated formula, which has been termed the Buddhist confession of faith. This formula, constantly on the lips of devout Buddhists and carved on their monuments, is apparently intended to give expression to a thought similar to that underlying the Chain of Causation. It appears first in the history in connection with the conversion of two of the greatest of the early disciples of the Buddha, Sâriputta and Moggallâna[1]; and in each case the recitation of the words by the venerable monk Assaji is said to have aroused in the mind of the hearer a clear understanding of the fact that "whatever is subject to origination is subject also to cessation or destruction":—

> "Laws or conditions of existence that arise from a cause, the cause of these the Buddha declared, and also the destruction of them. Such truths the great Teacher uttered."[2]

The relation between the statement of doctrine and the conclusion drawn is not at first sight

[1] *Mahâv.*, i. 23. 5, 10; Warren, p. 87 ff.; cp. *supra*, p. 217.

[2] *Ye dharmâ hetu-prabhavâ hetum teshâm Tathâgatah Hy avadat teshâm c'a yo nirodha evam-vâdî Mahâ-S'ramanah.* Cp. *S. B. E.*, xiii. p. 144 ff.; Kern, p. 25; Monier Williams, p. 104.

altogether clear. The link between the two is perhaps to be found in the series of the Nidânas, already discussed. The middle term as it were that brings them into dependence upon one another is the consideration that existence with its attendant misery was by the Buddha shown to have been brought about by the operation of certain causes, and was thereby proved to be terminable when those causes ceased to act. Or, in other words, the way of escape from the evils of life was pointed out in the destruction or suppression of the causes of life itself. It is however strange that this formula and the Chain of Causation are never in the books brought into direct connection. And it is possible therefore that there are here preserved in fragmentary and scarcely intelligible form indications that point to a more truly philosophical and consistent, a less material theory of the universe,—a theory which endeavoured to trace all things backwards and upwards to the one great primitive cause of all.

Buddhist Materialism.—In these doctrines and formulæ there is no explicit contradiction or dissent from the current Brâhmanical speculations, and nothing out of harmony with the tendencies of Hindu thought. They run parallel to, if they are not actually derived from forms of Indian philosophy which have persisted to the present day. It is otherwise with the Buddha's teaching concerning the origin and nature of the living being, and his denial of the existence of a soul. Here he came into conflict,—it can hardly have been undesignedly,—with the most acceptable and wide-spread of Hindu beliefs. In some of the books he is represented as setting aside, on the ground that they do not conduce to immediate profit, such questions as the identity of the *âtman*, the self or soul, with the body, of a future existence, or of the eternity of the visible world. Elsewhere however a more than merely agnostic position is taken up, and a distinct denial is given to the proposition that there is present in the living being anything beyond the body and its material constituents.[1] The Buddha therefore was here confronted with the problem of how to explain life and the perpetuation of life with all its miseries and alternations of fortune on purely materialistic principles, and without

[1] See especially the well-known comparison of the chariot and its parts in the Milinda-panha, 26–28 ; *S. B. E.*, xxxv. p. 43 ff. There appears to be no sufficient reason for refusing to ascribe to the Buddha himself the origination at least of this materialistic teaching. That it was developed and systematized by his successors is probable. Its apparent want of connection with the doctrine of the four Noble Truths etc. is no sufficient argument against its conception within the same Oriental mind.

postulating a spiritual author or cause of all.

Skandhas.—The solution offered is briefly as follows. The living being is constituted out of two or more of the five groups of elements, termed *skandhas.* These are *rupa,* form; *vedanâ,* feeling or sensation; *sanjnâ,* perception; *samskâra,* predisposition; *vijnâna,* consciousness, or thought. The first group contains four primary and twenty-four derivative "forms," the primary being the familiar earth, air, fire, and water. The second and third groups have each five divisions. To the fourth group are assigned fifty-one, and to the last, the most important group, eighty-nine parts or elements.[1] All five *skandhas* are present in the human being, but a less number in any one of the lower animals. They unite together at birth to form the living sentient creature, and in death are again dissolved and perish. Apart from them no existence is possible; and when the combination is broken up at death the individual ceases to be. It is however distinctly denied that either singly or in combination the skandhas *are* the individual. Such views as that "Sensation is my *âtman,*" self or *ego,* are qualified as heretical; while

[1] A complete list taken from the Visuddhi-Magga is given by Warren, p. 487 ff.

at the same time the idea of the existence of any *âtman* independent of the skandhas is strenuously rejected.[1] There is therefore no "soul" which in its individual and personal identity endures through many births. In fact since the mode of combination of the skandhas undergoes incessant change, the living being of the present moment is not strictly speaking the

[1] For the denial of the identity of the skandhas with the living being see *Mahâv.*, i. 6. 38–41, *Mahâ-Nidâna-Sutta*, 256. 21. The passages bearing on the non-existence of an *ego* are collected in Warren, p. 129 ff. One of the most definite is from the *Visuddhi-Magga*, ch. xviii :—

"Just as the word 'house' is but a mode of expression for wood and other constituents of a house, surrounding space in a certain relation, but in the absolute sense there is no house . . . in exactly the same way the words 'living entity' and 'Ego' are but a mode of expression for the presence of the five attachment groups, but when we come to examine the elements of being one by one, we discover that in the absolute sense there is no living entity there to form a basis for such figments as 'I am,' or 'I'; in other words, that in the absolute sense there is only name and form. The insight of him who perceives this is called knowledge of the truth.

"He however who abandons this knowledge of the truth and believes in a living entity must assume either that this living entity will perish or that it will not perish. If he assume that it will not perish, he falls into the heresy of the persistence of existences; or if he assume that it will perish, he falls into that of the annihilation of existences. . . . To say 'The living entity persists' is to fall short of the truth; to say 'It is annihilated' is to outrun the truth."

same as in the moment past or in the moment of the future.[1] This last speculation however, which is in reality only the logical conclusion of the doctrine of the *skandhas*, is probably a later refinement.

The five groups are sometimes classified into two divisions, *rûpa* or form standing over against the other four, which are collectively termed *nâma*. The living being is then said to consist of *nâmarûpa*, name and form.[2] The former includes all the mental and subjective qualities, the latter the external bodily or objective. From the "nâma" or mental group moreover it is possible for the wise and self-restrained man to win freedom in the present life. Not so with respect to the "form" group. From this deliverance only comes at the moment of death.

Karma.—The dissolution of the *skandhas* which takes place at death is immediately followed by a re-constitution. Thus a new individual arises in this or in some other world through the combining together afresh of the groups whose union had been momentarily broken up. The link between the new and the old is *karma*, action, or rather,—since the word is without an English equivalent,—action together with all its

[1] *Visuddhi-Magga*, viii.

[2] Cp. *Milinda-panha*, ii. 2. 6; *S. B. E.*, xxxv. p. 71 f.

inevitable consequences, good and evil. The individual perishes, utterly and for ever; but his *karma* lives on, and by its power is effected a new combination of the *skandhas* in a new living being, who is heir to the accumulated effects of all the actions of his predecessors, or, as it may be more loosely expressed, of his own deeds in former existences. There is however strictly speaking no "self" which passes from the one existence into the other. Only *karma* continues. And as long as *karma* is unexhausted, so long by an inevitable law will the series of re-births persist, each new life being the direct consequence of the activities bodily and mental of the preceding. There is a real break in the continuity of existence; and this break explains the loss of all memory of the events of previous lives. But the effects of all action pass from one to the other, and in the new existence the penalty must be paid for former wrong-doing, even as the reward will be reaped for kindly and virtuous deeds. Buddhas however, being possessed of omniscience, are acquainted with and can recall the occurrences not only of their own former existences, but those also of others.

Re-Birth.—It is evident therefore how widely, in spite of superficial resemblance, the Buddhist theory of re-births differs from the Hindu doctrine of metempsychosis or transmigration. In Buddhism there is no spirit or soul, no *âtman* or self, that "migrates." All is purely mechanical, the result of self-acting laws, which neither require nor submit to interference from without. Into the origin or meaning of these laws the Buddha did not stay to inquire. If the accounts given by the Buddhist historians and commentators themselves are to be accepted, he distinctly set aside all such inquiries as irrelevant, refused to be drawn into metaphysical discussions, and in effect declared that these and similar questions were beyond the lawful scope, if not beyond the competence of the human intellect. A further point of difference consisted in the limitation of the possibilities of re-birth to the six orders of living beings. The Hindu theory, which extends indefinitely downwards the limits of conscious life, so as to include plants and stones and the humblest objects of creation, has no counterpart in Buddhism.

Escape from Re-Birth.—From this dependence of re-birth upon karma acting on and through the skandhas it at once follows that a way of escape from existence with its attendant evils lies open, if the power of karma can be broken. If the force which compels a re-constitution of the elements of being can be destroyed, and its effects annulled, there will be no coming together again of the skandhas, and no renewal of existence after death. This then is theoretically the aim of every sincere and devout Buddhist, to extricate himself from the mechanical round of re-births, to break the chain of karma, so that the bitter fruits of action may cease to be gathered, and he may reach a state of untroubled and serene repose. The means by which the end may be attained is to be found in the Noble Eight-fold Path.[1] He who has become enlightened, knows and endeavours to tread in this path, has escaped from the ignorance which is the root of all misery, and has entered upon the road which leads to rest, to *nirvâna*. The ignorance which is thus the spring and cause of all suffering is not of course ignorance in general, but ignorance of the special truths which the Buddha taught. Destroy ignorance, and the process of karma will be arrested, there will be no more fruit of action, and therefore for that individual no further re-birth. Hence ignorance is the first term in the Chain of Causation[2]; and "on ignorance depends karma." It is however expressly laid down that ignorance is not an uncaused primary cause; ignorance "arises," and itself has a cause. For all

[1] *Supra*, p. 278 f. [2] *Supra*, p. 280 ff.

practical purposes however ignorance stands at the beginning, the *fons et origo* of all. What lay behind and beyond the Buddha himself did not care, and forbade his followers to speculate:—

> "As I have told you, O monks, the first beginning of ignorance cannot be discerned, nor can one say 'Before a given point of time there was no ignorance, it came into being afterwards.' Nevertheless, O monks, it can be discerned that ignorance possesses a definite dependence."[1]

A similar statement is made with regard to the craving for existence, the second starting-point in the Chain of Causation.[2] And it is further explained that ignorance is the cause of the karma, which results in unhappy craving or desire of that which leads to happy states of existence.

Different Kinds of Karma.—The Buddha however was not so unreasonable as to demand from his followers abstinence from all action as the necessary condition under which they might make for themselves a way of escape from the circle of re-births. Nor did he for a moment profess himself to practise such abstinence. As might be expected there are different kinds of *karma*. Some actions are meritorious, and others the contrary; some

[1] *Visuddhi-Magga*, xvii.; Warren, p. 170 ff.

[2] Cp. *supra*, p. 283.

karma is productive, and another class is destructive; *karma* in some depends directly upon ignorance, while in other cases other immediate causes are in operation.[1] But the leading and most important distinction as regards the future is that not all actions entail results which must be worked out in a new life. Actions performed without craving or "attachment" do not give rise to a re-constitution of the *skandhas*, and so do not issue in another existence. They are "barren," not "fruitful"; and as far as the future is concerned, it is immaterial whether they are performed or not. Through the teaching of the Buddha this freedom from craving may be gained; and what is thenceforth done by the saint or enlightened man produces no consequences in another birth. The works however of ordinary men are joined with ignorance and attachment, and cause trouble and suffering after death. This subject, admittedly a difficult one, is repeatedly discussed in the Buddhist books:—

"This truth, ^Ananda, that on attachment depends existence is to be understood in this way. Suppose, ^Ananda, there were utterly and completely no attachment at all of any one to anything, as namely the attachment of sensual pleasure, the attachment of heresy, the attachment of fanatical conduct, the

---

[1] See Warren, pp. 179 ff., 245 ff., 495 f.

attachment of the assertion of an Ego;—if there were nowhere any attachment, pray, on the cessation of attachment would there be any existence?"

"Nay, verily, Reverend Sir."

"Accordingly, Ânanda, here we have in attachment the cause, the occasion, the origin, and the dependence of existence."[1]

There are three conditions, O monks, under which deeds are produced. And what are the three? Covetousness hatred and infatuation are the three conditions under which deeds are produced.

When a man's deeds, O monks, are performed through covetousness hatred or infatuation, are caused by or originate in covetousness etc., wherever his personality may be, there those deeds ripen, and wherever they ripen, there he experiences the fruition of those deeds, be it in the present life, or in some subsequent one.

. . . .

There are three conditions, O monks, under which deeds are produced. And what are the three? Freedom from covetousness hatred and infatuation are the three conditions under which deeds are produced.

When a man's deeds, O monks, are performed without covetousness hatred or infatuation, are caused or originate without covetousness etc., then, inasmuch as covetousness etc. is gone, those deeds are abandoned, uprooted, pulled out of the ground like a palmyra tree, and become non-existent and not liable to spring up again in the future.[2]

'Bhante Nâgasena,' said the king, 'are there any who die without being born into another existence?'

'Some are born into another existence,' said the elder, 'and some are not born into another existence.'

---

[1] *Mahâ-Nidâna-Sutta*, 245, 1; Warren, p. 205.

[2] *Anguttara-Nikâya*, iii. 33. 1; abbreviated from Warren, p. 215 ff.

'Who is born into another existence, and who is not born into another existence?'

'Your majesty, he that still has the corruptions is born into another existence; he that no longer has the corruptions is not born into another existence.'

'But will you, bhante, be born into another existence?'

'Your majesty, if there shall be in me any attachment, I shall be born into another existence; if there shall be in me no attachment, I shall not be born into another existence.'[1]

'Bhante Nâgasena,' said the king, 'does a man know when he is not to be born into another existence?'

'Assuredly, your majesty, a man knows when he is not to be born into another existence.'

'Bhante, how does he know it?'

'He knows it from the cessation of all cause or reason for being born into another existence.'[2]

'Bhanto Nâgasena,' said the king, 'when you say "round of existence," what is that?'

'Your majesty, to be born here and die here, to die here and be born elsewhere, to be born there and die there, to die there and be born elsewhere,—this, your majesty, is the round of existence.'[3]

Nirvâna.—These truths it is the office of a Buddha to make known in the world, to preach anew doctrines which are as continually being overlooked and neglected. The external and individual means however by which alone this wisdom can be apprehended is intense con-

[1] *Milinda-panha*, ii. 1. 6; *S. B. E.*, vol. xxxv. p. 50.

[2] *Ib.* ii. 2. 2; *S. B. E.*, p. 65.

[3] *Ib.* iii. 6. 9; *S. B. E.*, p. 120.

centration of mind and thought. This was of course a familiar Indian device, and no novelty as taught by Gautama. Every man must for himself assimilate the truths proclaimed, must work out his own salvation, must practise the meditation and self-culture which alone can lead to inward peace and deliverance from the bondage of karma and re-birth. He who has reached this state, wherein desire and lust have ceased to have power over him, and no renewal of existence will accordingly take place after death, is said to have attained *nirvâna*, a restful untroubled state, in which there is no more present or prospective misery and pain. To gain *nirvâna* was the goal which the Buddha set before his followers as the supreme end of their efforts and longings. It was clearly an end attainable in the present life. Gautama himself professed to be in enjoyment of *nirvâna*. And in the sacred books a similar claim is made for many of his early disciples.

To define more closely and to expound in psychological terms the nature of *nirvâna* is not easy. The word signifies literally "blown out," "extinguished"; that is, the fire of lust, the clinging to existence. But in reality no more highly technical term is to be found in the entire vocabulary of Buddhism; and upon its precise meaning and content very much has been written. What *nirvâna* is not however can at once and very simply be stated. It is not extinction or annihilation. Neither is it a condition of mere trance or dreamless repose, in which all the activities of the body and mind are suspended. Either definition is incompatible with the claim to the enjoyment of *nirvâna* in the present life. But it is that condition of being in which all actions are performed without "clinging" or "attachment"; in which therefore no fruits of action are produced, *karma* is inoperative, and after their dissolution no re-combination of the elemental groups can occur. The Buddhist saint who has attained *nirvâna* still acts and thinks. But his actions and thoughts end with themselves, and there is no aftermath. The terms in which this attainment is recorded are found repeated without variation in several passages of the sacred books:—

The venerable Sona remaining alone and separate, earnest, zealous, and resolved, attained ere long to that supreme goal of the higher life for the sake of which noble youths go out from all and every household gain and comfort to become houseless wanderers,—yea, that supreme goal did he, by himself, and while yet in this visible world, bring himself to the knowledge of, and continue to realise, and to see face to face! And he became conscious that re-birth was at an end, that the higher life had been fulfilled, that all that should be done had been accomplished, and that after this present life there would be no beyond.[1]

Beyond *nirvâna* moreover there is a further and final emancipation, which can only be reached at and through death. This is *parinirvâna*, complete nirvâna. At this stage the force of the strongest and most persistent of the skandhas, the *rûpa* or form-group, is finally broken. The other four,—sensation, perception, predisposition, and consciousness, collectively the name-group,—give place earlier; and from the yoke of these deliverance may be obtained in the present life. This state or condition of deliverance is *nirvâna*; and when it has once been reached, no re-combination of the skandhas is possible. There remains only the form-group. This last link with an organised body is dissolved in death.[2]

Buddhist Sects.—The "History of Doctrine" of Buddhism remains unwritten, for want of sufficient materials on which to found historical and chronological conclusions. The records speak of numerous sects; but on the precise

[1] *Mahâv.*, v. 1. 18; cp. *Cullav.*, xi. 1. 15, *Mahâ-parin. Sutta*, v. 68.

[2] Cp. Warren, *Buddhism in Translations*, p. 155 ff., and the whole section on "Sentient Existence."

distinctions of doctrine and practice, or the period of their rise and fall, little or no light is afforded. The great cleavage which has persisted from the earliest times to the present day is into the two schools of North and South, or, what is not quite the same thing, the *Mahâyâna* and the *Hînayâna*. The doctrines of the former, while paramount in the countries bordering on India on the north, in China and in Japan, have found their way into Ceylon, and exercised a considerable influence on the Buddhism of the island. Hînayâna sacred books on the other hand have been met with as far north as Tibet. The distinction between the two is mainly doctrinal; for practice and the habits of the people vary greatly in the different Buddhist lands. The *Mahâyâna* system taught a kind of speculative theism, with which were united especially in Tibet elements of mysticism and fable, derived in large part from the ancient popular religions of the country. This system was moreover tolerant, gentler and more human than its rival, the Hînayâna; and permitted greater freedom to the individual both in action and belief than did the simpler agnosticism and stern but unattractive morality of primitive Buddhism. The name was therefore given to it of *Mahâyâna*, or the "Great

Vehicle," because it offered to convey all or any to heaven on easy terms; while the *Hînayâna*, or "Little Vehicle," practically confined salvation to the elect few. Thus the spirit of the Mahâyâna, if more lax, was undoubtedly more liberal than the orthodox doctrine as represented by the Hînayâna. And this characteristic appears in its many deities, who are generally compassionate and ready to exert themselves for the benefit of men.[1]

Origin of Mahâyâna School.—The rise of the two schools, their historical beginnings and growth, can only be doubtfully traced. If the heretical views maintained and condemned at Vais'âlî actually resulted in the formation of an independent sect, then the Mahâyâna may fairly be regarded as a development of the school or party of the Mahâsanghikas.[2] In the later Councils again of Patna and Jâlandhara it is possible to recognise mere partisan assemblies, connected the one with Hînayâna, the other with Mahâyâna teaching and tendencies. Later still the Chinese monks and pilgrims found the two schools existing and flourishing side by side in India, each with

[1] Kern, p. 124 f.; Waddell, *Buddhism of Tibet*, pp. 10 ff., 124 f.; Monier Williams, pp. 158 ff., 188 f.

[2] *Supra*, p. 224 f.

large monasteries and many adherents; but a general if slight movement was apparent in favour of the more popular system, which seemed as though in course of time it would supplant its rival. In the early traditional history of the Mahâyâna, the most prominent figure is *Nâgârjuna*, who is often regarded as its founder. He was the thirteenth or fourteenth in succession of the Buddhist patriarchs, Mahâ Kas'yapa the President of the Râjagriha Council being the first. Most probably he lived about the middle of the second century of our era. He taught, or is said to have taught, a "Middle Way" between the doctrines of the reality, and of the deceptiveness or illusory character of existence; and to have therefore called his system *Mâdhyamika*, or *Mâdhyamayâna* the "Middle Vehicle." The name is known and recognised in Tibet, but not elsewhere.[1] His authorship is claimed for the well-known Mahâyânist work the *Prajnâ-Pâramitâ*, "perfection in wisdom," containing mystical teaching on the origin and nature of being.[2] He is further said to have travelled

[1] Waddell, *ll. supra cc.*; Legge, *Fâ-Hian*, p. 14.

[2] The Sanskrit form of the text has been published by Max Müller in *Anecdota Oxoniensia*, Aryan Series, vol. i. pt. 3; and translated in *S. B. E.*, vol. xlix. He refers to it as "the

extensively in Southern India, and to have held the office of patriarch for no less than sixty years.

Philosophical Schools.—It is usual to enumerate eighteen schools or sects of Buddhists as existing in India in the early centuries of the Christian era. This number is given for example by Hiuen-Tsiang,[1] and in the Ceylon chronicles. In the *Sarva-dars'ana-sangraha*[2] also, dating from the middle of the fourteenth century, a brief epitome of Buddhist views is included in the summary of Indian philosophies. These sects are however in most instances little more than names to modern students, and have left no direct descendants either in the north or south. Their differences appear to have been largely metaphysical, and subordinate to the great division into the two schools of the Mahâyâna and Hînayâna, to one or other of which they were attached. That the precise number moreover was ill defined, and depended more upon the mode of enumeration than upon any broad and gene-

most widely read Buddhist text in Japan." Cp. Waddell, pp. 11, 125.

[1] Beal, i. p. 80.

[2] "Collection" or "review of all opinions," by Mâdhavâc'ârya; translated by E. B. Cowell and A. E. Gough, 2nd ed., London, 1894. See the account of the "Bauddha" system, p. 12 ff.

rally recognised distinctions, is shown by the fact that reference is sometimes made to thirty-two sects, and in one passage at least the existence of ninety-six is asserted. The four principal schools of thought, of which the others were probably mere sub-divisions, were the *Mâdhyamika* and *Yogâc'âra*, belonging to the Mahâyâna, and the *Vaibhâshika* and *Sautrântika*, which adhered to the Hînayâna. The *Vaibhâshika* traced its origin back to Râhula, son of Gautama. The two first taught a more or less consistent and complete idealism, and though technically Mahâyânists, occupied in reality a position nearer to the agnostic views of primitive Buddhism. According to the *Mâdhyamika* school nothing really exists, all things including nirvâna itself are *mâyâ*, illusion. The *Yogâc'âra* allow the existence of *vijnâna*, consciousness, but of nothing else besides; and have therefore been named *Vijnânavâdins*, or Sensationalists. These were in close relations with the Hindu philosophical schools of the Vedânta and the Yoga respectively. The *Vaibhâshika* and *Sautrântika* expounded a realist, or as it has been termed "presentationalist" philosophy, teaching that the universe with all its phenomena had an actual and real existence. They differed in the method by which they supposed this universe to be apprehended by the senses; the former asserting that objects are known immediately and in themselves, the latter mediately and through the intervention of images.[1] With regard also to the canonical Scriptures these two schools were at variance. The adherents of the Vaibhâshika acknowledged the authority of the Abhidharma but rejected the Sûtras; their opponents reversed the order, accepting the Sûtras but refusing the Abhidharma. Of further sub-divisions, those of the Vaibhâshika appear to have been the most important. They were four in number, namely Sarvâstivâda, Mahâsanghika, Sammatîya, and Sthavira. Of the two first named, Fâ-Hian says that he found copies of their rules in the Mahâyâna monastery at Patna, which he transcribed and translated into Chinese.

The latest of the Chinese travellers I-Tsing belonged himself to the Sarvâstivâda school, of the practices of which his book is a minute account. He makes brief mention of the Mâdhyamika and Yogâc'âra, which he says are the only two schools of the Mahâyâna existing in India. His "four principal schools

[1] Compare the curious parallel in the difference of views of the Vadagalais and Tengalais, *supra*, p. 155 f.

of continuous tradition," which he apparently intends to be understood belonged to the Hînayâna, correspond to the four sub-divisions above named; but the terms Vaibhâshika and Sautrântika are not met with in his work. The Sarvâstivâda was found to be the most influential and wide-spread, greatly predominating in the north of India, while the followers of the Sthavira were in the majority in the south. As to the difference between Hînayâna and Mahâyâna, I-Tsing declares that both "are perfectly in accord with the noble doctrine. . . . Both equally conform to truth and lead us to Nirvâna." The only distinction which he names is that the former eschews the worship of Boddhisattvas and the reading of Mahâyâna sûtras, practices which by the latter are regularly and statedly observed.[1]

[1] I-Tsing, Introduction, pp. 7 ff., 14 f.

MONASTICISM

THE most characteristic external feature of Buddhism was the *Sangha*, or Order of monks, which, modified and controlled by circumstances and by the disposition and habits of the people, has maintained itself in a more or less distinct form in every country in which the Buddhist faith has taken root. That this feature was really primitive, and not a later addition grafted on a philosophical stem, all available evidence tends to prove. The earliest Buddhist writings pre-suppose the existence of the Order, and found upon it their ecclesiastical system and rule. The address of the edict of king As'oka[1] is to a community not recently called into being, but possessed of a recognised status and a collection of sacred books. The *Sangha* also formed with the Buddha himself and the Dharma or sacred Law a kind of Buddhist triad, sculptured representations of which have been found, whereon the Sangha is depicted as a man holding a lotus, the

[1] *Supra*, p. 230 ff.

symbol of perfection and purity. This triad is the familiar Buddhist *tri-ratna*, the "three jewels," or "three honoured ones."[1]

Gautama Buddha moreover enjoined renunciation of the world as a necessary condition of salvation. The earliest Buddhist community therefore was conceived of as a community of monks, a religious order of men who were striving to attain the perfect life, and as a means to that end had withdrawn themselves from the world and worldly desires. And the earliest canonical books are concerned with the regulating of the lives of the members of the Order. This idea of separation from the world as a step towards spiritual enlightenment was not of course peculiar to Buddhism; it was familiar to the thought and practice of the rival Brâhmanical faith. In the Buddhist scheme however it was as it were organised, and made the centre and mainspring of a great ecclesiastical system. The members of the Sangha were termed *Bhikshus* or beggars; a name that amongst the Brâhmans was already employed technically to denote one who had entered upon the fourth *âs'rama* or period of life, and was dependent

[1] See the drawing of the sculpture from Buddha Gayâ in Monier Williams, *Buddhism*, p. 485, and cp. *ib.* p. 177 note.

entirely upon alms. No caste restrictions were placed upon entrance to the Order, although the greater number of the early members appear to have been Brâhmans. By the side of the monks was established an order of nuns, or *Bhikshunîs*; the foundation of which, although carried back by tradition to Gautama himself, must probably be ascribed to a later age.[1] Outside of both was the community of laymen. Thus the whole ecclesiastical system existed for and was subservient to the monk.

Rules of Admission.—Within the Sangha the only distinctions recognised were those of age and merit. The elders or *Sthaviras* governed; the *S'râmaneras*,[2] the novices or younger monks, were required to observe vows of abstinence and

[1] The tenth book of the *C'ullavagga* prescribes the duties and obligations of nuns, and relates the circumstances of the admission of women to the privileges of "the homeless state under the doctrine and discipline proclaimed by the Blessed One." Eight "chief rules" are laid down for their behaviour, especially towards the monks, and forms of admission similar to those in force in the male Sangha are appointed. The Buddha also is represented as consenting reluctantly to the request made on their behalf, and as prophesying the earlier extinction of the true religion in consequence of the permission given to women to retire from the world. *S. B. E.*, xx. p. 320 ff.; Warren, p. 441 ff.

[2] From the root *s'ram*, to exert oneself, to do penance or practise austerities.

to pledge themselves to implicit obedience. The latter might only be admitted with the consent of their parents in ordinary cases, and not before the age of fifteen.[1] At first the Buddha personally received all candidates into the Order; but later gave to the monks themselves the right to admit new members and to confer ordination, provided it were done formally and in a regularly constituted assembly.[2] The preliminary form of admission of the novice was termed *pravrajyâ*, a going forth, or retirement from the world. The ceremony appears at first to have been confined to a repetition of the "three-refuge" formula, namely:—I come for refuge to the Buddha, the Law, and the Order![3] and implied perhaps on the part of the boy or his guardians no more than a determination at some future time to become a monk. Later there were imposed upon them as upon the monks generally ten vows of abstinence, called the ten precepts, as follows:—abstinence from destroying life, from theft, from impurity, from falsehood, from strong drink; abstinence from eating at forbidden times, from dancing singing music and shows, from garlands scents and finery, from high or

[1] *Mahâv.*, i. 50 f., 54.   [2] *Ib.* i. 12, 28, 29.

[3] *Buddham s'aranam gac'c'hâmi, Dharmam s'aranam gac'c'hâmi, Sangham s'aranam ga'c'hâmi.*

broad couches, and from receiving gold or silver.[1] The first five abstinences were incumbent also upon Buddhist laymen. The second ceremony of initiation, which was the true ordination, was termed *upasampadâ*; and in order to be eligible for this the candidate must have already received *pravrajyâ*, and must be twenty years old.[2] The ordained monk became at once entitled to all the rights and privileges of the Order, and was provided with the usual alms-bowl and yellow vestments. The material and form of his clothing was carefully prescribed, and the outer robes at least were to be made in patches, like the rice-fields of Magadha.[3] It was then necessary for him to spend five years under a teacher, acquainting himself with all the details of doctrine and discipline. Besides the alms-bowl, the monk carried with him a razor and a water-strainer, the latter in order to avoid the sin of destroying any living thing while drinking; in later times also a rosary.

Life and Occupations.—The monks were accustomed to live in communities, originally in

[1] *Mahâv.*, i. 56; cp. Kern, p. 76 ff., Monier Williams, p. 126.

[2] *Mahâv.*, i. 49. 6; a detailed account of an ordination service held at Kandy will be found in Warren, p. 393 ff.

[3] *Mahâv.*, viii. 12

the open air without fixed abode or in simple mud huts, but later in large and elaborate monasteries, termed *vihâras.*[1] Their time was to be spent in meditation, in reciting and hearing prayers, and in the daily rounds to beg for food, for which however they were not allowed to make any request, as did the Brâhman students or ascetics. If it were given them voluntarily, they were to accept it with gratitude; if not, they moved on to another house. During *Vassa*, the season of the rains, they were forbidden to travel, except for short distances and on urgent business, lest their feet should crush and destroy animal life. The time for entering upon *Vassa* and the length of the period of retreat varied in different countries. In Ceylon it lasts for three months, and by a curious inversion of the original order and purpose, the monks then leave their monasteries, and either visit by invitation the house of some rich patron, or dwell in specially constructed sheds or booths.[2] Twice a month the Pâtimokkha was to be recited, on the *Uposatha* days, the days of abstinence or fasting,

[1] Whence the name of the district in Bengal, *Behar*, the land of monasteries. The word came to be used also to denote a temple.

[2] *Mahâv.*, iii. 1 ff.; compare Copleston, *Buddhism in Ceylon*, pp. 246 f., 446 ff.

and in the presence of at least four monks.[1] A simple and moral life was enjoined upon all with contentment and cheerfulness ; and all alike were bound by a strict vow of poverty.

Monasteries. — Although however the individual monk thus pledged himself to a life of simplicity and self-denial, no restriction was placed on the wealth or possessions that the monasteries might as corporations hold. In early and mediæval India especially the accounts of the Chinese pilgrims prove the great extent and influence of these institutions, which rivalled in power the religious orders of the Middle Ages in Europe. In Nepâl the rule of celibacy or of life in a monastery is no longer observed. The Buddhist preachers are married, and live as ordinary men. Sikhim appears to have received its Buddhism from Tibet, and its monks are adherents of the orthodox Tibetan church. The monasteries of Ceylon at one time rivalled those of India, both in influence and in reputation for learning and sanctity. They are now on a much smaller and humbler scale, rarely containing more than about a score of inmates. In the country districts often only two or three live together. The same institution has in Burma been the

[1] *Mahâv.*, ii. 4. 14, 26 ff.; *supra*, p. 244 f.

great organ of scholastic instruction. Every male Burman must at some time in his life be an inmate of a monastery; and all the boys go there to school, in most cases leaving at the expiration of their term much more indolent, and scarcely less ignorant than when they entered. They are taught to read and write Burmese, and a few Pâli texts are committed to memory. Those who adopt the monastic profession for life are termed *Pungis.* Of these last the time is spent in teaching, and in the service of the monasteries and temples.[1]

Buddhism in Tibet.—The most wealthy Buddhist communities are found in Tibet, where the monasteries are in possession of great wealth. Primitive superstitions also, nature and devil worship, have there maintained a powerful hold on the people, and have so controlled and modified the later religion of the Buddha that it is hardly recognisable. That the striking resemblance of Tibetan ritual, with its altars processions and incense, to the forms of the Roman Catholic and Greek churches, is due to early Nestorian missionaries, is now generally recognised. These men must have made their way

[1] W. R. Winston, *Four Years in Upper Burma*, chh. xi., xii. Under British rule this system of education, or absence of education, is of course rapidly breaking down.

into Tibet at a very early date; and the highly elaborate hierarchical system now existing in its origin and direction owes much to their teaching. The contrary influence however of native superstitions has been too strong in matters of belief. Between the two the simple characteristics of primitive Buddhism, which perhaps never had a real opportunity of establishing its hold upon the country, have been entirely overborne, so that Tibet is now probably the most superstitious and priest-ridden country in the world. "Primitive Lâmaism may therefore be defined as a priestly mixture of Sivaite mysticism, magic, and Indo-Tibetan demonolatry, overlaid by a thin varnish of Mahâyâna Buddhism. And to the present day Lâmaism still retains this character."[1]

Lâmas.—The monks in Tibet bear the name of *Lâmas*, "lofty" or "superior ones."[2] It is said that from 12 to 20 per cent. of the population are members of a monastic order.

[1] Waddell, p. 30.

[2] *Ibid.* p. 28. Dr. Waddell's is the standard and exhaustive work on the religion of Tibet, and is profoundly interesting to the student of religious thought and practice. To it I am almost entirely indebted for the following brief account. Compare S'rî S'arat C'handra Dâs, *Indian Pandits in the Land of Snow*, Calcutta, 1893; W. W. Rockhill, *Land of the Lâmas*, London, 1891.

The highest Lâmas are believed to be re-incarnations of the Buddha himself; and on the death of one of these his spirit enters into some little child, who is then sought out, and brought to the monastery with much pomp and ceremony. There are two chief or "Grand" Lâmas. The first and nominally supreme is the *Dalai*, the "vast" or "ocean" Lâma, who has his home and court at Lhasa, and is the acknowledged head of the Lâmaist church. He is supposed to be absolute sovereign of the whole country; and it is through him nominally that the Chinese exercise their control. The list of these Dalai Lâmas is carried back to the close of the fourteenth century of our era. They and their city are so carefully and jealously guarded that only one of them has ever been seen by an Englishman, by Mr. Manning in 1811[1]; and for more than fifty years no European has set foot in Lhasa. The second Grand Lâma is sometimes called the *Panchen* Lâma, the title signifying "Great Doctor."[2] His reputation for holiness stands even higher than that of his brother of Lhasa, because he is less involved in

[1] In Monier Williams, *Buddhism*, p. 331 ff., there is an interesting account of the Dalai Lâma's reception of S'arat C'handra Dâs.

[2] Waddell, p. 234.

political or secular affairs. He is moreover more accessible to Europeans, and has on several occasions received the visits of British travellers. His monastery is at Tashi-lhunpo, "the mass of glory," about 300 miles west by south of Lhasa. On the death of either of the Grand Lâmas, the other is charged with the duty of discovering and making known his successor. Besides these there are several other Grand Lâmas, less universally recognised and reverenced; one of whom resides in a monastery at Pekin. Beneath the Grand Lâmas come in regular gradation of office and rank the abbots, priests, deacons, and novices. The priest or monk corresponds to the bhikshu of India, the bhikkhu of Ceylon; he bears a title of equivalent meaning, *Ge-long*, is of at least twenty-five years of age, and is bound to observe all the rules of a fully ordained monk. The service of the monastery is completed by orders of lay-brethren. Outside of all are the ordinary laity, the "ignorant people," or "givers of alms."

Tibetan Sects.—The numerous and varied sects of Lâmaism are said to have first arisen from a reforming movement initiated by an Indian Buddhist monk *Atīs'a* in the first half of the eleventh century. His zeal was directed against the superstitions and practices of the ancient demonolatry, which had renewed their power over the people; and in his reform he aimed at the re-introduction of the Mahâyâna doctrines of a purer and more moral Buddhism. Between three and four centuries later his most prominent disciple and successor *Tson-k'apa* re-organised the sect or church founded by Atîs'a, and gave to it the title of *Ge-lug-pa*, or "the virtuous style." Thus restored and purified it became the established church of Tibet. The first Dalai Lâma is said to have been a nephew of Tson-k'apa.

Besides the Ge-lug-pa there are two other reformed sects, the *Kar-gyu-pa* and the *Saskya-pa* or *Sakya-pa*, both founded by pupils of Atîs'a in the latter half of the eleventh century under the inspiration of his teaching. These are more lax in their observances and mode of life than the Ge-lug-pa, and approach more nearly to the character of the old unreformed party. They also are divided into numerous sub-sects. It is only the monks of the established church who practise abstinence, and keep the vow of celibacy. Those who adhered to ancient usages and refused to follow Atîs'a bear the name of *Nin-ma-pa*, or "the old ones." Among them customs of sorcery and demon worship, derived from native and pre-Buddhistic sources, are rife. Of all the Lâmaistic sects the Nin-ma-pa is the furthest removed from primitive Buddhism, and the most lax in belief and practice.

Robes.—The robes worn by the members of the Order in Tibet are the three ordinary garments of a Buddhist monk, as prescribed by the Vinaya, with the addition of an undervest, trousers, and a hat. The colour however both of the robes and of the hat varies in the different sects. There is some evidence to show that even in the Southern church the distinctive Buddhist yellow is comparatively modern; and that in the Middle Ages in India the usual dress of the monk was red or reddish-brown.[1] In Tibet the Ge-lug-pa alone, the established church, may wear yellow robes; although in their case also the usual colour is red, but fastened by a yellow girdle. The hats differ in shape as well as in colour, and often convey by their form a symbolic or typical meaning. All the sects, with the exception of the Ge-lug-pa, have red hats; and the monks therefore of this sect are distinguished as "yellow hat," while the original unreformed

[1] Cp. Kern, p. 79; Waddell, p. 194 ff., with figures of the various kinds of hats worn. The change of colour from red to yellow is said to have been made by Tson-k'apa. According to the author of the *Sarva-dars'ana-sangraha*, "The skin garment . . . and the red vesture are adopted by the Bauddha (*i.e.* Buddhist) mendicants."

party, the Nin-ma-pa, are the "red-hat." The head-covering of the nuns is a skull-cap of red or yellow according to the sect.

Buddhism in China.—In China Buddhism has become more consistently theistic or polytheistic, and has accepted more unreservedly the character of a religion rather than a philosophy. The date of its formal introduction into the country is given as 62 A.D.; but Buddhist missionaries from India are said to have made their way thither more than two centuries previous to this time. Here as in early India the religion of the Buddha found itself in presence of strong and firmly established rivals. Its history therefore has been a history of adoption and compromise. Chinese Buddhism has taken under its protection native deities and forms of worship and belief, until it has lost all resemblance to the strict and severe system which Gautama expounded. The Buddhists of China are most liberal or lax in their creed and habits, and in many instances worship impartially at Taoist temples or Confucian shrines; while all alike pay honour to the tablets of their ancestors. The principal sect bears the name of the *Shin-shiu*, or sect of the "Pure Land," the western paradise of Amitâbha, and was established in the year 381 A.D. Its sacred books are the larger and smaller Sukhâvatî-vyûha.[1] The founder of this school and his disciples wrote a large number of Buddhist treatises, and translated many works from the Sanskrit. From all sources China possesses at the present day a rich and comparatively unexplored Buddhist literature.

Japan.—From China Buddhism was introduced into Japan in the year 552 A.D., but owing to the strong hold of *Shintôism*, the ancient native religion, upon the people, failed at first to make much progress. *Shintôism* is a kind of spirit worship, combining the worship of mythical heroes and ancestors with that of the powers of nature in a strange and elaborate ritual. In the ninth century a Buddhist monk named Ku-kai taught that the Shintô divinities were in reality incarnations of the Buddha; and this doctrine becoming widely accepted, the two sects lived and flourished side by side, mingling with one another, and using their temples in common. In 1868 Shintôism was adopted as the religion of the State, and for some years Buddhism declined. Both religions were set free from State control in 1884, and there has recently been a marked revival of Buddhist zeal and influence. There are ten or eleven principal

[1] *Supra*, p. 256 f.

sects,[1] of which the most important and popular, the sect of the "Pure Land," was founded in the twelfth century by the monk *Gen-ku* or *Hô-nen*, and revived after his death by his chief disciple *Shin-ran* in the year 1224. Both Gen-ku and Shin-ran are said to have originally belonged to the *Ten-dai* sect. Others of the numerous disciples of Gen-ku founded branch sects which still exist, but hold practically the same doctrine. The adherents of the Shin-shiu are the most liberal of the Buddhists of Japan. They allow the sacred books to be read in the language of the country, and do not insist on the celibacy of the monks. Of the other sects six do not accept the doctrine of the "Pure Land"; and some of them appear to belong rather to the Hînayâna school. According to the latest census of 1891 about 30 million out of the 45 million inhabitants of Japan are Buddhists, and of these a third belong to the

[1] The list of these is given as follows by a native Japanese scholar. Those marked * are followers of the "Pure Land" teaching; the years are the approximate or traditional dates of foundation:—Hossô, 660 A.D., afterwards included in the Shin-gon; Ten-dai,* 805 A.D.; Shin-gon, 816 A.D.; Yu-dzû-nen-butsu,* 1127 A.D.; Ziô-dŏ,* 1174 A.D.; Rin-zai, 1191 A.D.; Shin-shiu,* 1224 A.D.; Sô-tô, 1227 A.D.; Nic'i-ren, 1253 A.D.; Zi-shiu,* 1276 A.D.; Wô-baku, 1624 A.D.: see *Anecd. Oxon.*, vol. i. pt. ii., p. xviii. ff.

Shin-shiu sect. Both in China and Japan monasteries and images are very numerous, and some of the former are on a highly elaborate scale. Thus in a temple at Kyoto there are 33,333 statues of *Kwan-non,* the goddess of mercy, erected as a thank-offering by a former emperor on his recovery from sickness; and in the same country are found huge images of the Buddha in bronze, called *Daibutsus,* two at least of which are over 50 feet high.

MYTHOLOGY AND COSMOLOGY

MYTHOLOGY.—With the severe and simple doctrines of a primitive Buddhism it is improbable that the Oriental mind would long remain content. Accordingly at a comparatively early stage there was developed a rich mythology, which centred mainly around the person of the Buddha, the marvels of his life, and his words and deeds in former existences; and which by bringing them into some kind of relation to the person of the founder, succeeded in adopting under different names and with slightly changed characteristics most of the deities of Hinduism. So that a system, in theory and intention atheistic, became possessed of an elaborate hierarchy of angels and saints, gods and goddesses in all but name, who were made objects of worship. At the same time also the conception of Nirvâna as a practical end in view came to be obscured, and was allowed to fall into the background, being replaced by the desire to win one or other of the numerous heavens that rise above the earth, and to avoid the lower worlds or hells where all manner of torments awaited the evil-doer.

Cosmology.—According to Buddhist cosmology the universe in which we dwell is only one of many, each of which is divided into three regions or worlds, viz., *Kâmaloka*, or the world of desire, which is the lowest; *Rûpaloka*, or the world of form; and *Arûpaloka*, or the world of formlessness. Tibetan speculation carried the series yet higher; and above the Arûpaloka placed the world of the five celestial Jinas or *Dhyâni-Buddhas*,[1] crowned by the heaven of *'Adi-Buddha*, who is the first of all or primæval Buddha.[2] The Kâmaloka is sub-divided into the six *Devalokas*, or worlds of the gods, beneath which in descending order are the earth or the world of men; next that of the *As'uras*, or demons, dwelling below the earth; then the world of animals; of *Pretas* or ghosts, disembodied inhabitants of earth, the victims of hunger and thirst; and lowest of all the various hells, whose inhabitants suffer the extremes of torture in proportion to their several crimes. There are thus six forms of existence, and six only, through which a living being may pass. By painful accumulation of merit an inhabitant of one of the hells may in the course of ages win

[1] Cp. *infra*, p. 334 f. [2] Waddell, pp. 84 ff., 130 f., 336.

his way to a place among the gods; and conversely, an inhabitant of a Devaloka may fall so low as to find himself in hell. There is no escape or cessation save by a knowledge of the truth that the Buddha proclaims, through the destruction of *karma* and deliverance from re-birth.

The six Devalokas in their order upwards are as follows:—(1) The abode of the four *Mahârâjahs*, the guardians of the four quarters of the universe against the demons: these are on the east *Dhrita-râshtra*, the king of the Gandharvas; on the south Virûdhaka, the king of the Kumbhândas; on the west Virûpâksha, king of the Nâgas; on the north *Vais'ravana* or *Kuvera*, king of the Yakshas and god of riches. This lowest heaven is situated on the top of the mythical Mount Meru, 84,000 miles high, the centre and axis of the entire system.[1] (2) The *Trayastrims'a* heaven where Indra dwells and rules the abode of the "thirty-three" divinities. To this heaven the Buddha came to preach the law to his mother after her death; and in some of his previous existences he had himself been Indra. (3) The heaven of the *Yâmas*, the subjects of Yama, the king and lord of the dead. (4) The *Tushita* heaven, the home of the Bodhi-

[1] Cp. Waddell, *ll.cc.*, and the figures, pp. 79, 108, *al.*; Monier Williams, pp. 206 f., 213 f.; Kern, p. 57 ff.

sattvas, where Maitreya now presides.[1] The name signifies "gratified," "pleased," — the heaven therefore of the contented or satisfied ones. (5) The *Nirmâna-rati* heaven, the abode of the gods who delight in creating. (6) The *Paranirmita-vas'avarti* heaven, of the gods who control the creations of others, where Mâra, the great Tempter to evil, has his home.

Above these are the sixteen Rûpalokas, or the lower Brahmalokas, in which various classes of gods dwell. These are regions of true form, free from *kâma*, or desire; and are divided into four groups, corresponding to the four stages of *dhyâna*, or abstract meditation. He who practises the first kind of *dhyâna* will attain to a place in the lowest group, which consists of three heavens. The second and third *dhyânas* have each also three heavens. While the remaining seven are reserved for those who are proficient in the last stage of dhyâna, the *samâdhins* "completely absorbed," or *anâgâmins* "not returning."

Highest of all are the four *Arûpalokas*, the abodes of formless spirits, beings without material bodies, who are pure abstractions. Here are usually placed the Dhyâni Buddhas.

There are therefore altogether thirty-one

[1] *Infra*, p. 331 f.

abodes of living beings, the lowest of which are the hells. The number of the hells is given at 136, to meet the different grades of offenders. According to the Northern Buddhists there were eight principal hot hells, and as many cold.[1]

Buddhist Saints.—Gautama himself appears never to have laid claim to divine honours, or to have instructed his followers to look to him as a personal deliverer. His consistent teaching was that each man must work out his own salvation by observing the rules of conduct and discipline which the Buddha delivered. Precisely however as a divine character came to be ascribed to the Buddha, images of him to be made, and worship and prayers offered, so those of his disciples who had far advanced towards perfection became also objects of reverence and adoration. The steps or gradations of the path leading to nirvâna were duly marked out, and the highest position was occupied by those who having escaped from the round of re-births either have attained or are destined shortly to attain to Buddhahood; not all however who have escaped the grip of karma do actually become Buddhas in the world. In this pursuit of nirvâna or deliverance there are

[1] Waddell, p. 90 ff.; see *Abhidhammattha-Sangaha*, v. 2 ff., translated in Warren, p. 289 ff.

four progressive stages, which are further subdivided and defined. A Buddhist monk who is living in any one of the first three stages is termed a *S'râvaka*, a hearer or disciple. In the first stage he is free from passion, and can never be born again in a lower world than that of men; in the second he is subject to a single re-birth in that world; in the third he can only be re-born in a Brahmaloka. In the last or highest stage he will never enter upon a new birth, his karma is entirely destroyed, and he has already while still living attained to the great goal, nirvâna. The name applied to such men is *Arhat*, "noble" or "venerable" one; and all the earlier disciples of the Buddha were believed to have become *Arhats*. In the later history of Buddhism the use of the term was extended, and it was made generally applicable to all the great teachers or saints. *Arhats* were credited with supernatural faculties and powers, and especially with the possession of perfect wisdom. On a grade above these are the *Pratyekabuddhas*, "single" or "separate Buddhas," who have won salvation for themselves, but do not share the knowledge with others. They differ from true Buddhas, in that they are not absolutely omniscient; neither can they live upon earth at the same time as these. Above all, the head and crown of the universe of living beings are the *Buddhas* or the *^Adi-Buddha.*

Decline and Restoration of the True Religion.— A list of twenty-four or more Buddhas is given who preceded Gautama.[1] These all during their life-time preached the Law, and established the true religion. In course of time however men forgot the truth, and fell away into ignorance and sin. The same fate Gautama prophesied would overtake the community and religion founded by himself; and he even detailed the precise steps in the degeneration which would be followed. The final act would be the spontaneous gathering together of all the relics of all the saints under the great Bo-Tree, and their consumption by fire, amidst the lamentations of the gods and the neglect of men.[2] The ruin would be hastened in consequence of the admission of women into the Order.[3] After the lapse of 5000 years, with the disappearance of all knowledge of the truth, a new Buddha named *Maitreya* would appear, and restore the true religion unto men. At present he is dwelling

[1] *E.g.*, *Jâtaka*, i. 43, translated in Warren, p. 32 f.; or for the Northern tradition, *Sukhâv.-vyûha* 3, *S. B. E.*, xlix. pt. ii. p. 6 f.; Kern, p. 63 f.

[2] *Anâgata-Vamsa*, or History of Future Events; Warren, p. 481 ff.

[3] *C'ullav.*, x. 1. 6.

in the Tushita heaven, awaiting the right time of his revelation upon earth. As the future deliverer he receives the worship of all Buddhists.

Bodhisattvas.—A being who is thus destined to become a Buddha is termed a *Bodhisattva*, "one whose essence is wisdom"; and every Buddha in the earlier period of his existence has been a *Bodhisattva.* Gautama himself was in this position until the hour of his attainment of Buddhahood under the Bo-Tree. Lists of the Bodhisattvas with their names are found in the Buddhist books. In the Northern school especially the *Bodhisattvas* are most popular. And the title was given to other great saints, to whom were ascribed all the attributes and perfections of a true Bodhisattva, but who were not destined to appear as Buddhas upon earth. Their distinctive characteristic was that of mercy or compassion; and they were thus distinguished from the Arhats, who with a less human nature were qualified as cold and passionless. These Bodhisattvas were doubtless in many instances great teachers distinguished for their wisdom and influence, who during their life-time or after death came to be regarded with a superstitious reverence, and were practically deified.

In Northern Buddhism a triad of these divinities is early found, whose origin and history is altogether obscure. They were known to the Chinese pilgrims, and their cult must have been established in India at least some time before the visits of these monks.[1] On the other hand neither their names nor their office appear to have been recognised by the Buddhists of Ceylon, and in some of the oldest Northern books also they have no place. Their names are *Avalokites'vara*, "the lord who looks down," *i.e.* upon earth or men, also called *Padma-pâni*, "lotus-handed"; *Vajra-pâni*, "thunderbolt-handed"; and *Manju-s'rî*, "he of glorious splendour."[2] The first is the pitiful or compassionate lord, the most frequently invoked of all the deities of the Northern Buddhists. By the Tibetans the Dalai Lâma is regarded as an incarnation of Avalokites'vara. And in China and Japan his female counterpart has become the popular and universally worshipped "goddess of mercy," under the names of Kwan-yin and Kwan-non.[3] *Manju-s'rî* is the god of wisdom or of speech. *Vajra-pâni* is the wielder of the thunderbolt, the god

[1] See Fâ-Hian, ch. xvi.; Hiuen-Tsiang, in Beal, i. pp. 60, 127 f., 180, *al. passim.*

[2] Monier Williams, p. 195 ff.; Waddell, p. 354 ff., and figures at pp. 12, 13, 228.

[3] Compare the *S'akti* of the Hindus, *supra*, p. 166 ff.

of war, answering to the Hindu Indra. With these two others were later associated, making a total of five Bodhisattvas to correspond to the five Buddhas of the present age, namely Gautama himself with his three predecessors and Maitreya.

Dhyâni - Buddhas. — A further development peculiar to the Mahâyâna school was the conception of five *Dhyâni - Buddhas*, Buddhas of meditation, that is mystical or spiritual Buddhas. In Tibet these became the five celestial *Jinas*, evolved by meditation from the 'Adi-Buddha. In their origin therefore they were probably nothing more than metaphysical abstractions; but in practice their position is amongst the most highly honoured and widely reverenced divinities. They are different from Bodhisattvas, for they will never become Buddhas. And they also are provided with feminine consorts or counterparts. Unlike the Bodhisattvas however no reference is found to them in the records of the early travels of the Chinese monks. Of these Dhyâni-Buddhas the most popular and widely known was *Amitâbha* or *Amitâyus*,[1] "he of unbounded" or "infinite light"; the marvels and delights of whose paradise are expatiated upon in the sacred books of the Mahâyânists with an unrestrained wealth

[1] Cp. *supra*, p. 256 ff.

of imagery and fancy. He is spiritually the father of Avalokites'vara. And the Panchen Lâma is his living incarnation upon earth.

Thus practically there came to be five triads, each consisting of a Bodhisattva, a Buddha, and a Dhyâni-Buddha. The only triad however of any real significance and importance, or that has any hold upon the mind and reverence of the people, is that connected with the Buddha of history, viz.:—Avalokites'vara or Padma-pâni, Gautama Buddha, and Amitâbha.

Festivals.—By the Buddhists both of the North and South festivals and sacred days are observed, some at least of which have been borrowed from the Hindu calendar. Thus in Tibet and elsewhere the coming of the New Year is celebrated with public rejoicings. In Siam and Burma this takes the form of a Water Festival, a period of holiday and licence, when water is freely thrown about the streets and at the passers-by, and boat-racing is indulged in amidst great excitement. Elsewhere the same festival appears to mark the beginning of the rainy season. The close of this season, the season of the monastic retreat, was celebrated by a Feast of Lights, the Hindu Dîvâlî. And the anniversaries of the birth and death of Gautama Buddha, and of other Buddhas and holy men were duly observed. Most of the great temples and monasteries have further their own private or local celebrations, often attended by crowds of worshippers and of more than local reputation.

Sacred Objects.—Sacred objects also have never been wanting to Buddhist worship from the earliest period. Among the most important and widely spread of these is the *c'akra*, or *dharma-c'akra*, the "wheel of the law," a symbol intended to denote the endless circling of cause and effect, returning into one another. It is found depicted on early monuments, and was looked upon with reverence if not actually worshipped. The *dorje* or thunderbolt, the Sanskrit *vajra*, in the hands of Tibetan monks became an efficient instrument for driving away evil spirits.[1] In the same country one of the most prominent objects is the prayer wheel, found in every village and at every temple and shrine and in the hands of the lâmas of every sect, inscribed with the sacred and auspicious formula of prayer,—*Om mani padme hûm.* Literally translated this is, "Om, the jewel in the lotus, hûm"; and it is not therefore, properly speaking, a prayer at all, but an exclamation. The significance of the phrase

[1] It is figured for example in Waddell, p. 341, and often elsewhere.

has been much discussed, but apparently it refers to the supposed birth of Avalokites'vara, by whom the prayer was composed, from a lotus-flower. The mere repetition of the words secures unlimited merit, and an easy passage through the various forms of existence. It is probably by far the most frequently uttered formula of prayer in the world. Neither is it necessary actually to pronounce the words. Writing them upon a cylinder, which may then be turned by the wind or by machinery, is equally efficacious, and places to the credit of the Buddhist worshipper a store of merit without the necessity of personal exertion. The same formula inscribed on walls rocks and flags meets at every turn the eye of the traveller in Mongolia and Tibet.[1] It is worthy of especial notice that *Om*, the most sacred syllable of the

[1] The formula is generally believed to be of very considerable antiquity. Waddell gives a facsimile "in Indian characters of about the seventh century." It has not, so far as I am aware, been met with anywhere in India. Compare Monier Williams, p. 371 ff.; Waddell, p. 148 ff., with figures of prayer-wheels, pp. 45, 172, 218 *al.* The latter writer quotes a statement from one of the Tibetan chronicles:—"this formula 'is the essence of all happiness, prosperity, and knowledge, and the great means of deliverance'; for the *Om* closes re-birth amongst the gods, *ma* among the Titans, *ni* as a man, *pad* as a beast, *me* as a Tantalus, and *Hûm* as an inhabitant of hell."

Hindus, is thus equally holy to the followers of the Buddha. The Bo-Tree under which Gautama obtained Buddhahood, and other trees such as the mango, are also regarded as invested with peculiar sanctity. And the localities connected with his earthly life, as Kapilavastu Gayâ or Benares, have been centres of pilgrimage from the earliest times.

Relics.—The most sacred objects however are undoubtedly the relics of Buddhist saints; and among these, portions that were believed to have been preserved of the body of Gautama himself, or of articles used by him, naturally took the first place. For their protection and preservation solid structures of brick or stone were erected, in the centre of which the relic was placed within a casket. Buildings of this character, of greater or less dimensions, are found in all Buddhist countries, and in India the ruins of them are numerous. Several of the largest and most important have been excavated, as at Amarâvati and Bhattiprôlu in the Kistna District of South India, and recently at Piprâhwâ in the North near to Gautama's birthplace.[1] Originally merely hemispherical mounds they developed into elaborate

[1] See *Archæological Survey of India*, New Series, vols. vi., xv.; *J. R. A. S.*, 1898, p. 573 ff.

buildings which retained the same general form, but were often richly ornamented, provided with railings and a circular walk for the processions of pilgrims; and at the top a gilt canopy. The name applied to them was *stûpa* or *dâgaba*,[1] the latter term denoting at first the casket in which the relic was enshrined, and then extended to the entire building. It is still, as it has always been in Buddhist countries, a work of the greatest merit to raise a *stûpa*, even if no relic can be placed therein. Unfortunately the same merit does not attach to keeping them in repair; once built they are neglected, and allowed to fall into ruin. They are now often erected merely in honour of some saint, or to commemorate some event. In early times they were apparently always designed for the preservation of relics.

A third and almost synonymous term applied to these monuments was *c'aitya*, a "heap" or "pile." As distinguished from *stûpa*, the name *c'aitya* is said to be properly used only of an erection within a temple or hall, not in the open air. In Tibet the buildings are termed *ch'ortens*, and are more varied in form, presenting some-

[1] *Dâgaba* is probably a shortened form of *dhâtu-garbha*, "relic-receptacle"; which was again corrupted into "pagoda." *Stûpa*, through the Pâli *thûpa*, has become the modern *tope*.

times the appearance almost of stepped pyramids, with domes and capital. The celebrated Tooth-Temple at Kandy in Ceylon holds perhaps the most famous and venerated relic in the Buddhist world.[1]

The *dâgabas* or pagodas of Burma are very numerous, and some of them are of great size. The principal pagoda of Rangoon is higher than St. Paul's Cathedral, and a quarter of a mile in circuit. According to general belief there are here preserved hairs from Gautama's head, together with relics also of former Buddhas; and the temple is visited by crowds of pilgrims. Still larger is the Mengohn pagoda by the river-side above Mandalay, the foundations of which are said to cover an area of nearly five acres,—"the largest mass of solid brickwork in the world"; but which was never carried to completion. In Pegu and the lower country great numbers of Buddhist caves have been discovered, containing ancient sculptures and images; and a few brief and unimportant inscriptions have also been found.

Summary of Doctrine.—Buddhist teaching then, as represented by its earliest documents and traditions, starts from the position that

[1] See a description in Monier Williams, pp. 453 f., 500 ff.

man must work out his own salvation by the force of his own determination and will, apart from external or supernatural assistance. In this respect Gautama declared himself unable to render any aid to his disciples. It is the office of a Buddha to proclaim the truth,—truth into which the ordinary man is incapable of penetrating untaught: whether he hear and obey, and by acceptance of the revelation and submission to the doctrine and discipline, achieve deliverance from evil, depends upon himself alone. Evil moreover is not evil in a moral sense, but is summed up in the one word existence and in all that it implies. This deliverance consists in detachment from all the objects of sense, from all lust and craving for continuance of life; and is not to be attained by mere asceticism, but by overcoming the passions, and by resolutely pursuing a noble and virtuous course. It is ignorance that binds to existence, and that lies at the root of all suffering. The Buddha brings light and knowledge. But for the manner in which they profit or fail to profit by the light men are themselves alone responsible, and in the present or a future existence will themselves pay the penalty or enjoy the reward.

Into the deeper metaphysical questions that lie behind the practical needs of every-day life

Gautama appears to have consistently refused to enter. The abundant and almost riotous speculation of later developments of Buddhism is rooted elsewhere than in the Founder's teaching. Simply and sternly agnostic he took the gloomy view of life so universal in Indian thought; and taught not so much the overcoming of its evils and the bearing of its responsibilities, as the evasion of both. If his creed is to be summed up in philosophical terms it is agnostic rather than atheistic, practical and intensely pessimistic. At the same time he distinctly disavowed all sympathy with spiritual conceptions, and rejected the belief in a spiritual element in man or in the universe. But the taking up of this position appears to have been dictated rather by a dislike, perhaps constitutional, to metaphysical assertions, than by any positive materialistic prepossessions. For himself he disclaimed any honours or rights beyond those of a mere man, who having by his own exertions and merit attained to perfect knowledge has become the benefactor of the human race by preaching the truth and showing to them the way of salvation.

The primitive Buddhist ideal therefore is in many respects not unworthy of the high praise that has often been bestowed upon it. Of all non-Christian religions Buddhism approaches nearest to Christianity in the presentation and enforcement of a lofty code of morality. It is in the development and the working out of the details of the scheme that inconsistencies and short-comings arise. Nor is the reason far to seek. Buddhism failed and has always failed to supply a sufficient motive or encouragement for the pursuit of righteousness, or to render assistance to the disciple who has embarked in the prescribed course. That Gautama preached a selfish religion has often been made a charge against Buddhism. And of that charge neither the Founder nor those who later elaborated and extended his teaching can stand acquitted. The good works which a Buddhist does are avowedly for his own sake alone, for the accumulation of a store of merit for himself. The claims of self-interest are presented to him at every turn in his sacred books and in the teachings of his Church. But there is nothing higher or nobler, nothing to lift him above the ignominy of a self-centred life, or to inspire him with lofty ideals of disinterested service for his fellow-men.

Buddhism also was the first missionary religion, and won all its early triumphs through preaching. The zeal and devotion of the Buddhist monks who carried their Master's teaching into other lands, or who came to India to perfect their own knowledge of the Law which he had proclaimed, have rarely been excelled. Its missionary success was largely due to its doctrine of the absolute equality of all men, with equal opportunities and with equal prospects. In this respect it was like Muhammadanism. But the methods of the Buddhist preachers were always peaceable. Buddhism is probably the only great religion which has never persecuted. It has won its way by persuasion, but never by the sword; nor has it ever used its position or power to compel conformity to its precepts. The missionary glories of Buddhism however lie in the dim past. No modern propaganda is carried on. Among the Buddhists of Ceylon alone a revived interest has become apparent of recent years in their own sacred books, and in the defence of their faith. But the interest is largely literary, suggested and inspired by European example. Nor does it appear likely to spread, or to exercise a more than transient or local influence upon the future of a religion which, whatever its defects, has unquestionably done much to benefit the human race, and to introduce and perpetuate a higher standard of conduct and of life.

JAINISM

LITERATURE. GENERAL.—See Literature of Brâhmanism, etc.

TRANSLATIONS.—H. Jacobi, *Jaina Sûtras*, *S. B. E.*, vols. xxii. and xlv., Oxford, 1884 and 1895.

JAINISM

RELATION to Buddhism.—The precise relationship between Jainism and the religious system of the Buddha, already discussed, is still undetermined. The materials accumulated enable certain broad conclusions to be drawn; but beyond these it is not possible to go, to trace in detail the dependence of the one upon the other, or to assert their absolute independence. The general likeness of the two systems is obvious at a glance; their real dissimilarity only reveals itself on close inspection. The earlier view which regarded Jainism as a mere offshoot of Buddhism, and identified its reputed founder with Gautama Buddha, has ceased with clearer knowledge to be tenable. But on the other hand the resemblances, whether in early traditions, in doctrine or in organisation, are too close to be explicable by mere accident, or the play of similar forces working to similar results. The founder or reformer of Jainism can no longer be claimed as a mere reflex or double of the Buddha. The story of his life with all its coincidences and similarities is yet too distinct to admit of being any further confused with Buddhist histories. Whether or how far the portrait, dim enough at the best, is true to life may be fairly debated. It does not however represent the same original as is depicted in the traditions of the rival, and infinitely more important and successful faith.

Testimony of the Buddhist Books.—If reliance may be placed upon the statements of the Buddhist books, they themselves bear testimony to the reality and independent position of the teacher whom Jaina authorities name as the author of their religious creed. Among the opponents of the Buddha, whose views are represented as unsound and heretical, was one Nâtaputta of Vais'âlî, the head of the sect of the Niganthas or naked ascetics.[1] Nâtaputta, in Sanskrit Jnât*ri*putra, has been shown to be the same as *Mahâvîra* the founder of Jainism;[2] while *Nirgrantha*, "free from bonds" or "impediments," is the usual term in their sacred books for a Jaina monk. Nâtaputta is further said to have died shortly before Gautama himself.

[1] *Mahâvagga*, vi. 31. 2; *C'ullavagga*, v. 8. 1; *Sutta-Nipâta*, iii. 6: cp. Barth, p. 150, note 3.

[2] See note by Rhys Davids in *S. B. E.*, vol. xvii. p. 109; Hopkins, p. 283 and note.

Buddhist authorities do not however represent the Niganthas as a newly arisen sect. It has therefore been suggested with some probability that Nâtaputta should be looked upon rather as a reformer of existing views and practices than as the originator of a new school of thought. If this conclusion were correct, it would determine the question of precedence in favour of Jainism. In either case Mahâvîra must be regarded as an older contemporary of the Buddha.

Moreover while light is thus thrown upon Jaina history from Buddhist sources, the reverse is also true that occasionally the representations of the Buddhist books can be explained by facts noticed or preserved in Jaina records. For example, in the Buddhist accounts the heretical tendency of the men of Vais'âlî, and their indifference if not hostility to the Buddha, is very pronounced, but no explanation of their attitude is forthcoming. The missing link is supplied, and at the same time the truth of the Buddhist representation is confirmed by the Jaina narrative, in which this city appears as a centre and stronghold of the Jaina faith.

Relations to Brâhmanism.—The attitude moreover of the two religions towards the Brâhmanism by which they were surrounded appears to have been entirely different. In the Buddhist books the "true Brâhman" is never mentioned but with respect. Buddhism, though it preached different doctrines, ever lived in amity and tolerance with its great rival and mother; and there is not a particle of evidence to show that the supposed hostility between the two faiths was other than imaginary, or that persecution ever took place on either side. With Jainism the case was far otherwise. The legend of the transfer of the embryo of Mahâvîra from the womb of a Brâhman to that of a Kshatriya woman, because it was impossible for so great a prophet to be born "in low families, mean families, degraded families, poor families, indigent families, beggars' families, or brahmanical families,"[1] is an indication of ill-feeling or contempt slight but significant. The dislike appears also to have been fully reciprocated, in spite of the fact that in modern times at least Jaina practice approaches much more nearly to the Hindu model than Buddhism can ever have done.[2] It is possible that to the fact that it was a recognised opponent of established Brâhmanism the Jaina religion

[1] *Kalpa Sûtra*, 17; *S. B. E.*, xxii. p. 225.

[2] Compare the Râjputâna proverbs quoted from the Bombay Census Report in *Indian Antiquary*, vol. xxv. p. 147:—"It is better to jump into a well than to pass a Jain ascetic on the road." "Through the shadow of a Jain temple a Hindu may not run even to escape a tiger."

owed its immunity, when Buddhism died or was trampled out in India. More probably its comparative insignificance saved it. In modern India Jainism survives, and in theory at least holds a middle place between agnostic and materialistic Buddhism on the one hand, and on the other the idealism of the Brâhmans.

Numbers and Distribution.—According to the last census there were nearly one and a half millions of Jainas in the country, forming a half per cent. of the total population.[1] They exist mainly in the west and north, comparatively few being found in the south. In the southern districts they must at one time however have been more numerous, since it is stated that Tamil and Kanarese literature show considerable traces of Jaina influence.[2] The few that remain are generally in a humble position in life, employed in agriculture. Elsewhere they are most numerous in Ajmîr and Râjputâna generally, and in the native States of the Bombay Presidency, and occupy a better social position as tradesmen and merchants. Within the last ten years their numbers have increased at a considerably higher

[1] J. A. Baines, *General Report of the Census of India*, 1891, pp. 162, 172.

[2] See R. Caldwell, *Dravidian Grammar*, 2nd ed., 1875, Introd., pp. 86, 124, 129.

rate than the average of the population of India. This however may be largely or entirely due to greater accuracy of registration.

The Jinas.—The term *Jaina* or *Jain* signifies a follower of the *Jina*, the "victorious" or "conquering" one. *Jina* is the technical term for the teacher or founder of the *Jaina* religion, as the Buddha for that of the Buddhist. But both terms are used interchangeably as epithets, along with many others, of the head of the rival sect. According to the Jaina tradition there have been twenty-four *Jinas*, who all made their appearance in India, and each in turn revived the doctrine or truth taught by his predecessor, which had been forgotten in the course of time. Details of their lives are given in the *Kalpa Sûtra* ascribed to Bhadrabâhu, who is said to have lived in the fourth century B.C. In its present form the work is many centuries later, and contains large additions and amplifications. The only biography that is there given with any degree of completeness is that of Mahâvîra, the last of the Jinas and founder of the present religion; and of even this narrative two-thirds are taken up with the miraculous circumstances attending his birth. The remaining lives are very brief, and bear a strong resemblance to one another; increasing in the marvellousness of their details, until *Rishabha* the first Jina is reached, who taught the seventy-two sciences and the hundred arts, and lived for more than eight millions of years. It is thought that besides Mahâvîra there may have been preserved in *Pârs'va*, the Jina immediately preceding, some facts and tradition of a real historical personage.[1]

Life of Mahâvîra.—*Mahâvîra*, the founder or perhaps merely the reformer or restorer of the Jaina sect, was the son of a Kshatriya chieftain Siddhârtha, belonging to the Kâs'yapa clan, ruler of Kundagrâma in Videha. Kundagrâma has been identified with Kotigâma of the Buddhist books,[2] and was therefore situated not far from Vais'âlî. His mother Tris'alâ was sister to the king of Vais'âlî, and he is himself called Vais'âlika, an evident proof of the close connection of his family with this place. Through his mother Mahâvîra was also related to Bimbisâra, of the royal house of Magadha. The usual portents heralded and accompanied his birth. It is noticeable that in the "fourteen illustrious great dreams" which appeared to his mother was included that of a white elephant, as

[1] *S. B. E.*, vol. xxii. p. 217 ff.; the names of the twenty-four are given for example by Monier Williams, *Indian Wisdom*, p. 129 f. note 2.

[2] *Mahâv.*, vi. 29 f.; *Mah.îparin. S.*, ii. 1–5.

to the mother of Gautama. A ten days' festival was held to celebrate the birth of the child, and the name was given to him by his parents of *Vardhamâna*, "increaser" of wealth. He was also called *S'ramana*, or "ascetic," and *Mahâvîra*, the "great hero," because of his patience and endurance. This last name was bestowed upon him by the gods.

Few details of his life are given. When he was thirty years old his parents died, and in fulfilment of an earlier promise, and with the assent of his elder brother, he retired from the world, and like Gautama "perceiving . . . that the time for his Renunciation had come" he abandoned his position and wealth, and under an As'oka tree stripped himself of his ornaments, and after a two and a half days' solitary fast "entered the state of houselessness."[1] For thirteen months he continued to wear clothes, but afterwards lived as a naked ascetic, "neglecting his body." In the thirteenth year after again fasting for two and a half days he attained supreme wisdom, became a *Kevalin*, or Arhat, possessed of perfect knowledge; and thenceforth devoted himself to teaching, itinerating far and

[1] It is noticeable that all the Jinas, so far as is related, carry out the act of renunciation under the same species of tree, the As'oka.

wide, and succeeded in attaching to himself many disciples. At his death there are said to have been 1400 S'ramanas, *i.e.* Jaina monks or ascetics, 36,000 nuns, 159,000 lay-votaries, 318,000 female lay-votaries, and numbers of sages whose particular accomplishments are duly chronicled. In this work of teaching and preaching he spent thirty years, and died at Pâpâ at the age of seventy-two; or as the writer of the *Sûtra* phrases it, "became a Siddha, a Buddha, a Mukta, a maker of the end (to all misery), finally liberated, freed from all pains." The date of his death is given as 527 B.C. He is recorded to have had eleven *Ganadharas* or chief disciples, of whom only one survived him. These became the leaders or founders of nine distinct schools or *Ganas.*[1] In the Buddhist tradition also he is represented as having died before Gautama.

Jaina Sects.—The followers of Mahâvîra bore the name of *Nirgranthas,* "freed from bonds," ascetics. The title is found in one of the inscriptions of As'oka, and is therefore of early date. The names of many sub-divisions also, or sub-sects, are chronicled, with the time and occasion of their rise. Most of these however are now extinct. At the present day the Jaina

[1] See the names in Jacobi, *S. B. E.*, vol. xxii. pp. xvi., 286 ff.

monks are divided into two principal orders, viz.—the *S'vetâmbaras*, or "white-robed," and the *Digambaras*, "sky-clad," or naked. The former wear the garments of a monk, and are found chiefly in the north and west of India. The Jainas of the south are generally *Digambaras*, and with more or less strictness regularly go about unclothed, and make a virtue of dirt and uncleanliness. As an organised sect the *Digambaras* are said to have arisen towards the end of the first century of our era, under the leadership of a certain S'ivabhûti. The *S'vetâmbaras* represent the main body, from which the others separated. The practice however of so extreme asceticism must have existed among the Jaina sects long before the schism, as may be inferred from the tradition concerning the founder himself; and it is in fact derived from earlier Brâhmanism. The two sects differ further in their canon of sacred writings, and in the position adopted towards the admission of women into the monastic order. This the S'vetâmbaras permit; but there are no nuns among the Digambaras, and according to their creed women are incapable of attaining Nirvâna.

History and Character of Sacred Books.—In character the Jaina sacred books bear a strong resemblance to those of the Buddhists. The same subjects are discussed, and if with considerably less ability and interest, yet in much the same way. The tradition of the S'vetâmbaras places the earliest formal collection of writings in the time of Bhadrabâhu, in the first half of the fourth century B.C., when the monks of Pâtaliputra gathered together and arranged the twelve *Angas,* sections or departments of scripture. The *Angas* however according to the same tradition, which the Digambaras also accept, were preceded by fourteen other and older works, termed *Pûrvas*; of which four had been lost during or before the patriarchate of Bhadrabâhu. The death of the latter is placed by the S'vetâmbaras in the year 357 B.C., but by the Digambaras eight years earlier. He is credited not only with the compilation but also with the authorship of parts of the literature. The *Pûrvas* either in whole or in substance were inserted in the 12th *Anga,* called the *Drishtivâda*, which subsequently disappeared; and our only knowledge of them is derived from a brief table of contents found in the 4th *Anga.* Another tradition ascribes the composition of the *Pûrvas* to Mahâvîra himself, the *Angas* being the work of the Ganadharas. If these traditions could be accepted, they would throw back the origin of the Jaina literature to a very early date. They are however entirely unsupported. And the little that may be inferred from style and contents would point to a similar and perhaps contemporary origin with the older Pâli literature of the Buddhists. The language also of the books, a Prâkrit dialect, is said by Jacobi to approximate in character to the Pâli.

The final revision of the Canon, or *Siddhânta*, is said to have taken place at the Council of Valabhî[1] in the year 454 A.D. under the direction of Devarddhi, who in order to preserve the sacred texts had them committed to writing. The work of Devarddhi was therefore conservative, although he is also said to have enlarged the Canon by the incorporation of new treatises. According to other authorities the Jainas were in possession of written books at least three centuries earlier. The Canon as a whole is accepted only by the S'vetâmbaras. The Digambaras reject the Angas, and appear to have no

[1] An ancient capital city in Kâthiâwâr, the centre and home of a powerful Hindu dynasty from about 495 A.D. until the second half of the eighth century. See Cunningham, *Anc. Geography*, pp. 316 ff., 323, who identifies the site with the extensive ruins of Vamilapura, 18 miles west-north-west of Bhaunagar. Hiuen-Tsiang visited the town, and found a flourishing Buddhism with very many sectaries of different sorts; Beal, vol. ii. p. 266 ff. Cp. *S. B. E.*, xxii. pp. xxxvii., 270.

fixed or definite collection of their own of sacred scriptures.[1]

Doctrines.—Like the Buddhists the Jainas expounded a doctrine of Nirvâna, but in their sacred books and in their teaching an essentially different idea is conveyed by the term, based upon a different conception of the living being and its composition. The theory of the skandhas with its materialistic pre-suppositions is entirely unknown to Jaina philosophy. But on the contrary they maintain a kind of dualism

[1] The complete Canon, which is in reality only that of the S'vetâmbaras of the north, comprises fifty works, viz. 5 *Kalpa-sûtras*, and the 45 *^Agamas*, manuals of doctrine, or collections of sacred precepts. The latter are divided into :— 11 *Angas ;* 12 *Upângas*, supports or supplements to the *Angas* ; 4 *Mûlasûtras*, or fundamental sûtras ; 10 *Prakîrnakas*, or miscellaneous pieces ; and 8 *C'hedas*, or sections. See Barth, *Religions of India*, p. 147 note ; a slightly different arrangement in Monier Williams, *Indian Wisdom*, p. xxxvi. note 1. Prof. Hermann Jacobi has translated in *S. B. E.*, vols. xxii. and xlv., first the *^Ac'ârânga Sûtra*, a manual of conduct, the first of the 11 Angas, and the *Kalpa Sûtra*, consisting of five Lives of the Jinas ; and second, the *Uttarâdhyayana Sûtra*, and the *Sûtrakritânga Sûtra*. The title *Kalpa Sûtra* seems to be derived from the use of the word *kalpa* to denote the heaven or abode of the gods. The Digambara monks possess sacred writings of their own, but little or nothing appears to be known about them. In a report of his recent archæological journey across India to Nepâl, Mr. C. Bendall announces that he succeeded in obtaining at Jaipur some valuable Digambara MSS.

of soul and matter, which is most closely akin to the Sânkhya doctrine of the Brâhmans. All existing beings are composed of two parts *jîva* and *ajîva*, or soul and not-soul, which are the two supreme and ultimate realities of the universe, and are both eternal. The entanglement of the soul in matter, its enforced union with not-soul, is the source of all misery and the present distress. Nirvâna is the deliverance of the soul from this union, its release from bondage to things material, and entrance thereby into a state of unending felicity. Until this release is effected the soul passes from one body to another, through a succession of re-births, the possibilities of which are not limited as with the Buddhists to six orders of living beings only, but extend indefinitely downwards. Thus not only do animals and plants possess souls, but also the material elements and inanimate objects of all kinds. The Jaina re-birth therefore is a true transmigration. And the only contact with Buddhist teaching appears in the doctrine of "released" souls, that is souls which are still bound to matter by the one sense of touch, but which will never pass into another existence.

The way to attain nirvâna is revealed and taught by the *Jina* or *Tîrthakara*, who like the

Buddha restores to men the knowledge of the truth, forgotten through the lapse of time. Twenty-four *Jinas* have already appeared, of whom Mahâvîra was the last, the number corresponding to the twenty-four Buddhas of the present age. Jainism however recognises only two ages or eras, the *utsarpinî* or ascending, and the *avasarpinî* or descending, both of them of immense length. Each is sub-divided into six stages, and the world is now in the last stage but one of the "descending" era, which is an evil age. Nothing seems to be recorded or prophesied of future *Jinas*. The path of liberation or means of release is by the *tri-ratna*, the three gems, viz.:—right faith or intuition, right knowledge, right conduct. Right faith is explained to be absolute unquestioning faith in the teaching of the *Jina*; and right knowledge is a perfect understanding of the real nature of the soul. Knowledge itself again is of five kinds:—*mati*, simple apprehension; *s'ruta*, clear perception based on mati; *avadhi*, a knowledge of special objects, the fruit of right intuition; *manas-paryâya*, insight into the mind or thoughts of another; *kevala*, "pure" or perfect knowledge, that is omniscience. An *Arhat* is defined as one who has reached this state of perfect knowledge, and in whom by the help of the three jewels all obstacles to knowledge have been removed. It is therefore logically concluded that no being is omniscient from eternity. Right conduct finally is the conduct of one who acts with right faith and knowledge. This is also five-fold, corresponding to the five vows of the Jaina monk.[1]

This teaching or revelation of the Jina is otherwise expressed as the revelation of the *tattvas*, essences or first principles. Of these the two highest are jîva and ajîva, which contain in themselves the mystery of being. Others affirm that there are five *tattvas*:—*jîva*, or soul; *âkâs'a*, ether; *dharma*, law; *adharma*, not-law; *pudgala*, form. Others again give seven, or even nine *tattvas*.

Asceticism.—A further condition which must be fulfilled by the wise man who would achieve his own deliverance is the observance of ascetic rules and modes of life. Herein lay a deep and wide cleavage between the two faiths of the Buddha and the Jina. Gautama, having in his own person made trial of asceticism and found it wanting, discouraged it in his disciples. Mahâvîra set the example of living in the practice of extreme asceticism, with prolonged fasting. Such a life is characterised in the

[1] *Infra*, p. 364.

books as of great merit, and minute regulations are laid down for daily observance, whether in food drink or clothing, or in personal habits. The Jaina monk, who aspires to release from the body, after having passed through a series of re-births, must live for at least twelve years in strict asceticism, the number twelve being prescribed in imitation of the founder, who spent twelve years as a mendicant monk before his attainment of perfect knowledge.

Monastic Order.—The monastic institution however was more loosely organised among the Jainas than among the Buddhists; and greater freedom and personal independence appear always to have been allowed. No injunctions were given with respect to a common dwelling-place, and in this respect Jaina practice conformed to the Brâhmanical rather than to the Buddhist model. By the Digambaras the right of admission into the order was denied to women. The monks were divided into two classes, *yatis*, devotees or ascetics, and *s'râvakas*, hearers or disciples. Upon both practically the same discipline and obedience were enjoined. The monks were also termed, perhaps merely by their Brâhman opponents, *syâdvâdins*, literally "those who say 'it may be,'" from the position of uncertainty or agnosticism which they took up with regard to the metaphysical questions of the origin and nature of being.[1] The five principal vows or "renunciations" which they were called upon to observe were as follows[2]:—abstinence from destroying life, from falsehood, from taking that which is not given, from impurity and self-indulgence, and from "attachments" to worldly things. These are sub-divided each into five clauses, which define and particularise; and further minute directions are given throughout the sacred books for daily life and conduct. The precept of *ahimsâ* especially, that of doing no injury to any living being, is more scrupulously observed by the Jainas than by any other sect. This abstinence however from taking life does not apply to their own. Under certain circumstances, when the twelve necessary years of asceticism have been passed, religious suicide is not only innocent but an act of merit or even a duty; and in former times is said to have been of frequent occurrence.[3] Three vows of obedience also were incumbent upon all,—to the *Jina*, the *dharma* or law, and the *guru* the living representative or successor of the Jina.

[1] Cp. Barth, p. 148; *Sarva-dars'.*, p. 59 ff.
[2] *Âc'ârânga Sûtra*, ii. 15; *S. B. E.*, xxii. p. 202 ff.
[3] *Ib.* i. 7. 4–8.

Comparison of the five Jaina vows with those of the Buddhist[1] will at once show that the first four are the same although given in a different order. That neither sect however has borrowed directly from the other is rendered probable by the fact that the ancient Hindu law-books also prescribe five chief vows for the Brâhman ascetic, the first four of which are identical with the Buddhist or Jaina precepts. The fifth Brâhman vow is a pledge of generosity; upon which the Hindu commentator notes that although an ascetic has no property and so is apparently precluded from being liberal, still he possesses books which he may give away. It was perhaps the inappropriateness of this injunction which led Buddhist and Jaina teachers to substitute another. In both instances the dependence of the later orders is upon the earlier, not upon one another.[2]

Dress and Equipment.—The equipment of the Jaina monk was in some respects slightly more

[1] *Supra*, p. 311 f.

[2] See a detailed discussion of the relation of the vows of the three orders by H. Jacobi in *S. B. E.*, vol. xxii. p. xxii. ff. The Brâhman vows are given from Baudyâyana in *S. B. E.*, vol. xiv. p. 279, as follows:—"Abstention from injuring living beings, truthfulness, abstention from appropriating the property of others, continence, liberality." Cp. Gautama iii. 11 ff.; *S. B. E.*, vol. ii[2]. p. 193 f.

elaborate than that of the Buddhist. A single plain garment or robe is prescribed for a monk, four for a nun. The Digambaras dispense with clothes altogether; thus presenting a great contrast to the members of the Buddhist order, who are at all times decently clad. In no case may he accept as a gift robes specially made or prepared for him, but if those offered are old or dirty they should be gratefully received. In addition to his robe or robes the monk carries a single alms-bowl, which must not be of expensive materials, a broom with which to sweep the ground before him lest he tread unawares upon any living creature, and a veil over the mouth to prevent the unconscious swallowing of insect life. Like the Buddhists also the Jainas observe Vassa, not moving abroad for four months during the rains, or travelling from place to place[1]; they practise fasting regularly, and go on pilgrimage. The chief place of resort for Jaina pilgrims is Pârasnâth Hill, in the Hazâribâgh

[1] This practice also has been supposed to be borrowed from Brâhmanism. "An ascetic must not change his residence during the rainy season." Gaut. iii. 13; *S. B. E.*, ii². p. 193: cp. Baudhy. ii. 6. 11. 20. This notice is however as far as my knowledge goes quite isolated, and there are no further traces of a Brâhman observance of Vassa. It is possible that the mere physical difficulty of journeying in the rainy season may have contributed to give rise to the practice.

District, Bengal, where are numerous Jaina temples, and where ten out of the twenty-four Jinas are said to have attained Nirvâna.[1]

Jaina approaches to Hinduism.—The Jainas of the present day, although in theory atheistic, have drawn so near to the surrounding Hinduism as to be practically idolatrous. They have adopted many of the Hindu divinities, and in addition to the Jina pay divine honours to his chief disciples the Ganadharas. There exists also among them a female or goddess cult, similar to that of the Hindu S'akti. Many Jaina images and temples are met with in India, especially in the south; and at one time the sect must have been much more numerous and powerful than it is at the present. The Jainas reject the Veda, but are said to observe caste distinctions. Nevertheless there is now amongst them a distinct movement towards Hinduism, and a tendency to group themselves amongst the

[1] Pârasnâth is a corruption of Pârs'vanâtha, the name of the Jina preceding Mahâvîra. He was the last of the ten who here attained Nirvâna, and the hill was therefore named after him. For an account of Pârasnâth see the *Gazetteer of India, s.v.*, where it is stated that 10,000 pilgrims frequent the place every year, and that new shrines are still occasionally erected. The height of the hill is about 4500 ft. There is an interesting narrative of an ascent of Pârasnâth in the year 1848 in Sir J. Hooker's *Himâlayan Journals*, chap. i.

many sects of the dominant religion. Brâhman priests also are found officiating in Jaina temples.

Comparison with Buddhism and Brâhmanism.—A comparison therefore of Jainism with Brâhmanism on the one hand and Buddhism on the other leads to the conclusion that it is in reality nearer to the former both in constitution and practice than to the latter. The resemblances to Buddhism, striking as they are, lie in great part upon the surface; the underlying differences penetrate to the very heart and centre of the two systems. The lives of the two founders, if Mahâvîra may be termed a founder, so curiously alike in their general course, diverge entirely in detail; and where they touch, the history and portraits harmonise on the supposition that they represent distinct and opposing teachers, but are almost inexplicable if the one is a mere reflex or repetition of the other. Similarly the regulations and later history of the monastic order, the speculations and conclusions of the leaders of thought on either side, moved on parallel or slightly divergent but by no means on coincident lines. And the Church Councils of each sect, in the little that is really known of them, appear to resemble one another in nothing save in the one circumstance that they were Councils of the ecclesia. It is evident however that the two movements of Buddhism and Jainism had their origin in one and the same cause, namely a revolt from the domineering spirit and exclusive claims of the Brâhmans. Both had their roots in the more ancient system, and in different ways sought emancipation from its yoke. Nor were they alone in this desire for liberty. Others made the same attempt, and like them were stigmatised as heretics by the adherents of the orthodox faith. These two creeds and philosophies however have survived in systematised form. The others have perished, or have been drawn back again into a comprehensive Hinduism. Jainism also is retrograding, and as it seems with accelerating pace. Buddhism alone has always stood its ground, and while borrowing has remained more markedly independent. There is evidence also that in the Middle Ages, in parts at least of India, the two faiths were by no means so unequally matched in influence and number of adherents as might be inferred from their respective positions at the present day. Jaina literature is dreary and uninteresting. But in its subjects and general treatment it bears a strong resemblance to the Buddhist; and both work on lines familiar to the older literature of India.

Conclusions.—All the available evidence therefore points to the same conclusion. The Buddhist and Jaina systems have many characteristics and doctrines in common, and have probably in the past modified and influenced one another to a considerable extent. These resemblances however are mainly due to their common origin. The points of contact between the two religions are precisely those in which each is indebted to a pre-existing Brâhmanism. The likeness is that of a common descent. But while Jainism diverged comparatively little, and after a long resistance is now succumbing to the attractions of its surroundings, Buddhism rapidly hardened into an elaborate system with greater independence and originality, and moving on broader and more generous lines secured for itself a position and extent of influence which has enabled it to more than rival the mother faith from which it sprang.

INDEX

The figures refer to the pages. Where more than one number is given, the BLACK TYPE indicates the principal reference.

The Preacher's Magazine

UNION FOR BIBLICAL AND HOMILETIC STUDY.

A CORRESPONDENCE COLLEGE FOR BIBLE STUDENTS.

MOTTO: "*Study to show thyself approved unto God, a workman that needeth not to be ashamed, rightly dividing the word of truth.*"—2 TIMOTHY ii. 15.

President—
REV. ARTHUR E. GREGORY.

Secretary—
REV. J. A. CLAPPERTON, M.A., Addingham, Leeds.

Members may join at any time. Membership is open to all Christian workers.

THE SUBSCRIPTION IS ONLY SIXPENCE PER ANNUM, but Members who can afford it are invited to give a larger sum, in order to meet the expenses of Prizes, etc., and to provide poorer Members with Text-Books at a further reduction.

The Preacher's Magazine contains the "Monthly Chronicle of the U.B.H.S."

If you wish to join the Union, send your Name and Address to the General Secretary, with Postal Order or Stamps for your Subscription and the Text-Books you require.

Special arrangements can be made to meet the needs of local Classes. Those who are already conducting such Classes, or desire to start them, are invited to communicate with the General Secretary.

BOOKS FOR BIBLE STUDENTS—continued.

SYSTEMATIC THEOLOGY.

THE THEOLOGICAL STUDENT. A Handbook of Elementary Theology. By J. ROBINSON GREGORY. 2s. 6d. Eleventh Thousand.

An Explanatory Index of Theological Terms and a very full List of Questions for Self-Examination add greatly to the practical value of the book.

CHURCH HISTORY.

FROM MALACHI TO MATTHEW: Outlines of the History of Judea from 440 to 4 B.C. By R. WADDY MOSS. 2s. 6d. Third Thousand.

IN THE APOSTOLIC AGE. THE CHURCHES AND THE DOCTRINE. By R. A. WATSON, M.A., D.D. 2s. 6d.

A MANUAL OF MODERN CHURCH HISTORY. By W. F. SLATER, M.A. 2s. 6d. Second Thousand.

A HISTORY OF LAY PREACHING IN THE CHRISTIAN CHURCH. By JOHN TELFORD, B.A. 2s. 6d.

THE CHURCH OF THE WEST IN THE MIDDLE AGES. Two Vols. From Gregory the Great to Clement the Fifth. By HERBERT B. WORKMAN, M.A. 2s. 6d. each.

CHRISTIAN EVIDENCES.

SCRIPTURE AND ITS WITNESSES: Outlines of Christian Evidence. By Professor J. SHAW BANKS. 2s. 6d.

THE SACRED LANGUAGES.

AN INTRODUCTION TO THE STUDY OF HEBREW. By J. T. L. MAGGS, B.A., B.D. 5s.

AN INTRODUCTION TO THE STUDY OF NEW TESTAMENT GREEK. By J. HOPE MOULTON, M.A., late Fellow of King's College, Cambridge, and Master in the Leys School. 3s. Second Thousand.

A FIRST READER IN NEW TESTAMENT GREEK. By J. HOPE MOULTON, M.A. 6d. net.

The above two books can be had bound together in one Volume, 3s. 6d.

TRANSLATIONS AND REFERENCES TO MOULTON'S FIRST READER IN NEW TESTAMENT GREEK. 1s. net. *Only to be had by direct application to the Publishers.*

BIBLICAL CRITICISM.

THE AGE AND AUTHORSHIP OF THE PENTATEUCH. By WILLIAM SPIERS, M.A., F.G.S. 3s. 6d. Second Thousand.

HOMILETICS.

THE LAY PREACHER'S HANDBOOK: First Steps in Homiletics. By C. O. ELDRIDGE, B.A. 2s. Sixth Thousand.

LONDON: C. H. KELLY, 2, CASTLE STREET, CITY ROAD, E.C.

BY THE REV. J. SHAW BANKS—*continued.*

SCRIPTURE AND ITS WITNESSES. Outlines of Christian Evidence. Second Thousand. Small crown 8vo, 2s. 6d.

"May be commended to the student for the clearness and ability with which it is written, and its thorough understanding of the exact problems that the Christian apologetic has to solve at the present day."—*Leeds Mercury.*

"Professor Banks writes with strong but calm conviction of the strength of his case, and his book is one to produce or confirm an intelligent faith in Christ and His gospel. This is a book which every young preacher ought to have."—*Preachers' Magazine.*

"Professor Banks has a lucid and interesting style, and brings to his task both scholarship and good sense. . . . The book is well fitted to give the general reader an intelligent standing-ground for his faith, while offering him a glimpse of the great questions which the advanced theological thought of to-day is debating."—*Christian World.*

"An admirable introduction to the study of Christian evidences. . . . A careful and accurate book."—*Light and Leading.*

"We have read this book with intense pleasure and profit, and heartily commend it to all thoughtful readers."—*Sword and Trowel.*

CHRISTIANITY AND THE SCIENCE OF RELIGION. Demy 8vo, paper covers, 1s.; cloth, 2s.

"Marked by compression, incisiveness, and force."—*Watchman.*

"Mr. Banks possesses in a rare degree the faculties of logical keenness and close observation. The lecture is well reasoned throughout, and is a worthy contribution to the defensive literature of the Christian Church."—*Hastings and St. Leonards News.*

"A very able discussion of a great subject."—*Sheffield and Rotherham Independent.*

THREE INDIAN HEROES: William Carey, the Missionary; Henry Havelock, the Soldier; Henry Lawrence, the Statesman. Portraits and Illustrations. Small crown 8vo, 1s.

A PREACHER'S LIBRARY. Hints on Theological Reading. Third Edition, Revised and Enlarged. Demy 8vo, paper covers, 1s.

"A standard book on books. Its aim is practical, and, within its own range, you will not find a safer guide."—*Expository Times.*

A PREACHER'S GENERAL READING. Companion to "A Preacher's Library." Demy 8vo, paper covers, 6d.

"Books like these are very valuable. Hundreds will thank Mr. Banks for a difficult task well executed."—*Christian.*